JIRA Essentials
Third Edition

Use the features of JIRA to manage projects and
effectively handle bugs and software issues

Patrick Li

BIRMINGHAM - MUMBAI

JIRA Essentials
Third Edition

First published: May 2011

Second published: April 2013

Third edition: April 2015

Production reference: 1220415

Published by Packt Publishing Ltd.
Livery Place
35 Livery Street
Birmingham B3 2PB, UK.

ISBN 978-1-78439-812-5

www.packtpub.com

Credits

Author
Patrick Li

Reviewers
Mizan Ali Sayed
Miroslav Králik
Heiko Lübbe
Sabina Şerbu

Commissioning Editor
Taron Pereira

Acquisition Editor
Harsha Bharwani

Content Development Editor
Arwa Manasawala

Technical Editor
Saurabh Malhotra

Copy Editor
Charlotte Carneiro

Project Coordinator
Danuta Jones

Proofreaders
Safis Editing
Lauren E. Harkins
Paul Hindle
Joanna McMahon

Indexer
Hemangini Bari

Production Coordinator
Nilesh R. Mohite

Cover Work
Nilesh R. Mohite

About the Author

Patrick Li is a cofounder and senior engineer at AppFusions. AppFusions is an expert in developing and packaging integrated solutions for many enterprise applications and platforms, including IBM Connections, Jive, Atlassian, Google Apps, Box, Dropbox, and more.

He has worked in the Atlassian ecosystem for over 8 years, developing products and solutions for the Atlassian platform and providing expert consulting services. He is one of the top contributors to the Atlassian community, providing answers and advices on forums such as Atlassian Answers and Quora.

He has extensive experience in designing and deploying Atlassian solutions from the ground up and customizing existing deployments for clients across verticals, such as healthcare, software engineering, financial services, and government agencies.

I would like to thank all the reviewers for their valuable feedback and also the publishers and coordinators for their help and support in making this happen. Lastly, I would like to thank my family, especially my wife Katherine, for encouraging me along the way.

About the Reviewers

Mizan Ali Sayed is an Atlassian expert who has extensive experience in implementing, customizing, and supporting Atlassian tools, mainly JIRA and Confluence. He also has experience in training small, medium, and large teams on JIRA and JIRA administration.

He is active within the Atlassian community and has published free add-ons on the Atlassian Marketplace. He has previously reviewed two books on JIRA administration and development by Packt publishing. Mizan has won the Star Employee Award for 3 consecutive years.

You can reach him at `mizanalisayed@gmail.com`.

> First and foremost, I would like to thank my wife. She has been my inspiration and motivation for continuing to improve my knowledge and moving my career forward. I also thank my wonderful daughter, Aaminah, for always making me smile. I'd like to thank my parents for allowing me to follow my ambitions throughout my childhood.
>
> My co-workers, especially Amrut Bhonsle, showed me the ropes in IT. Without this knowledge, I wouldn't have ventured into learning about JIRA and other Atlassian tools.

Miroslav Králik is a young professional focusing on ITIL-based ITSM, with a passion for helping clients succeed and getting them excited about making their products, services, and processes better. He is currently working at a multinational integrated digital agency, where he leads a technical team and is responsible for EMEA web applications, maintenance and support services.

He has been using, administrating, and developing custom plugins and scripts for JIRA for 3 years at many different companies.

He is also one of the cofounders of Next Kickoff, an SRO, a lean start-up company based in Prague that focuses on solving specific domain problems.

Miroslav can be found on LinkedIn (`https://www.linkedin.com/in/mikralik`).

I would like to thank my girlfriend, Maria, for her support and understanding when I have worked evenings and nights. I would also like to thank all my current and former colleagues that I have had the pleasure of working with, and a special thanks to my colleague and friend, Kaveh, for "transferring" all the knowledge while working together over the past few years.

Heiko Lübbe has been working with JIRA, on a daily basis, since 2007. He has worked in different roles, as an end user with ticket-based workflows, setting up and introducing JIRA, JIRA administration, JIRA migration, as a project manager, and a Scrum master. As a freelance consultant, Mr. Lübbe works with many different companies, from small Internet companies to big multinational companies, but always with JIRA.

He presented "Using JIRA for project management" at the Berlin/Brandenburg PMI Chapter meeting in 2012.

He is still working as a senior technical IT project manager on a freelance basis in Berlin, Germany.

Sabina Şerbu has a PhD in distributed systems from the University of Neuchâtel, Switzerland, and an MSc in computer science from the Politehnica University of Bucharest, Romania.

Sabina has been working in the areas of networking and document management, and she is often involved in academic projects. She has hands-on and managerial experience with JIRA and has been an active reviewer for conferences and technical documentation.

Sabina Şerbu can be found at `www.sabinaserbu.ch`.

www.PacktPub.com

Support files, eBooks, discount offers, and more

For support files and downloads related to your book, please visit www.PacktPub.com.

Did you know that Packt offers eBook versions of every book published, with PDF and ePub files available? You can upgrade to the eBook version at www.PacktPub.com and as a print book customer, you are entitled to a discount on the eBook copy. Get in touch with us at service@packtpub.com for more details.

At www.PacktPub.com, you can also read a collection of free technical articles, sign up for a range of free newsletters and receive exclusive discounts and offers on Packt books and eBooks.

https://www2.packtpub.com/books/subscription/packtlib

Do you need instant solutions to your IT questions? PacktLib is Packt's online digital book library. Here, you can search, access, and read Packt's entire library of books.

Why subscribe?

- Fully searchable across every book published by Packt
- Copy and paste, print, and bookmark content
- On demand and accessible via a web browser

Free access for Packt account holders

If you have an account with Packt at www.PacktPub.com, you can use this to access PacktLib today and view 9 entirely free books. Simply use your login credentials for immediate access.

Instant updates on new Packt books

Get notified! Find out when new books are published by following @PacktEnterprise on Twitter or the *Packt Enterprise* Facebook page.

Table of Contents

Preface   **xi**

Chapter 1: Getting Started with JIRA   **1**

The JIRA architecture   **1**

  High-level architecture   2

    Web browsers   3

    Application services   3

    Data storage   3

  The JIRA installation directory   3

  The JIRA home directory   4

System requirements   **5**

  Hardware requirements   5

  Software requirements   6

    Operating systems   6

    Java platforms   7

    Databases   7

    Application servers   8

Installation options   **8**

Installing and configuring JIRA   **9**

  Installing Java   10

  Installing MySQL   12

  Preparing MySQL for JIRA   12

  Installing JIRA   14

    Obtaining and installing JIRA   14

    Installing MySQL driver   19

    The JIRA setup wizard   19

    Starting and stopping JIRA   26

Post-installation configurations   **27**

  Increasing JIRA's memory   27

  Changing JIRA's port number and context path   29

Configuring HTTPS   29
Summary   **31**
Chapter 2: Project Management   **33**
The JIRA hierarchy   **33**
Project category   34
Project   35
Issue   35
Field   35
Project permissions   **36**
Creating projects   **37**
Changing the project key format   39
Importing data into JIRA   **40**
Importing data through CSV   41
Project user interfaces   **46**
Project Browser   **47**
The Summary tab   48
The Issues tab   48
The Road Map tab   49
The Change Log tab   49
The Versions and Components tab   49
The Source and Reviews tab   50
Project Administration   **50**
The Summary tab   51
The Components tab   52
Creating components   53
Managing components   53
Component lead and default assignee   53
The Versions tab   54
Creating versions   54
Managing versions   55
Other tabs   56
The Help Desk project   **57**
Creating a new project category   57
Creating a new project   58
Assigning a project to a category   59
Creating new components   59
Putting it together   60
Summary   **61**
Chapter 3: Issue Management   **63**
Understanding issues   **64**
JIRA issue summary   **64**

Working with issues   **66**
    Creating an issue   66
    Editing an issue   68
    Deleting an issue   69
    Moving an issue between projects   70
    Casting a vote on an issue   72
    Receiving notifications on an issue   73
    Assigning issues to users   74
    Sharing issues with other users   75
Issue linking   **76**
    Enabling issue linking   76
    Creating link types   76
    Linking issues with other issues   78
    Linking issues with remote contents   79
Issue cloning   **80**
Time tracking   **81**
    Configuring time tracking   81
    Specifying original estimates   83
    Logging work   83
Issues and comments   **85**
    Adding comments   85
    Managing your comments   86
    Permalinking a comment   86
Attachments   **87**
    Enabling attachments in JIRA   87
    Attaching files   89
    Attaching screenshots   90
Issue types and subtasks   **90**
    Creating issue types   92
    Deleting issue types   92
    Subtasks   93
       Enabling subtasks   93
       Creating subtasks   94
       Issue type schemes   94
Issue priorities   **97**
The help desk project   **98**
    Adding new issue types   98
    Creating an issue type scheme   99
    Putting it together   100
Summary   **100**

Chapter 4: Field Management   101

Built-in fields   102
Custom fields   102
Custom field types   102
Standard fields   103
Advanced fields   104
Searchers   105
Custom field context   105
Managing custom fields   106
Adding a custom field   107
Editing/deleting a custom field   109
Configuring a custom field   111
Adding custom field contexts   112
Configuring select options   113
Setting default values   114
Field configuration   114
Adding a field configuration   116
Editing/deleting a field configuration   116
Copying a field configuration   117
Managing field configurations   117
Field description   118
Field requirement   119
Field visibility   119
Field rendering   120
Screens   122
Field configuration scheme   122
Managing field configuration schemes   122
Adding a field configuration scheme   123
Editing/deleting a field configuration scheme   124
Copying a field configuration scheme   124
Configuring a field configuration scheme   125
Associating a field configuration scheme with a project   126
The Help Desk project   127
Setting up a custom field   128
Setting up the field configuration   129
Setting up a field configuration scheme   129
Putting it together   130
Summary   132

Chapter 5: Screen Management   133

JIRA and screens   133
Working with screens   135
Adding a new screen   137
Editing/deleting a screen   137

Copying a screen 138
Configuring screens 138
  Adding a field to a screen 139
  Deleting a field from a screen 140
Using screen tabs 140
  Adding a tab to a screen 141
  Editing/deleting a tab 142
Working with screen schemes **143**
Adding a screen scheme 144
Editing/deleting a screen scheme 145
Copying a screen scheme 146
Configuring a screen scheme 146
  Associating screens to issue operations 147
  Editing/deleting an association 148
Issue type screen scheme **148**
Adding an issue type screen scheme 149
Editing/deleting an issue type screen scheme 150
Copying an issue type screen scheme 150
Configuring an issue type screen scheme 151
  Associating issue types to screen schemes 151
  Editing/deleting an association 152
Associating an issue type screen scheme with a project 152
The Help Desk project **153**
Setting up screens 154
Setting up screen schemes 156
Setting up issue type screen schemes 157
Putting it together 158
Summary **159**
Chapter 6: Workflows and Business Processes **161**
Mapping business processes **161**
Understanding workflows **162**
Managing workflows 164
Issue statuses 165
Transitions 165
  Triggers 166
  Conditions 166
  Validators 167
  Post functions 167
Using the workflow designer 168
Authoring a workflow 170
  Adding a trigger to a transition 174
  Adding a condition to a transition 175

Adding a validator to a transition	176
Adding a post function to a transition	178
Updating an existing workflow	179
Workflow schemes	**180**
Creating a workflow scheme	182
Configuring a workflow scheme	182
Assigning an issue type to a workflow	183
Editing/deleting an association	185
Activating a workflow scheme	186
Extending workflow with workflow add-ons	**187**
JIRA Suite Utilities	187
JIRA Workflow Toolbox	187
JIRA Misc Workflow Extensions	187
Workflow Enhancer for JIRA	188
Script Runner	188
The Help Desk project	**188**
Setting up workflows	189
Setting up workflow schemes	191
Putting it together	192
Summary	**194**
Chapter 7: E-mails and Notifications	**195**
JIRA and e-mail	**195**
Mail servers	**196**
Working with outgoing mails	**197**
Adding an outgoing mail server	197
Disabling outgoing mail	200
Enabling SMTP over SSL	200
Sending a test e-mail	201
Mail queues	**202**
Viewing the mail queue	203
Flushing the mail queue	204
Manually sending e-mails	**204**
Events	**206**
Adding a mail template	207
Adding a custom event	210
Firing a custom event	210
Notifications	**212**
The notification scheme	**213**
Adding a notification scheme	214
Editing a notification scheme	214
Deleting a notification scheme	215

Copying a notification scheme   215
Managing a notification scheme   216
  Adding a notification   216
  Deleting a notification   218
Assigning a notification scheme   218
Troubleshooting notifications   **220**
Incoming e-mails   **221**
Adding an incoming mail server   222
Mail handlers   223
  Creating a new issue or adding a comment to an existing issue   224
  Adding a comment with the entire e-mail body   225
  Adding a comment from the non-quoted e-mail body   225
  Creating a new issue from each e-mail message   225
  Adding a comment before a specified marker or separator in the e-mail body   226
  Adding a mail handler   226
  Editing and deleting a mail handler   228
The Help Desk project   **228**
Setting up mail servers   229
Setting up custom events   229
Setting up a notification scheme   230
Setting up notifications   231
Putting it together   231
Summary   **232**
Chapter 8: Securing JIRA   **233**
User directories   **233**
Managing user directories   235
Connecting to LDAP   236
Users   **238**
User Browser   239
Adding a user   240
Enabling public signup   242
Enabling CAPTCHA   243
Groups   **244**
Group Browser   245
Adding a group   246
Editing group memberships   246
Deleting a group   248
Project roles   **248**
Project Role Browser   248
Adding a project role   249
Editing a project role   249
Deleting a project role   250

Managing default members   250
Assigning project role members   251
JIRA permissions hierarchy   **253**
Global permissions   254
JIRA system administrator versus JIRA administrator   255
Configuring global permissions   255
Granting global permissions   256
Revoking global permissions   257
Project permissions   258
Permission schemes   260
Applying a permission scheme   265
Issue security   266
Issue security scheme   266
Adding an issue security scheme   267
Configuring an issue security scheme   267
Applying an issue security scheme   271
Troubleshooting permissions   **271**
Workflow security   **272**
The Help Desk project   **273**
Setting up groups   273
Setting up user group association   273
Setting up permission schemes   274
Setting up permissions   274
Putting it together   275
Summary   **276**
Chapter 9: Searching, Reporting, and Analysis   **277**
Search interface and options in JIRA   **277**
Issue navigator   278
Basic search   279
Advanced search with JQL   280
Quick search   283
Working with search results   284
Switching result views   284
Exporting search results   284
Customizing the column layout   285
Sharing search results   286
Filters   **286**
Creating a filter   287
Managing filters   287
Editing and sharing a filter   288
Subscribing to a filter   290
Deleting a filter   291
Changing the ownership of a filter   292

Reports	**293**
Generating a report	294
Dashboard	297
Managing dashboards	297
Creating a dashboard	298
Editing and sharing a dashboard	299
Deleting a dashboard	299
Configuring a dashboard	299
Setting a layout for the dashboard	300
Gadgets	300
Placing a gadget on the dashboard	301
Moving a gadget	303
Editing a gadget	303
Deleting a gadget	304
The Help Desk project	**304**
Setting up filters	304
Setting up dashboards	305
Setting up gadgets	306
Putting it together	306
Summary	**307**
Chapter 10: JIRA Service Desk	**309**
Introducing JIRA Service Desk	**309**
Installing JIRA Service Desk	310
Getting started with JIRA Service Desk	311
Creating a new service desk	313
Branding your customer portal	315
Service desk users	**316**
Adding an agent to service desk	317
Adding a customer to service desk	318
Adding a collaborator to service desk	319
Request types	**319**
Setting up request types	319
Organizing request types into groups	320
Setting up fields	321
Setting up workflow	323
Service-level agreement	**325**
Setting up an SLA	325
Setting up custom calendars	328
Queues	**329**
Creating a new queue	330
Creating knowledge base articles	**331**
Summary	**333**

Chapter 11: Advanced Features   335

JIRA Agile   335
Getting JIRA Agile   336
Starting with JIRA Agile   337
Working with boards   338
  Creating a new board   339
Working with Scrum boards   341
  Working with epics   341
  Working with sprints   343
Working with Kanban boards   345
  Setting up column constraints   345
  Releasing a version   346
Setting JIRA Agile as the home page   347
Issue collector   348
Setting up an issue collector   349
Embedding the issue collector   350
Summary   352
Index   353

Preface

Over the years, JIRA has grown from a simple bug tracking system designed for engineers to manage their projects to an all-purpose issue tracking solution. As it has matured over time, JIRA has become more than an application, it has transformed into a platform, with a suite of other products that are built on it, enabling it to adapt and deliver value to a wide variety of use cases.

JIRA 6 is the latest major release of JIRA and its product family. It comes with new features that include support for service desk applications and enhancements made to existing features such as providing flexible and robust workflow design and agile methodology support. In this book, we will cover all the basics of JIRA and its core capabilities as a feature-rich, issue-tracking system, as well as add-ons that add additional features to the JIRA platform.

Packed with real-life examples and step-by-step instructions, this book will help you become a JIRA expert.

What this book covers

This book is organized into eleven chapters. The first chapter starts with setting up your own JIRA, and the subsequent chapters will introduce key features and concepts. With each chapter, you will learn important concepts such as business processes, workflows, e-mails, and notifications. You will also have the opportunity to put your newly-acquired knowledge into practice by following a live JIRA sample implementation.

Chapter 1, Getting Started with JIRA, serves as the starting point of the book and aims to guide you to set up a local copy of a JIRA application that will be used throughout the book. For seasoned JIRA experts, this will both refresh your knowledge and also introduce you to the changes in JIRA 6. By the end of this chapter, you should have a running JIRA application.

Chapter 2, Project Management, covers how to set up projects and project-related administration tasks in JIRA. The concept of schemes is also introduced as it is the core concept of JIRA administration.

Chapter 3, Issue Management, covers everything related to issue creation and the operations that can be performed on an issue (excluding workflow transitions). Furthermore, this chapter touches on the various aspects of issues, as they are the focal point of JIRA. This chapter also serves as an opportunity to show and allow you to set up dummy data that will be used by the sample project.

Chapter 4, Field Management, covers how JIRA collects data through the use of fields and how to expand on this ability through the use of custom fields. This chapter then continues with the various behaviors that can be configured for fields.

Chapter 5, Screen Management, builds on the preceding chapter and explores the concept of screens and how users can create and manage their own screens. This chapter ties in all the previous chapters to show the power behind JIRA's screen design capabilities.

Chapter 6, Workflows and Business Processes, explores the most powerful feature offered by JIRA, workflows. The concept of issue life cycles is introduced, and various aspects of workflows explained. This chapter also explores the relationship between workflows and other various JIRA aspects that have been previously covered, such as screens. The concept of JIRA extensions is also briefly touched in the sample project, using some popular free extensions.

Chapter 7, E-mails and Notifications, focuses on how to get automatic e-mail notifications from JIRA and explores the different settings that can be applied. This is a very important and powerful feature of JIRA and also a critical part of the example project featured in this book. This chapter also ties in the workflow chapter and explains in detail how JIRA manages its notification mechanism.

Chapter 8, Securing JIRA, focuses on the different security control features offered by JIRA. As this topic affects all aspects of JIRA, all previous topics are touched on, explaining how security can be applied to each. It also covers LDAP integration, where you can hook up your JIRA with an existing LDAP system for user management.

Chapter 9, Searching, Reporting, and Analysis, focuses on how data captured in JIRA can be retrieved to provide various types of reporting features. It also covers the changes introduced in JIRA 6.

Chapter 10, JIRA Service Desk, covers the new JIRA Service Desk product, an add-on to transform JIRA into a fully-fledged service desk solution. It looks at installing add-ons, setting up service desks, and defining custom SLA metrics.

Chapter 11, *Advanced Features*, covers advanced features that can help to change your JIRA into more than just a traditional issue tracking system. It looks at how you can run agile projects with JIRA through the use of JIRA Agile and how you can turn JIRA into an effective feedback collection system.

What you need for this book

The installation package used in this book will be the Windows Installer standalone distribution, which you can get directly from Atlassian at `http://www.atlassian.com/software/jira/download`.

You will also need additional software, including Java SDK, which you can get from `http://www.oracle.com/technetwork/java/javase/downloads/index.html` and MySQL, which you can get from `http://dev.mysql.com/downloads`.

Who this book is for

If you want to get started with JIRA, and learn how to install, use, and manage your instance, then this is the perfect book for you.

You will need to be familiar with basic computer operations, specifically the system on which you will use JIRA, and software project management. Familiarity with agile methodologies such as Scrum will also be useful. For the first chapter, we will assume you are familiar with the operating system you are going to install JIRA on.

Conventions

In this book, you will find a number of text styles that distinguish between different kinds of information. Here are some examples of these styles and an explanation of their meaning.

Code words in text, database table names, folder names, filenames, file extensions, pathnames, dummy URLs, user input, and Twitter handles are shown as follows: "open the `server.xml` file in a text editor from the `JIRA_INSTALL/conf` directory."

A block of code is set as follows:

```
<Resource name="mail/JiraMailServer"
  auth="Container"
  type="javax.mail.Session"
  mail.smtp.host="mail.server.host"
  mail.smtp.port="25"
  mail.transport.protocol="smtp"
```

```
    mail.smtp.auth="true"
    mail.smtp.user="username"
    password="password"
/>
```

Any command-line input or output is written as follows:

```
grant all on jiradb.* to 'jirauser'@'localhost' identified by
  'jirauser';
```

New terms and **important words** are shown in bold. Words that you see on the screen, for example, in menus or dialog boxes, appear in the text like this: "select the **Simple Issue Tracking** project template and click on the **Next** button."

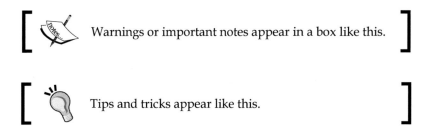

> Warnings or important notes appear in a box like this.

> Tips and tricks appear like this.

Reader feedback

Feedback from our readers is always welcome. Let us know what you think about this book—what you liked or disliked. Reader feedback is important for us as it helps us develop titles that you will really get the most out of.

To send us general feedback, simply e-mail feedback@packtpub.com, and mention the book's title in the subject of your message.

If there is a topic that you have expertise in and you are interested in either writing or contributing to a book, see our author guide at www.packtpub.com/authors.

Customer support

Now that you are the proud owner of a Packt book, we have a number of things to help you to get the most from your purchase.

Downloading the color images of this book

We also provide you with a PDF file that has color images of the screenshots/diagrams used in this book. The color images will help you better understand the changes in the output. You can download this file from `http://www.packtpub.com/sites/default/files/downloads/8125EN_ColoredImages.pdf`.

Errata

Although we have taken every care to ensure the accuracy of our content, mistakes do happen. If you find a mistake in one of our books—maybe a mistake in the text or the code—we would be grateful if you could report this to us. By doing so, you can save other readers from frustration and help us improve subsequent versions of this book. If you find any errata, please report them by visiting `http://www.packtpub.com/submit-errata`, selecting your book, clicking on the **Errata Submission Form** link, and entering the details of your errata. Once your errata are verified, your submission will be accepted and the errata will be uploaded to our website or added to any list of existing errata under the Errata section of that title.

To view the previously submitted errata, go to `https://www.packtpub.com/books/content/support` and enter the name of the book in the search field. The required information will appear under the **Errata** section.

Piracy

Piracy of copyrighted material on the Internet is an ongoing problem across all media. At Packt, we take the protection of our copyright and licenses very seriously. If you come across any illegal copies of our works in any form on the Internet, please provide us with the location address or website name immediately so that we can pursue a remedy.

Please contact us at `copyright@packtpub.com` with a link to the suspected pirated material.

We appreciate your help in protecting our authors and our ability to bring you valuable content.

Questions

If you have a problem with any aspect of this book, you can contact us at `questions@packtpub.com`, and we will do our best to address the problem.

1
Getting Started with JIRA

In this chapter, we will start with a high-level view of JIRA, going through each of the components that make up the overall application. We will then examine the various deployment options, system requirements for JIRA 6, and platforms/ software that are supported. Finally, we will get our hands dirty by installing our very own JIRA 6 from scratch, with the newly improved installation wizard. In the end, we will also cover some post-installation steps, such as setting up SSL to secure your new instance.

By the end of this chapter, you will have learned about the following:

- The overall architecture of JIRA
- The basic hardware and software requirements to deploy and run JIRA
- Platforms and applications supported by JIRA
- Installing JIRA and all of the required software
- Post-installation configuration options to customize your JIRA

The JIRA architecture

Installing JIRA is simple and straightforward. However, it is important for you to understand the components that make up the overall architecture of JIRA and the installation options available. This will help you make an informed decision and be better prepared for future maintenance and troubleshooting.

High-level architecture

Atlassian provides a comprehensive overview of the JIRA architecture at `https://developer.atlassian.com/display/JIRADEV/JIRA+Architectural+Overview`. However, for day-to-day administration and usage of JIRA, we do not need to go into details; the information provided can be overwhelming at first glance. For this reason, we have summarized a high-level overview that highlights the most important components in the architecture, as shown in the following figure:

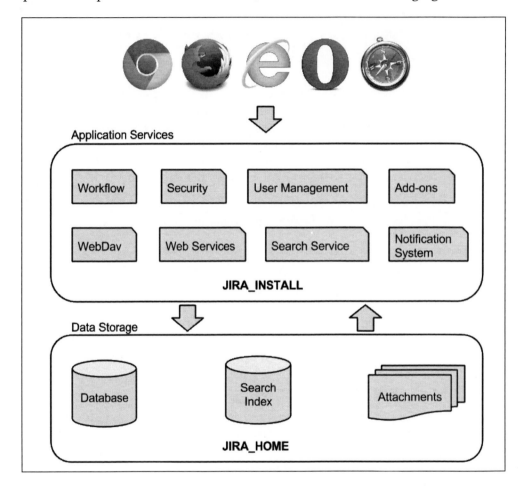

Web browsers

JIRA is a web application, so there is no need for users to install anything on their machines. All they need is a web browser that is compatible with JIRA. The following table summarizes the browser requirements for JIRA:

Browsers	Compatibility
Internet Explorer	8.0 (not supported with JIRA 6.3)
	9.0, 10.0, 11.0
Mozilla Firefox	Latest stable versions
Safari	Latest stable versions on Mac OSX
Google Chrome	Latest stable versions
Mobile	Mobile Safari
	Mobile Chrome

Application services

The application services layer contains all the functions and services provided by JIRA. These services include various business functions, such as workflow and notification, which will be discussed in depth in *Chapter 6, Workflows and Business Processes* and *Chapter 7, E-mails and Notifications*, respectively. Other services such as REST/Web Service provide integration points to other applications The OSGi service provides the base add-on framework to extend JIRA's functionalities.

Data storage

The data storage layer stores persistent data in several places within JIRA. Most business data, such as projects and issues, are stored in a relational database. Content such as uploaded attachments and search indexes are stored in the filesystem in the JIRA_HOME directory, which we will talk about in the next section. The underlying relational database used is transparent to the users, and you can migrate from one database to another with ease as referenced at `https://confluence.atlassian.com/display/JIRA/Switching+Databases`.

The JIRA installation directory

The JIRA installation directory is where you install JIRA. It contains all the executable and configuration files of the application. JIRA neither modifies the contents of the files in this directory during runtime, nor does it store any data files inside the directory; the directory is used primarily for execution. For the remainder of the book, we will be referring to this directory as `JIRA_INSTALL`.

The JIRA home directory

The JIRA home directory contains key data and configuration files that are specific to each JIRA instance, such as JIRA's database connectivity details. As we will see later in this chapter, setting the path to this directory is part of the installation process.

There is a one-to-one relationship between JIRA and this directory. This means each JIRA instance must and can have only one home directory, and each directory can serve only one JIRA instance. In the old days, this directory was sometimes called the data directory. It has now been standardized as the JIRA Home. It is for this reason that, for the rest of the book, we will be referring to this directory as JIRA_HOME.

The JIRA_HOME directory can be created anywhere on your system, or even on a shared drive. It is recommended to use a fast disk drive with low network latency to get the best performance from JIRA.

This separation of data and application makes tasks such as maintenance and future upgrades an easier process. Within JIRA_HOME, there are several subdirectories that contain vital data, as shown in the following table:

Directory	Description
data	This directory contains data that is not stored in the database. For example, uploaded attachment files.
export	This directory contains the automated backup archives created by JIRA. This is different from a manual export executed by a user; manual exports require the user to specify where to store the archive. We will cover this in *Chapter 10, JIRA Service Desk*.
import	This directory contains the backups that can be imported. JIRA will only load the backup files from this directory.
log	This directory contains the JIRA logs.
plugins	This directory is where the installed add-ons are stored. In the previous versions of JIRA, add-ons were installed by copying the add-on files to this directory manually; however in JIRA 5, you will no longer need to do this, unless specifically instructed to do so. Add-ons will be discussed further in the later chapters.
caches	This directory contains cache data that JIRA uses to improve its performance at runtime. For example, search indexes are stored in this directory.
tmp	This directory contains temporary files created at runtime, such as file uploads.

When JIRA is running, the JIRA_HOME directory is locked. When JIRA shuts down, it is unlocked. This locking mechanism prevents multiple JIRA instances from reading/writing to the same JIRA_HOME directory and causing data corruption.

JIRA locks the JIRA_HOME directory by writing a temporary file called jira-home. lock into the root of the directory. During shutdown, this file will be removed. However, sometimes JIRA may fail to remove this file, such as during an ungraceful shutdown. In this case, you can manually remove this locked file to unlock the directory so that you can start up JIRA again.

 You can manually remove the locked file to unlock the JIRA_HOME directory if JIRA fails to clean it up during shutdown.

System requirements

Just like any other software application, there is a set of base requirements that need to be met before you can install and run JIRA. Therefore, it is important for you to be familiar with these requirements so that you can plan out your deployment successfully. Note that these requirements are for a behind-the-firewall deployment, also known as the **JIRA Server**. Atlassian also offers a Cloud-based alternative called **JIRA Cloud**, available at https://www.atlassian.com/software#cloud-products.

The cloud version of JIRA is similar to the behind-the-firewall JIRA deployment in most areas, and it is perfect for organizations that do not want to have the overhead of the initial setup and just want to get up and running quickly. One major limitation of JIRA Cloud is that you cannot use many of the third-party add-ons available. If you want to have all the power and flexibility of the JIRA Server and worry-free server management, you may consider managed hosting for JIRA offered by third-party vendors.

Hardware requirements

For evaluation purposes, where there will only be a small number of users, JIRA will run happily on any server that has a 1.5 GHz processor and 1 GB to 2 GB of RAM. As your JIRA usage grows, a typical server will have a quad core 2 GHz CPU and 4 GB of RAM dedicated to the JIRA application.

For production deployment, as in most applications, it is recommended that you run JIRA on its own dedicated server. There are many factors that you should consider when deciding how much resource to allocate to JIRA, and also keep in mind how JIRA will scale and grow. When deciding on your hardware needs, you should consider the following:

- Number of users in the system
- Number of issues and projects in the system
- Number of concurrent users, especially during peak hours

It can be difficult at times to estimate these figures. As a reference, a server running with 2.0+ GHz of dual/quad CPU and 1 GB of RAM will be sufficient for most instances with around 200 users.

Officially, JIRA only supports x86 hardware and 64-bit derivatives of it. When running JIRA on a 64-bit system, you will be able to allocate more than 4 GB of memory to JIRA, a limit if you are using a 32-bit system. If you are planning to deploy a large instance, it is recommended that you use a 64-bit system.

Software requirements

JIRA has four requirements when it comes to software. It needs a supported operating system and a Java environment. It also needs an application server to host and serve its contents and a database to store all of its data. In the following sections, we will discuss each of these requirements and the options that you have to install and run JIRA with.

Operating systems

JIRA supports most of the major operating systems, so the choice of which operating system to run JIRA on becomes a matter of expertise, comfort, and in most cases, existing organization's IT infrastructure and requirements.

The operating systems supported by Atlassian are Windows and Linux. There is a JIRA distribution for Mac OSX, but it is not officially supported. With both Windows and Linux, Atlassian provides an executable installer wizard package, which bundles all the necessary components to simplify the installation process (only available for standalone distribution).

There are minimal differences when it comes to installing, configuring, and maintaining JIRA on different operating systems. If you do not have any preferences and would like to keep the initial cost down, Linux is a good choice.

Java platforms

JIRA is a Java-based web application, so it needs to have a Java environment installed. This can be a **Java Development Kit (JDK)** or a **Java Runtime Environment (JRE)**. The executable installer that comes with Windows or Linux contains the necessary files and will install and configure the JRE for you. However, if you want to use the archive distributions, you will need to make sure that you have the required Java environment installed and configured.

JIRA 6 requires Java 7 or later. If you run JIRA on an unsupported Java version, including its patch version, you may run into unexpected errors. The following table shows the supported Java versions for JIRA:

Java platforms	Support status
Oracle JDK/JRE	Java 7 — JIRA 6 and later
	Java 8 — JIRA 6.3 and later

Databases

JIRA stores all its data in a relational database. While you can run JIRA with HyperSQL Database (HSQLDB), the in-memory database that comes bundled with JIRA, it is prone to data corruption. You should only use this to set up a new instance quickly for evaluation purposes, where no important data will be stored. For this reason, it is important that you use a proper database such as MySQL for production systems.

Most relational databases available on the market today are supported by JIRA, and there are no differences when you install and configure JIRA. Just like operating systems, your choice of database will come down to your IT staff's expertise, experience, and established corporate standards. If you run Windows as your operating system, then you might probably want to go with the Microsoft SQL Server. On the other hand, if you run Linux, then you should consider Oracle (if you already have a license), MySQL, or PostgreSQL.

The following table summarizes the list of databases that are currently supported by JIRA. It is worth mentioning that both MySQL and PostgreSQL are open source products, so they are excellent options if you are looking to minimize your initial investments.

Database	Support Status
MySQL	MySQL 5.x (excluding 5.0)
	Requires JDBC Connector/J 5.1
PostgreSQL	PostgreSQL 8.4 and newer
	Requires PostgreSQL Driver 8.4.x
Microsoft SQL Server	SQL Server 2005 and newer
	Requires JTDS 1.2.4 driver
Oracle	Oracle 11g
	Requires Oracle 11.2.x driver
HSQLDB	Bundled with standalone distribution, for evaluation only

Take a special note of the driver's requirement on each database, as some drivers that come bundled with the database vendor (for example, the SQL Server) are not supported.

Application servers

JIRA 6 officially only supports Apache Tomcat as the application server. While it is possible to deploy JIRA into other application servers, you will be doing this at your own risk, and is not recommended.

The following table shows the versions of Tomcat that are supported by JIRA 6:

Application server	Support Status
Apache Tomcat	Tomcat 6.0.32 — JIRA 6 and 6.1
	Tomcat 7.0.47 — JIRA 6.2 and newer

Installation options

JIRA comes in two distributions: the standalone and WAR distributions. The only difference is that the standalone distribution comes bundled with Apache Tomcat, an in-memory database, and Java, if you use the executable installer version. The WAR distribution, on the other hand, contains only the JIRA web application.

As you can see, the standalone distribution comes with everything required to get JIRA installed. The standalone distribution comes in two flavors: an executable installer and a ZIP archive. The executable installer provides a wizard-driven interface that will walk you through the entire installation process. It even comes with a Java installer to save you some time. The ZIP archive flavor contains everything except for a Java installer, which means you will have to install Java yourself. You will also need to perform some post-installation steps manually, such as install JIRA as a service. However, you do get the advantage of learning what really goes on under the hood.

The WAR distribution is for more advanced users who are familiar with the Java EE application deployment model. With the WAR distribution, you have to make the necessary changes to the configuration files, build your own deployable JIRA, and then deploy it to an application server; in this case, Tomcat. The advantage of using WAR distribution is that it is very easy for you to version control all the changes you make to the standard distribution files, which makes future upgrades much easier.

Installing and configuring JIRA

Now that you have a good understanding of the overall architecture of JIRA, the basic system requirements, and the various installation options, we are ready to deploy our own JIRA instances.

In the following exercise, we will be installing and configuring a fresh JIRA instance that will be ready for a small production team. We will be performing our installation on a Windows platform with a MySQL database server. If you are planning to use a different platform or database, please refer to the vendor documentation on installing the required software for your platform.

In this exercise, you will:

- Install a fresh instance of JIRA
- Connect JIRA to a MySQL database

We will continue to use this JIRA instance in our subsequent chapters and exercises as we build up our help desk implementation.

For our deployment, we will be using the following:

- JIRA standalone distribution 6.3.1
- MySQL 5.6.19
- Microsoft Windows 7

Installing Java

Since we will be using the installer package with Java bundled, you can skip this section. If you are using the ZIP archive or WAR distribution, you need to make sure you have Java installed on your system.

JIRA 6 requires **Java Runtime Environment (JRE)** version 7 or a newer run. You can verify the version of Java you have by running the following command in a Command Prompt:

`java -version`

The preceding command tells us which version of Java is running on your system as shown in the following screenshot:

If you do not see a similar output, then chances are you do not have Java installed. You will need to perform the following steps to set up your Java environment:

To install JDK on your system, simply perform the following steps:

1. Download the latest JDK from `http://www.oracle.com/technetwork/java/javase/downloads/index.html`.

    At the time of writing, the latest version of Java 8 is JDK 8 Update 11.

2. Double-click on the downloaded installation file to start the installation wizard.

3. Select where you would like to install Java, or you can simply accept the default values. The location where you install JDK will be referred to as `JAVA_HOME` for the rest of the book.

4. Create a new environment variable named JAVA_HOME with the value set to the full path of where you installed Java. You can do this as follows:

    1. Open the System Properties window by holding down your *Windows* key and press the *Pause* key on your keyboard.

    2. Select the **Advanced system settings** option.

    3. Click the **Environment Variable** button from the new popup.

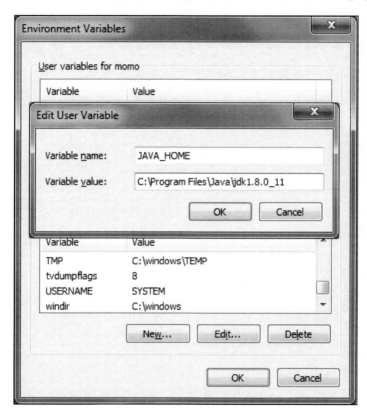

5. Edit the PATH environment variable and append the following to the end of its current value:

    `;%JAVA_HOME%\bin`

6. Test the installation by typing the following command in a new command prompt:

    `java -version`

This will display the version of Java installed if everything is done correctly. In Windows, you have to start a new command prompt after you have added the environment variable to see the change.

Installing MySQL

The next step is to prepare an enterprise database for your JIRA installation. JIRA requires a fresh database. If during the installation process, JIRA detects that the target database already contains any data, it will not proceed. If you already have a database system installed, then you may skip this section.

To install MySQL, simply perform the following steps:

1. Download MySQL from `http://dev.mysql.com/downloads`, select MySQL Community Server, and then select the MSI installer for Windows.

 At the time of writing, the latest version of MySQL is 5.6.19.

2. Double-click on the downloaded installation file to start the installation wizard.

3. Click on **Install MySQL Products** on the welcome screen.

4. Read and accept the license agreement and click the **Next** button.

5. Select the **Server only** option on the next screen. If you are an experienced database administrator, you can choose to customize your installation. Otherwise, just accept the default values for all subsequent screens.

6. Configure the MySQL root user password. The username will be `root`. Do not lose this password, as we will be using it in the next section.

7. Complete the configuration wizard by accepting the default values.

Preparing MySQL for JIRA

Now that you have MySQL installed, you need to first create a user for JIRA to connect MySQL with, and then create a fresh database for JIRA to store all its data:

1. Start the MySQL Command Line Client by navigating to **Start | All Programs | MySQL | MySQL Server 5.6 | MySQL 5.6 Command Line Client**.

2. Enter your MySQL root user password you set during installation.

3. Use the following command to create a database:

```
create database jiradb character set utf8;
```

4. Here, we are creating a database called `jiradb`. You can name the database anything you like. As you will see later in this chapter, this name will be referenced when you connect JIRA to MySQL. We have also set the database to use UTF-8 character encoding, as this is a requirement for JIRA. You need to ensure that the database uses the InnoDB storage engine to avoid data corruption, by using the following command:

```
grant all on jiradb.* to 'jirauser'@'localhost' identified by
   'jirauser';
```

5. We are doing several things here. First, we create a user called `jirauser` and assign the password `jirauser` to him. You should change the username and password to something else.

6. We have also granted all the privileges to the user for the `jiradb` database that we just created so that the user can perform database operations, such as create/drop tables and insert/delete data. If you have named your database something other than `jiradb` in step 5, then make sure you change the command so that it uses your database name.

7. This allows you to control the fact that only authorized users (specified in the preceding command) are able to access the JIRA database to ensure data security and integrity.

8. To verify your setup, exit the current interactive session by issuing the following command:

```
quit;
```

9. Start a new interactive session with your newly created user:

```
mysql -u jirauser -p
```

10. You will be prompted for a password, which you have set up in the preceding command as `jirauser`.

11. Use the following command:

```
show databases;
```

12. This will list all the databases that are currently accessible by the logged-in user. You should see `jiradb` among the list of databases.

13. Examine the `jiradb` database by issuing the following commands:

```
use jiradb;
show tables;
```

14. The first command connects you to the `jiradb` database, so all of your subsequent commands will be executed against the correct database.

15. The second command lists all the tables that exist in the `jiradb` database. Right now, the list should be empty, since tables have been created for JIRA, but don't worry — as soon as we connect to JIRA, all the tables will automatically be created.

Installing JIRA

With the Java environment and database prepared, you can now move on to installing JIRA. Normally, there are only two steps:

- Download and install the JIRA application
- Run through the JIRA setup wizard

Obtaining and installing JIRA

The first step is to download the latest stable release of JIRA. You can download Atlassian JIRA from `http://www.atlassian.com/software/jira/download`.

The Atlassian website will detect the operating system you are using and automatically suggest the installation package for you to download. If you intend to install JIRA on a different operating system than the one you are currently on, make sure you select the correct operating system package.

As mentioned earlier, with Windows, there is a Windows installer package and a self-extracting ZIP package. For the purpose of this exercise, we will use the installer package (Windows 64-bit Installer):

1. Double-click on the downloaded installation file to start the installation wizard, and click the **Next** button to continue.

2. Select the **Custom Install** option and click the **Next** button to continue. Using the custom installation will let us decide where to install JIRA and also many configuration options.

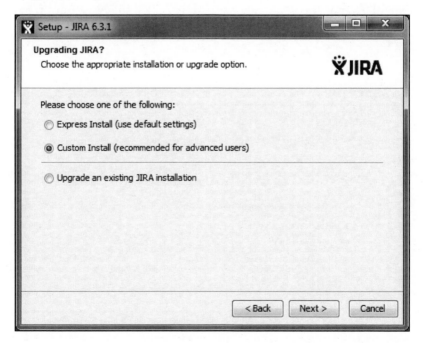

3. Select the directory where JIRA will be installed. This will become the JIRA_ INSTALL directory. Click the **Next** button to continue.

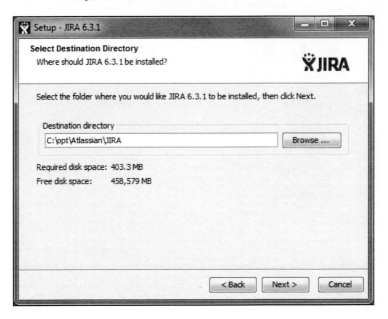

4. Select where JIRA will store its data files, such as attachments and log files. This will become the JIRA_HOME directory. Click the **Next** button to continue.

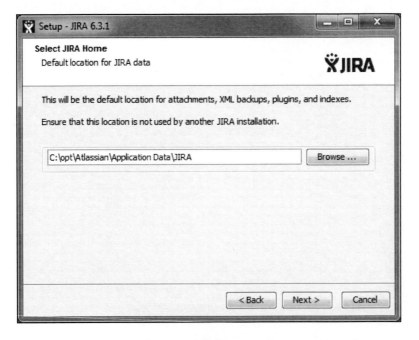

5. Select where you would like to create shortcuts to the Start menu, and click the **Next** button to continue.

6. In the **Configure TCP Ports** step, we need to select the port on which JIRA will be listening for incoming connections. By default, JIRA will run on port 8080. If 8080 is already taken by another application or you want JIRA to run on a different port such as port 80, select the **Set custom value for HTTP and Control ports** option and specify the port numbers you want to use. Click the **Next** button to continue.

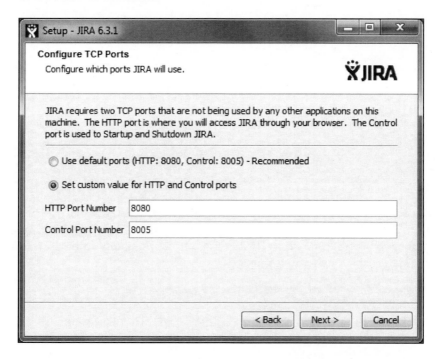

7. For the last step, select whether you would like JIRA to run as a service. If you enable this option, JIRA will be installed as a system service and can be configured to start automatically with the server.

8. Click the **Install** button to start the installation.

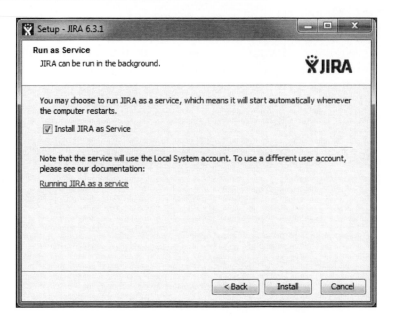

9. Once the installation is complete, check the **Launch JIRA 6.3.1 in browser** option and click **Finish**. This will close the installation wizard and open up your web browser to access JIRA. This might take a few minutes to load as JIRA starts up for the first time.

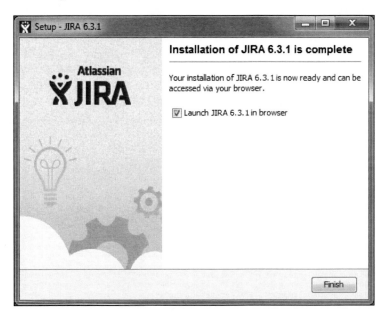

Since we need to install the MySQL database driver for JIRA, we are launching JIRA in the browser now to verify that the installation was successful.

Installing MySQL driver

JIRA does not come bundled with the MySQL database driver, so we have to install it manually. You can download the required driver from `http://dev.mysql.com/downloads/connector/j/`. Once downloaded, you can install the driver by copying the driver jar file into the `JIRA_INSTALL/lib` directory. After that, you need to restart JIRA. If you have installed JIRA as a Windows service in step 9, please see the *Starting and stopping JIRA* section.

 Make sure you select the **Platform Independent** option and download the jar or tar archive.

The JIRA setup wizard

JIRA comes with an easy-to-use setup wizard that will walk you through the installation and configuration process in six simple steps. You will be able to configure the database connections, default language, and much more. You can access the wizard by opening `http://localhost:<port number>` in your browser, where the `<port number>` is the number you have assigned to JIRA in step 6 of the installation.

In the first step of the wizard, you will be asked to select **Server Language** and what database JIRA should connect to.

The server language will determine what language will be used when users access JIRA. You will see that as soon as you make a change from the drop-down list, JIRA will automatically change its onscreen text to the selected language.

The database connection setting will determine what database JIRA will use. If you select the **Built In** option, JIRA will use its bundled in-memory database, which is good for evaluation purposes. If you want to use a proper database, such as in our case, you should select the **My Own Database** option.

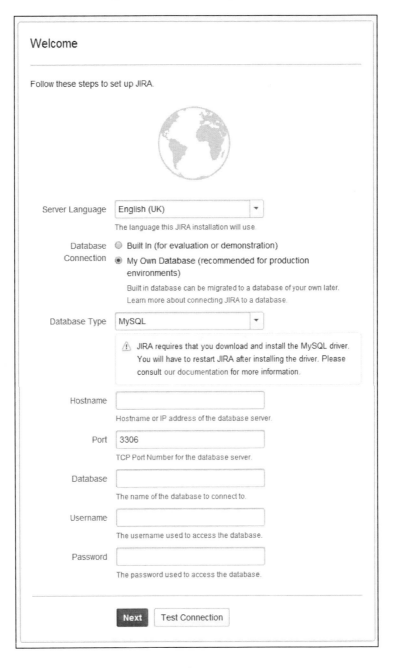

The **Built In** option is great to get JIRA up and running quickly for evaluation purposes.

After you have selected the **My Own Database** option, the wizard will expand for you to provide the database connection details. If you do not have the necessary database driver installed, JIRA will prompt you for it, as shown in the preceding screenshot.

Once you have filled in the details for your database, it is a good idea to first click on the **Test Connection** button to verify that JIRA is able to connect to the database. If everything is set up correctly, JIRA will report back with a success message. You should be able to move onto the next step by clicking the **Next** button. This may take a few minutes, as JIRA will now create all the necessary database objects. Once this is done, you will be taken to step 2 of the wizard.

In the second step, you will need to provide some basic details about this JIRA instance. Once you have filled in the required properties, click on **Next** to move on to step 3 of the wizard.

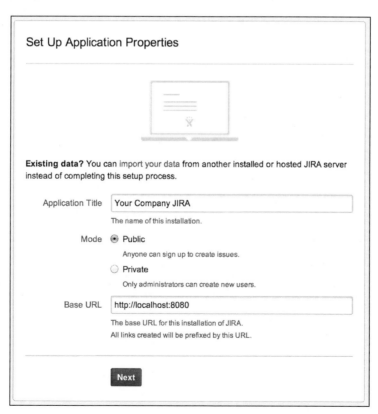

In the third step, you need to select whether you want to install only JIRA, or if you would like to install additional add-ons. In this example, we will be installing JIRA only, so select the **I'm using JIRA for project tracking** option and click on **Next**. You can install these additional add-ons later.

In the fourth step, we need to provide a license key for JIRA. If you have already obtained a license from Atlassian, you can select **I have a JIRA key** option. Then cut and paste it into the **License Key** text box. If you do not have a license, you can generate an evaluation license by selecting either **I have an account but no key** option if you have an account on `https://my.atlassian.com`, or by selecting **I don't have an account** to register a new account with Atlassian. Evaluation license will grant you access to JIRA's full set of features for one month.

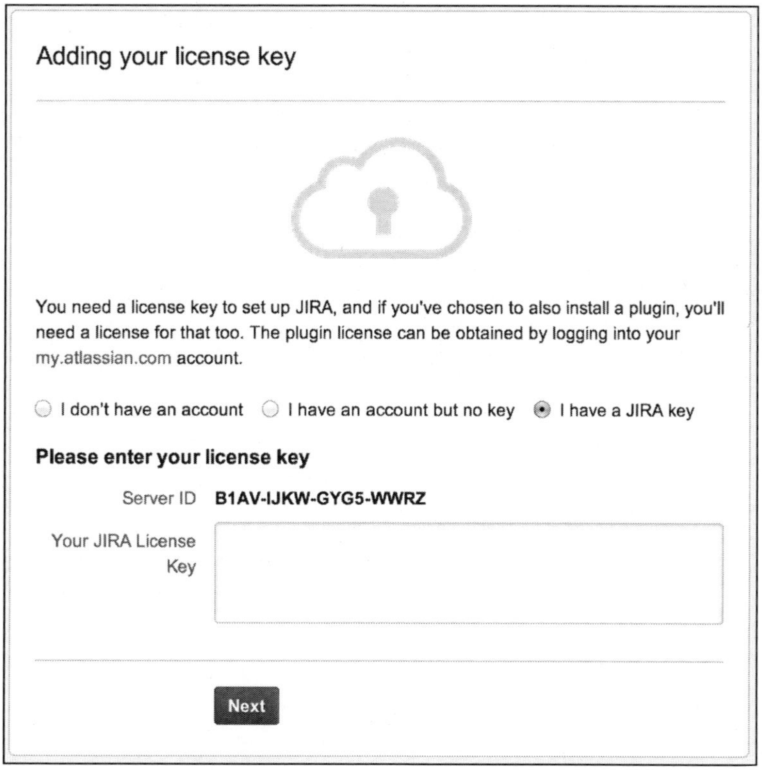

Adding your license key

You need a license key to set up JIRA, and if you've chosen to also install a plugin, you'll need a license for that too. The plugin license can be obtained by logging into your my.atlassian.com account.

○ I don't have an account   ○ I have an account but no key   ● I have a JIRA key

Please enter your license key

Server ID   **B1AV-IJKW-GYG5-WWRZ**

Your JIRA License Key

Next

In the fifth step, you will be setting up the administrator account for JIRA. It is important that you keep the account details somewhere safe and do not lose the password. Since JIRA only stores the hashed value of the password instead of the actual password itself, you will not be able to retrieve it. However, there are methods for you to reset the password if you do lose it, as we will see in *Chapter 10, JIRA Service Desk*. Fill in the administrator account details and click on **Next** to move on to the last step.

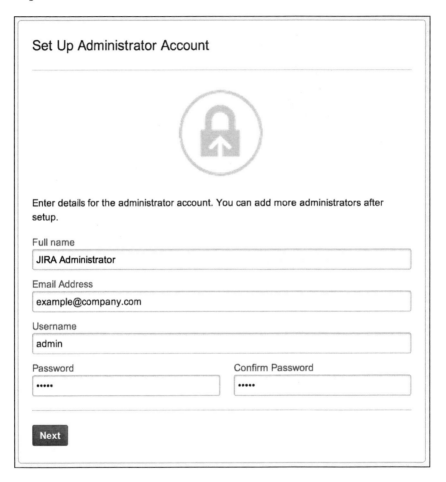

This account is important and it can help you troubleshoot and fix problems later on. Do not lose it!

In the sixth and final step, you can set up your e-mail server details. JIRA will use the information configured here to send out notification e-mails. Notification is a very powerful feature in JIRA and one of the primary methods for JIRA to communicate with the users. If you do not have your e-mail server information handy, you can skip this step now by selecting the **Later** option and clicking on **Finish**. You can configure your e-mail server settings later, as you will see in *Chapter 7, E-mails and Notifications*.

Congratulations! You have successfully completed your JIRA setup, and you will be taken directly to your new JIRA instance.

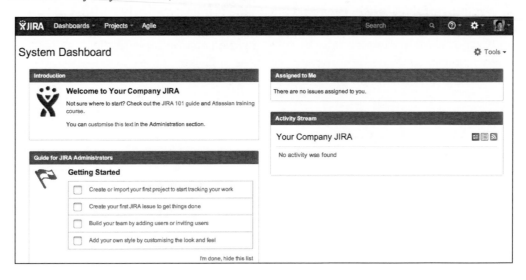

Starting and stopping JIRA

Since JIRA is installed as a Windows service, you can start, stop, and restart it via the Windows services console, by navigating to **Start** | **Control Panel** | **Administrative Tools** | **Services**. In the services console, look for Atlassian JIRA, and you will be able to stop and start the application, as shown in the following screenshot:

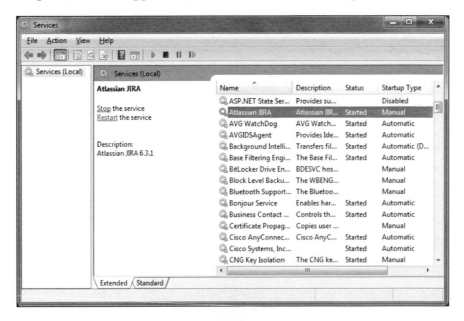

Post-installation configurations

The post-installation configuration steps are optional, depending on your needs and environment. If you set up JIRA for evaluation purposes, you probably do not need to perform any of the following steps, but it is always a good practice to be familiar with these as a reference.

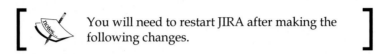

> You will need to restart JIRA after making the following changes.

Increasing JIRA's memory

The default memory setting for JIRA is usually sufficient for a small-to medium-sized deployment. As JIRA's adoption rate increases, you will find that the amount of memory allocated by default is no longer enough. If JIRA is running as a Windows service we described in this chapter, you can increase the memory as follows:

1. Find the JIRA Windows service name. You can do this by going to Windows services console and double clicking on **Atlassian JIRA** service. The service name will be the part after //RS// in the **Path to executable** field, for example JIRA150215215627.

2. Open a new command prompt and change the current working directory to `JIRA_INSTALL/bin` directory.

3. Run the following command, substitute in the actual service name for JIRA:

   ```
   tomcat7w //ES//<JIRA Windows service name>
   ```

4. Select the **Java** tab, update the **Initial memory pool** and **Maximum memory pool** size, and click on **OK**.

5. Restart JIRA to apply the change.

If you are not running JIRA as a Windows service, you need to open the setenv. bat file (for Windows) or the setenv.sh (for Linux) file in the JIRA_INSTALL/bin directory. Then, locate the following lines:

```
set JVM_MINIMUM_MEMORY="384m"
set JVM_MAXIMUM_MEMORY="768m"
```

Change the value for the two parameters and restart JIRA. Normally, 4 GB (4096m) of memory is enough to support a fairly large instance of JIRA used by hundreds of users.

  Make sure you have enough physical RAM available before allocating instances to JIRA.

Changing JIRA's port number and context path

As a part of the installation process, the installation wizard prompted us which port JIRA should listen for incoming connections. If you have accepted the default value, it is port 8080. You can change the port setting by locating and opening the `server.xml` file in a text editor in the `JIRA_INSTALL/conf` directory. Let's examine the relevant contents of this file:

```
<Server port="8005" shutdown="SHUTDOWN">
```

This line specifies the port for command to shutdown JIRA/Tomcat. By default, it is port 8005. If you already have an application that is running on that port (usually another Tomcat instance), you need to change this to a different port:

```
<Connector port="8080" protocol="HTTP/1.1">
```

This line specifies which port JIRA/Tomcat will be running on. By default, it is port 8080. If you already have an application that is running on that port, or if the port is unavailable for some reason, you need to change it to another available port:

```
<Context path="/jira" docBase="${catalina.home}/atlassian-jira"
  reloadable="false" useHttpOnly="true">
```

This line allows you to specify the context that JIRA will be running under. By default, the value is empty, which means JIRA will be accessible from `http://hostname:portnumber`. If you decide to specify a context, the URL will be `http://hostname:portnumber/context`. In our example here, JIRA will be accessible from `http://localhost:8080/jira`.

Configuring HTTPS

By default, JIRA runs with a standard, non-encrypted HTTP protocol. This is acceptable if you are running JIRA in a secured environment, such as an internal network. However, if you plan to open up access to JIRA over the Internet, you will need to tighten up security by encrypting sensitive data, such as usernames and passwords that are being sent, by enabling HTTPS (HTTP over SSL).

For a standalone installation, you will need to perform the following tasks:

- Obtain and install a certificate
- Enable HTTPS on your application server (Tomcat)
- Redirect traffic to HTTPS

First, you need to get a digital certificate. This can be obtained from a certification authority, such as VeriSign (CA certificate), or a self-signed certificate generated by you. A CA certificate will not only encrypt data for you, but also identify your copy of JIRA to the users. A self-signed certificate is useful when you do not have a valid CA certificate and you are only interested in setting up HTTPS for encryption. Since a self-signed certificate is not signed by a Certification Authority, it is unable to identify your site to the public, and users will be prompted with a warning that the site is untrusted when they first visit it. However, for evaluation purposes, a self-signed certificate will suffice until you can get a proper CA certificate.

For the purpose of this exercise, we will create a self-signed certificate to illustrate the complete process. If you have a CA certificate, you can skip the following steps.

Java comes with a handy tool for certificate management called **keytool**, which can be found in the JIRA_HOME\jre\bin directory if you are using the installer package. If you are using your own Java installation, then you can find it in JAVA_HOME\bin.

To generate a self-signed certificate, run the following commands from a command prompt:

```
keytool -genkey -alias tomcat -keyalg RSA
keytool -export -alias tomcat -file file.cer
```

This will create a keystore (if one does not already exist) and export the self-signed certificate (file.cer). When you run the first command, you will be asked to set the password for the keystore and Tomcat. You need to use the same password for both. The default password is changeit. You can specify a different password of your choice, but you then have to let JIRA/Tomcat know, as we will see later.

Now that you have your certificate ready, you need to import it into your trust store for Tomcat to use. Again, you will use the keytool application in Java:

```
keytool -import -alias tomcat -file file.cer
  JIRA_HOME\jre\lib\security\cacerts
```

This will import the certificate into your trust store, which can be used by JIRA/Tomcat to set up HTTPS.

To enable HTTPS on Tomcat, open the server.xml file in a text editor from the JIRA_INSTALL/conf directory. Locate the following configuration snippet:

```
<Connector port="8443" maxHttpHeaderSize="8192" SSLEnabled="true"
maxThreads="150" minSpareThreads="25" maxSpareThreads="75"
enableLookups="false" disableUploadTimeout="true"
acceptCount="100" scheme="https" secure="true"
```

```
clientAuth="false" sslProtocol="TLS"
  useBodyEncodingForURI="true"/>
```

This enables HTTPS for JIRA/Tomcat on port 8443. If you have selected a different password for your keystore, you will have to add the following line to the end of the preceding snippet, before the closing tag:

```
keystorePass="<password value>"
```

The last step is to set up JIRA so that it automatically redirects from a non-HTTP request to an HTTPS request. Find and open the web.xml file in the JIRA_INSTALL/atlassian-jira/WEB-INF directory. Then, add the following snippet to the end of the file, before the closing </web-app> tag:

```
<security-constraint>
  <web-resource-collection>
    <web-resource-name>all-except-attachments</web-resource-name>
    <url-pattern>*.js</url-pattern>
    <url-pattern>*.jsp</url-pattern>
    <url-pattern>*.jspa</url-pattern>
    <url-pattern>*.css</url-pattern>
    <url-pattern>/browse/*</url-pattern>
  </web-resource-collection>
  <user-data-constraint>
    <transport-guarantee>CONFIDENTIAL</transport-guarantee>
  </user-data-constraint>
</security-constraint>
```

Now, when you access JIRA with a normal HTTP URL, such as http://localhost:8080/jira, you will be automatically redirected to its HTTPS equivalent, https://localhost:8443/jira.

Summary

JIRA is a powerful and yet simple application, as reflected by its straightforward installation procedures. You have a wide variety of options to choose how you would like to install and configure your copy. You can mix and match different aspects, such as operating systems and databases, to best suit your requirements. The best part is that you can have a setup that is comprised entirely of open source software that will bring down your cost and provide you with a reliable infrastructure at the same time.

In the next chapter, we will start to explore various aspects of JIRA. The following chapters, starting with projects, will talk about key concepts in any JIRA installation.

2
Project Management

JIRA initially started off as a bug tracking system, helping software development teams to better track and manage the problems/issues in their projects. Over the years, JIRA has improved its features to add support for Scrum and Kanban through the JIRA Agile add-on. This enables projects to be managed through both the traditional waterfall model and newer agile methodologies.

In this chapter, we will start with a high-level view of the overall hierarchy on how data is structured in JIRA. We will then take a look at the various user interfaces that JIRA has for working with projects, both as an administrator and an everyday user. We will also introduce permissions for the first time in the context of projects and will expand on this in later chapters.

By the end of this chapter, you will learn the following:

- How JIRA structures content
- Different user interfaces for project management in JIRA
- How to create new projects in JIRA
- How to import data from other systems into JIRA
- How to manage and configure a project
- How to manage components and versions

The JIRA hierarchy

Like most other information systems, JIRA organizes its data in a hierarchical structure. At the lowest level, we have **field**, which are used to hold raw information. Then the next level up, we have **issue**, which are like a unit of work to be performed.

An issue will belong to a project, which defines the context of the issue. Finally, we have **project category**, which logically group similar projects together. We will discuss each of these levels in the forthcoming sections. The figure in the following illustrates the hierarchy we just talked about:

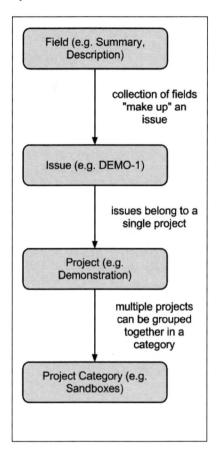

Project category

Project category is a logical grouping for projects, usually of similar nature. Project category is optional. Projects do not have to belong to any category in JIRA. When a project does not belong to any category, it is considered uncategorized. The categories themselves do not contain any information; they serve as a way to organize all your projects in JIRA, especially when you have many of them.

Project

In JIRA, a **project** is a collection of issues. Projects provide the background context for issues by letting users know where issues should be created. Users will be members of a project, working on issues in the project. Most configurations in JIRA, such as permissions and screen layouts, are all applied on the project level.

It is important to remember that projects are not limited to software development projects that need to deliver a product. They can be anything logical, such as the following:

- Company department or team
- Software development projects
- Products or systems
- A risk register

Issue

Issues represent work to be performed. From a functional perspective, an issue is the base unit for JIRA. Users create issues and assign them to other people to be worked on. Project leaders can generate reports on issues to see how everything is tracking. In a sense, you can say JIRA is issue-centric.

We will be looking at issues in more detail in *Chapter 3, Issue Management*. For now, you just need to remember three things:

- An issue can belong to only one project
- There can be many different types of issues
- An issue contains many fields that hold values for the issue

Field

Fields are the most basic unit of data in JIRA. They hold data for issues and give meaning to them. Fields in JIRA can be broadly categorized into two distinctive categories, namely, system fields and custom fields. They come in many different forms, such as text fields, drop-down lists, and user pickers. Fields and the topics related to them are discussed in more depth in *Chapter 4, Field Management*. For now, you just need to remember three things:

- Fields hold values for issues
- Fields can have behaviors (hidden or mandatory)
- Fields can have a view and structure (text field or drop-down list)

Project permissions

Before we start working with projects in JIRA, we need to first understand a little bit about permissions. **Permission** is a big topic, and we will be covering that in detail in *Chapter 8, Securing JIRA*. For now, we will briefly talk about the permissions related to creating and deleting, administering, and browsing projects.

In JIRA, users with the JIRA administrator permission will be able to create and delete projects. By default, users in the **jira-administrators** group have this permission, so the administrator user we created during the installation process in *Chapter 1, Getting Started with JIRA*, will be able to create new projects. We will be referring to this user and any other users with this permission as **JIRA Administrator**.

For any given project, users with the **Administer Project** permission for that project will be able to administer the project's configuration settings. As we will see in the later sections of this chapter, this means that users with this permission will have access to the Project Administration interface for a given project. This allows them to update the project's details, manage versions and components, and decide who will be able to access this project. We will be referring to users with this permission as the Project Administrator. By default, the JIRA Administrator will have this permission.

If a user needs to browse the contents of a given project, then he must have the **Browse Project** permission for that project. This means that the user will have access to the Project Browser interface for the project. By default, the JIRA Administrator will have this permission.

As you have probably realized already, one of the key differences in the three permissions is that the JIRA Administrator's permission is global, which means it is global across all projects in JIRA. The Administer Project and Browse Project permissions are project-specific. A user may have the Administer Project permission for project A, but only Browse Project permission for project B. As we will see in *Chapter 8, Securing JIRA*, this separation of permissions allows you to set up your JIRA instance in such a way that you can effectively delegate permission controls, so you can still centralize control on who can create and delete projects, but not get over-burdened with having to manually manage each project on its own settings. Now with this in mind, let's first take a quick look at JIRA from the JIRA Administrator user's view.

Creating projects

To create a new project, the easiest way is to select the **Create Project** menu option from the **Projects** drop-down menu from the top navigation bar. This will bring up the create project dialog. Note that, as we explained, you need to be a **JIRA Administrator** (such as the user we created during installation) to create projects. This option is only available if you have the permission.

When creating a new project in JIRA, we need to first select the type of project we want to create, from a list of **project templates**. Project template, as the name suggests, acts as a blueprint template for the project. Each project template has a predefined set of configurations such as issue type and workflows. For example, if we select the **Simple Issue Tracking** project template, and click on the **Next** button.

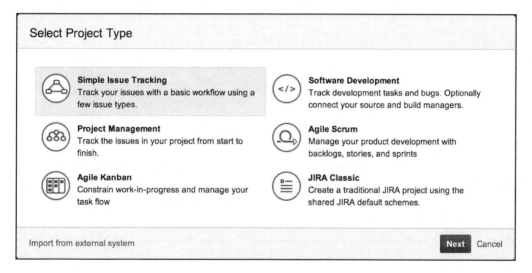

Select Project Type

Simple Issue Tracking
Track your issues with a basic workflow using a few issue types.

Software Development
Track development tasks and bugs. Optionally connect your source and build managers.

Project Management
Track the issues in your project from start to finish.

Agile Scrum
Manage your product development with backlogs, stories, and sprints

Agile Kanban
Constrain work-in-progress and manage your task flow

JIRA Classic
Create a traditional JIRA project using the shared JIRA default schemes.

Import from external system

Next   Cancel

JIRA will show us the issue types and workflow for the **Simple Issue Tracking** template. If we select a different template, then a different set of configurations will be applied. For those who have been using JIRA since JIRA 5 or earlier, **JIRA Classic** is the template that has the classic issue types and classic JIRA workflow. Clicking on the **Select** button will accept and select the project template.

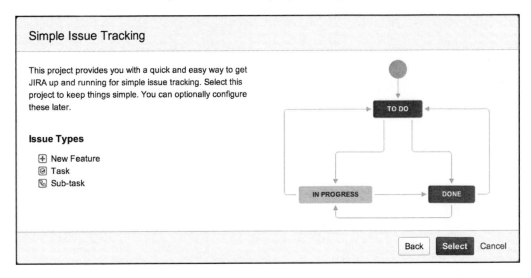

For the last step, we need to provide the new project's details. JIRA will help you validate the details, such as making sure the project key conforms to the configured format. After filling in the project details, click on the **Submit** button to create the new project.

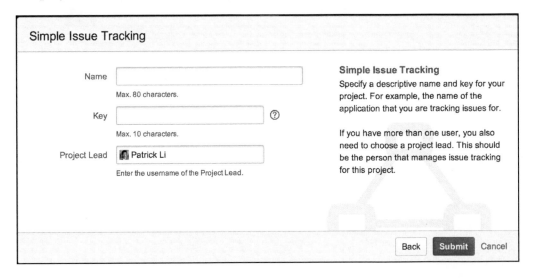

The following table lists the information you need to provide when creating a new project:

Field	Description
Name	A unique name for the project.
Key	A unique identity key for the project. As you type the name of your project, JIRA will auto-fill the key based on the name, but you can change the autogenerated key with one of your own. Starting from JIRA 6.1, the project key is not changeable after the project is created. The project key will also become the first part of the issue key for issues created in the project.
Project Lead	The lead of the project can be used to auto-assign issues. Each project can have only one lead. This option is available only if you have more than one user in JIRA.

Once you have created the new project, you will be taken to the **Project Browser** interface, which we will discuss in the forthcoming sections.

Changing the project key format

When creating new projects, you may find that the project key needs to be in a specific format and length. By default, the project key needs to adhere to the following criteria:

- Contain at least two characters
- Cannot be more than 10 characters in length
- Contain only characters, that is, no numbers

You can change the default format to have less restrictive rules.

 These changes are for advanced users only.

First, to change the project key length perform the following steps:

1. Browse to the JIRA Administration console.
2. Select the **System** tab and then the **General Configuration** option.
3. Click on the **Edit Settings** button.

4. Change the value for the **Maximum project key size** option to a value between 2 and 255 (inclusive), and click on the **Update** button to apply the change.

Changing the project key format is a bit more complicated. JIRA uses a regular expression to define what the format should be. To change the project key format use the following steps:

1. Browse to the JIRA Administration console.
2. Select the **System** tab and then the **General Configuration** option.
3. Click on the **Advanced Settings** button.
4. Hover over and click on the value (**([A-Z][A-Z]+)**) for the **jira.projectkey. pattern** option.
5. Enter the new regular expression for the project key format, and click on **Update**.

There are a few rules when it comes to setting the project key format:

*   The key must start with a letter
*   All letters must be uppercase, that is (A-Z)
*   Only letters, numbers, and the underscore character can be used

Importing data into JIRA

JIRA supports importing data directly from many popular issue-tracking systems, such as Bugzilla, GitHub, and Trac. All the importers have a wizard-driven interface, guiding you through a series of steps. These steps are mostly identical with few differences. Generally speaking, there are four steps when importing data into JIRA that are as follows:

1. Select your source data. For example, if you are importing from CSV, it will select the CSV file. If you are importing from Bugzilla, it will provide Bugzilla database details.
2. Select a destination project where imported issues will go into. This can be an existing project or a new project created on the fly.
3. Map old system fields to JIRA fields.
4. Map old system field values to JIRA field values. This is usually required for select-based fields, such as the priority field, or select list custom fields.

Importing data through CSV

JIRA comes with a CSV importer, which lets you import data in the comma-separated value format. This is a useful tool if you want to import data from a system that is not directly supported by JIRA, since most systems are able to export their data in CSV.

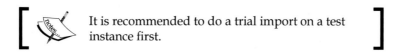 It is recommended to do a trial import on a test instance first.

Use the following steps to import data through a CSV file:

1. Select the **Import External Project** option from the **Projects** drop-down menu.

2. Click on the **Import from Comma-separated Values (CSV)** importer option. This will start the import wizard.

3. First you need to select the CSV file that contains the data you want to import, by clicking on the **Choose File** button.

4. After you selected the source file, you can also expand the **Advanced** section to select the file encoding and delimiter used in the CSV file. There is also a **Use an existing configuration** option, we will talk about this later in this section.

5. Click on the **Next** button to proceed.

6. For the second step, you need to select the project you want to import our data into. You can also select the **Create New** option to create a new project on the fly.

7. If your CSV file contains date-related data, make sure you enter the format used in the **Date format** field.

8. Click on the **Next** button to proceed.

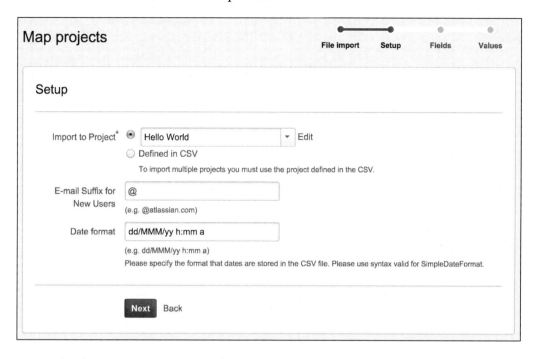

9. For the third step, you need to map the CSV fields to the fields in JIRA. Not all fields need to be mapped. If you do not want to import a particular field, simply leave it as **Don't map this field** for the corresponding **JIRA** field selection.

10. For fields that contain data that needs to be mapped manually, such as for select list fields, you need to check the **Map field value** option. This will let you map the CSV field value to the JIRA field value, so they can be imported correctly. If you do not manually map these values, they will be copied over as is.

11. Click on the **Next** button to proceed.

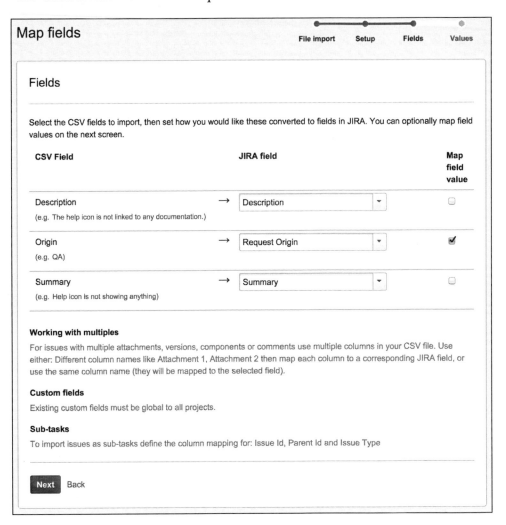

12. For the last step, you need to map the CSV field value to the JIRA field value. This step is only required if you have checked the **Map field value** option for a field in step 10.

13. Enter the JIRA field value for each CSV field value.

14. Once you are done with mapping field values, click on the **Begin Import** button to start the actual import process. Depending on the size of your data, this may take some time to complete.

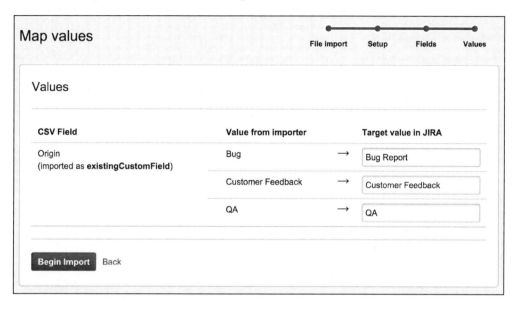

15. Once the import process completes, you will get a confirmation message that tells you the number of issues that have been imported. This number should match the number of records you have in the CSV file.

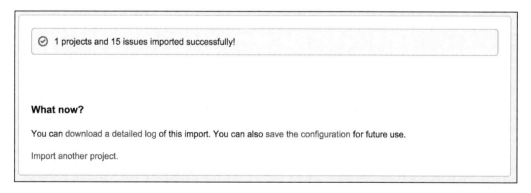

On the last confirmation screen, you can click on the **download a detailed log** link to download the full log file containing all the information for the import process. This is particularly useful if the import was not successful.

You can also click on the **save the configuration** link, which will generate a text file containing all the mappings you have done for this import. Even if you need to run a similar import in the future, you can use this import file so that you will not need to manually re-map everything again. To use this configuration file, check the **Use an existing configuration file** option in step one.

As we can see, JIRA's project importer makes importing data from other systems simple and straightforward. However, you must not underestimate its complexity. For any data migration, especially if you are moving off one platform and onto a new one, such as JIRA, there are a number of factors you need to consider and prepare for. The following list summarizes some of the common tasks for most data migrations:

- Evaluate the size and impact. This includes how many records you will be importing and also the number of users that will be impacted by this.

- Perform a full gap analysis between the old system and JIRA, such as how the fields will map from one to the other.

- Set up test environments for you to run test imports on to make sure you have your mappings done correctly.

- Involve your end users as early as possible, and have them review your test results.

- Prepare and communicate any outages and support procedure post-migration.

Project user interfaces

There are two distinctive interfaces for projects in JIRA. The first interface is designed for everyday users, providing useful information on how the project is going with graphs and statistics, called Project Browser.

The second interface is designed for project administrators to control project configuration settings, such as permissions and workflows, called Project Administration.

Since you created your first project, the first interface you see will be Project Browser, we will start our discussion around this interface and then move on to the Project Administration interface.

Project Browser

Project Browser is the interface most users will be using with JIRA. It acts as the home page of the project, providing useful information, such as issue statistics, recent user activities, and information from other connected systems, such as source control and continuous integration.

To access the Project Browser interface, simply select the project from the Project's drop-down or the project's list via the **View All Projects** option. Note that you will also need to have the Browse Project permission.

The preceding screenshot shows an example project with sample data such as release dates already set up, as shown in the following screenshot:

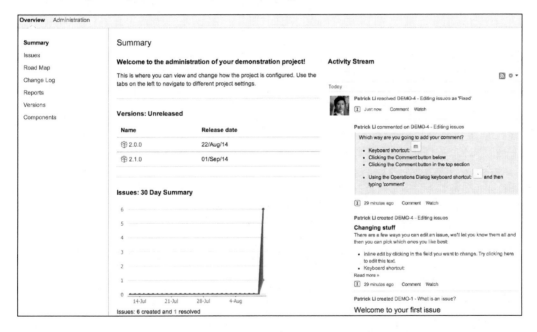

The Project Browser is made up of several tabs and the description of these tabs are as follows:

Project Browser tab	Description
Summary	Displays a quick overview of the project. You can also access predefined reports and search filters directly here.
Issues	Displays a breakdown of issues in the project grouped by attributes, such as priority and status.
Road Map	Displays all the unreleased versions for the project.
Change Log	Displays all the released versions for the project.
Versions	Displays the summary of unreleased versions of the project. This tab is only available when versions are configured.
Components	Displays the summary of components and their related issues. This tab is only available when components are configured for the project.
Labels	Displays all the available labels in the project. Labels can be assigned to issues as tags.

The Summary tab

The **Summary** tab provides you with a single-page view into the project you are working on. It provides you with a quick glance of the project with key information, including the following:

- Project summary description
- A 30-day summary graph showing created issues (red) versus resolved issues (green)
- Unreleased versions and their release dates
- Recent activities performed on the issues in this project
- Summary graph showing issues created versus issues resolved

The Issues tab

The **Issues** tab provides users with a nice breakdown of issues within the project. Issues are broken down and grouped by several key factors, such as priority and assignee, giving users a quick overview of the project's state. For example, **Unresolved: By Assignee** lets you know how many open issues are being assigned to each user, allowing the project team to better plan their resource allocation, as shown in the following screenshot:

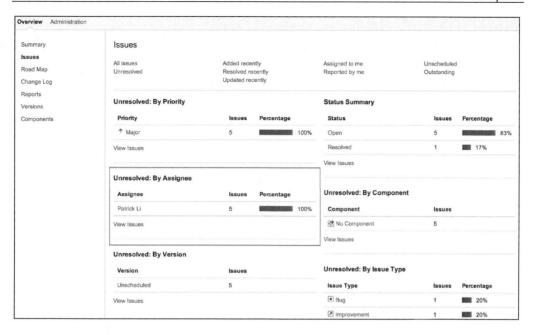

The Road Map tab

The **Road Map** tab breaks down issues based on the versions they belong to. If you have set up versions in JIRA, then this tab will show you the upcoming unreleased versions and issues that need to be completed before the version can be released.

The Change Log tab

Similar to the **Road Map** tab, the **Change Log** tab breaks down issues based on versions. The difference is that the **Change Log** tab shows the versions that have already been released. This is very useful when you have to go back and check what has been achieved and completed for each of the past versions that provide you with a lot of changes.

The Versions and Components tab

The **Versions** and **Components** tab list all the available versions and components that have been configured for this project, respectively. If the user is also the project administrator, then there will be links for the user to add new versions and components, respectively.

The Source and Reviews tab

The **Source** and **Reviews** tab require you to have the Altassian FishEye, Stash, and Crucible applications to be installed. Once installed, the tabs will pull in data from the applications and display them. If you do not have the required applications installed and configured, the tabs will prompt you to install the applications. FishEye and Stash are great tools to manage your code repositories — from browsing code contents to reviewing commits and changes. Stash is specially designed to support **distributed version control system (DVCS)** repositories such as Git. Crucible is another application from Atlassian that allows your developers to collaborate with code reviews. Installing and configuring FishEye, Stash, and Crucible are beyond the scope of this book.

Project Administration

The Project Administration interface is where project administrators can manage the settings and configurations of their projects. For example, you can change the project's name, select what issue types will be available for the project, and manage a list of components within the project. Only users with the Administer Projects permission for a given project will be able to access this interface.

To access the Project Administration interface use the following steps:

1. Go to the project browser for the project you want to administer.
2. Select the **Administration** tab. If you do not see the tab, then you do not have the necessary permission.

From the Project Administration interface, if you are a JIRA Administrator (such as the user created during installation) you will be able to perform the following key operations:

- Update project details, such as project name, description, and avatar
- Manage what users see when working on the project, such as issue types, fields, and screens
- Control permission settings and notifications
- Manage the list of available components and versions

 If you are not a JIRA Administrator (that is, you do not have the JIRA Administrator global permission), you can only view the current project's configuration. We will cover permissions in *Chapter 8, Securing JIRA*.

The preceding key operations are shown in the following screenshot:

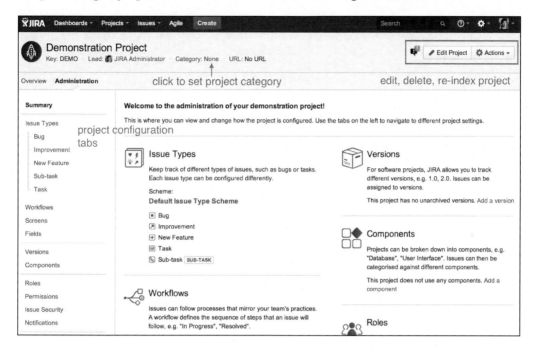

JIRA 6 has made many improvements to this interface. As we will see in later chapters when talking about configurations such as issue types and screens, not only does JIRA tell us what configuration schemes are being used by the project, but also their details. It also lets us make changes on the spot.

The Summary tab

The first group consists of a single tab, the **Summary** tab. On this tab, JIRA displays a single-page view on all the current configuration settings for the project. Not all the settings will have their own tabs. Those that do not have a tab will also be shown here, on the **Summary** tab.

On this tab, you can do the following:

- Update the project's general information, including the project key (only available after JIRA 6.1)
- Set the project's category
- Re-index the project
- Delete the project

The Components tab

The **Components** tab is where project administrators can manage the components for their projects. Components can be thought of as subsections that make up the full project. In a software development project, components can be various modules that the final product comprises. As shown in the following screenshot, there are three components configured in the current project:

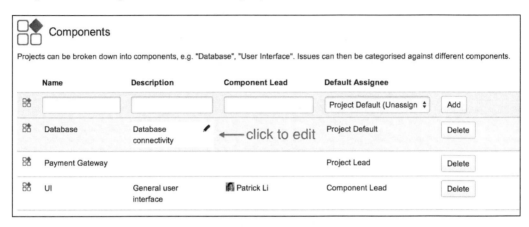

In JIRA, components are project-specific. This means that components from one project cannot be used in a different project. This also allows each project to maintain its own sets of components. A component has four pieces of information, as shown in the following table:

Field	Description
Name	This is a unique name for the component.
Description	This is an optional description to offer more explanation on what the component is for.
Component Lead	This is an optional field where you can select a single user as the lead for the component. For example, in a software project, this can be the main developer for the component.
Default Assignee	This tells JIRA when an issue is created without the assignee being selected. If the issue has a component, then JIRA will auto-assign the issue to the selected default assignee.

Creating components

Unlike some older versions of JIRA, you can create new components directly from the **Components** tab:

1. Browse to the **Components** tab for the project.
2. Provide a unique name for the component. JIRA will let you know whether the name is already taken.
3. Provide a short description for the new component.
4. Select a user to be the lead of the component. Just start typing and JIRA will prompt you with options that meet the criteria.
5. Select the default assignee option for the component.
6. Click on **Add** to create the new component.

Once you have created the new component, it will be added to the list of existing components. When a component is first created, it will be placed at the top of the list. If you refresh the page, the list will then be ordered alphabetically.

Managing components

If you want to edit a component's name or any other details, all you need to do is hover your mouse over the component's name, and you will see that the name field is highlighted. Click on the name to make the field editable, make your changes, and click on **Update**. If you want to delete a component, all you have to do is to click on the **Delete** button next to the target component.

Component lead and default assignee

As explained in the preceding section, one of the useful features of components is the ability to assign a default assignee to each individual component. This means, when a user creates an issue and sets the assignee as **Automatic**, JIRA will be able to automatically assign the issue based on the component selected. This is a very powerful feature for organizations where members of various teams often do not know each other. Therefore, when it comes to assigning issues at creation time, it is difficult to decide who to assign it to. With this feature, it can be set up so that the lead of the component becomes the default assignee and the issues raised can then be delegated to other members of the team.

For our demo project, each of the supported systems has a system expert, which is represented as the lead of the respective component. When the business user logs a ticket and selects a component, the ticket will go directly to the lead. This setup is also flexible enough. If the user knows who to best assign the ticket to, he or she can directly assign the ticket to a member of the team and the automatic assignment will not take place.

> If the issue has more than one component with a default assignee, the assignee for the first component in alphabetical order will be used.

The Versions tab

Like the **Components** tab, the **Versions** tab allows project administrators to manage versions for their projects. Versions serve as milestones for a project. In project management, versions represent points in time. While for projects that are not product-oriented, versions may seem to be something that is less relevant; versions can still be valuable at managing and tracking the progress of issues and work.

As with components, versions also have a number of attributes, as shown in the following table:

Field	Description
Name	This is a unique name for the version.
Description	This is an optional description to offer more explanation on what the version is for.
Release Date	This is an optional date that will be marked as the scheduled date to release the version. Versions that are not released according to the release date will have the date highlighted in red.

Creating versions

Creating new versions is as simple as providing the necessary details for the new version and clicking on the **Add** button:

1. Browse to the **Versions** tab for the target project.
2. Provide a unique name for the version (for example, 1.1.0, v2.3). JIRA will let you know whether the name is already taken.
3. Provide a short description for the new version.

4. Select the date for when the version starts and will be released by using the date picker.

5. Click on **Add** to create the new version.

Unlike components, versions will not be ordered automatically by JIRA, so you will have to manually maintain the order. To change the order of versions, all you have to do is hover your mouse pointer over to the left of the version, and you will be able to drag the version up and down the list.

Managing versions

Just like managing components, the **Versions** tab uses the in-place editing feature. You just need to click on the field of the version you want to change, and click on **Update** to apply.

When you hover over a version, you will notice that there is a little cog icon to the right. If you click on that, you will have the options to do the following:

Option	Description
Release	This will mark the version as released; meaning it is completed or shipped. When you release a version, JIRA will automatically check to make sure that all the issues are completed for the selected version. If these are incomplete, you will be prompted to either ignore those issues or push them to a different version. If the version has already been released, it will change to **Unrelease**.
Build and Release	This is similar to the **Release** option, but it also performs a build through Atlassian Bamboo, if there are any software codes. The version will only be released if the build is successful. This option is not available if the version is already released.
Archive	This will mark the version as archived; meaning that the version is stored away until further notice. When a version is archived, you cannot release or delete it until it is unarchived.
Delete	This will delete the version from JIRA. Again, JIRA will search for issues that are related to this version and prompt you as to whether you would like to move these issues to a different version.

The options discussed in the preceding table can be seen in the following screenshot:

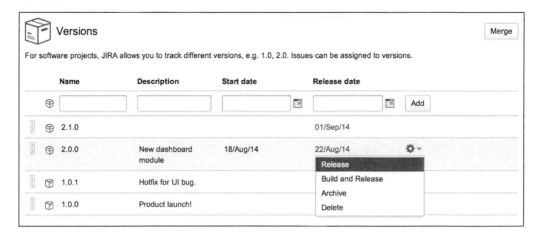

There is also a merge versions feature that allows you to merge multiple versions together. Merging versions will move issues from one version to another.

Other tabs

There are a number of other tabs on the Project Administration interface. We will not get into the details for these tabs as they will each be covered in their own chapters later. We will, however, take a quick tour to look at what each tab does, as shown in the following table:

Tab	Description
Issue Types	This controls the types of issues that users can create for the project. For example, this may include **Bugs**, **Improvements**, and **Tasks**.
	Issue Types will be covered in *Chapter 3, Issue Management*.
Workflows	This controls the workflow issues that we will go through. Workflows consist of a series of steps that usually mimic the existing processes that are in place for the organization.
	Workflows will be covered in *Chapter 6, Workflows and Business Processes*.
Screens	**Screens** are what users see when they create and edit issues in JIRA.
	Screens will be covered in *Chapter 5, Screen Management*.

Tab	Description
Fields	**Fields** are what JIRA uses to capture data from users when they create issues. JIRA comes with a set of default fields, and the JIRA administrator is able to add additional fields as needed.
	Fields will be covered in *Chapter 4, Field Management*.
Roles	The project administrators can define roles in the project and assign users to them. These roles can then be used to control permissions and notifications.
	Roles will be covered in *Chapter 8, Securing JIRA*.
Permissions	As we have already seen, permissions define who can perform certain tasks or have access in JIRA.
	Permissions will be covered in *Chapter 8, Securing JIRA*.
Issue Security	JIRA allows users to control who can view the issues they created, by selecting the issue security level.
	Issue security will be covered in *Chapter 8, Securing JIRA*.
Notifications	JIRA has the ability to send out e-mail notifications when certain events occur. For example, when an issue is updated, JIRA can send out an e-mail to alert all users who participate on the issue of the change.
	Notifications will be covered in *Chapter 7, E-mails and Notifications*.

The Help Desk project

Now that we have seen all the key aspects that make up a project, let's revisit what we learned so far and put it to practice. In this exercise, we will be setting up a project for our support teams:

- A new project category for all support teams
- A new project for our help desk support team
- Components for the systems supported by the team
- Versions to better manage issues created by users

Creating a new project category

Let's start by creating a project category. We will create a category for all of our internal support teams and their respective support JIRA projects.

Please note that this step is optional as JIRA does not require any project to belong to a project category:

1. Log in to JIRA with a user who has JIRA Administrator's permission.
2. Browse to the JIRA administration console.
3. Select the **Projects** tab and **Project Categories**.
4. Fill in the fields as shown in the following screenshot.
5. Click on **Add** to create the new project category.

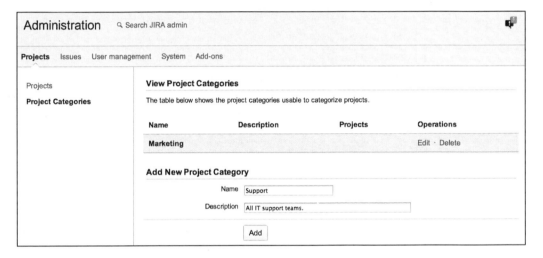

Creating a new project

Now that we have a project category created, let's create a project for our help desk support team. To create a new project, perform the following steps:

1. Bring up the create project dialog by selecting the **Create Project** option from the **Projects** drop-down menu.
2. Select the **Simple Issue Tracking** project template.
3. Name our new project as Global Help Desk and accept the other default values for **Key** and **Project Lead**.
4. Click on the **Submit** button to create the new project.

You should now be taken to the Project Browser interface of your new project.

Assigning a project to a category

Having created the new project, you need to assign the new project to your project category, and you can do this from the Project Administration interface:

1. Select the **Administration** tab.
2. Click on the **None** link next to **Category**, on the top left of the page, right underneath the project's name.
3. Select the new **Support** project category we just created.
4. Click on **Select** to assign the project.

Creating new components

As discussed in the earlier sections, components are subsections of a project. This makes logical sense for a software development project, where each component will represent a software deliverable module. For other types of project, components may first appear useless or inappropriate.

It is true that components are not for every type of project out there, and this is the reason why you are not required to have them by default. Just like everything else in JIRA, all the features come from how you can best map them to your business needs.

The power of a component is more than just a flag field for an issue. For example, let's imagine that the company you are working for has a range of systems that need to be supported. These may range from phone systems and desktop computers to other business applications. Let's also assume that our support team needs to support all of the systems. Now, that is a lot of systems to support. To help manage and delegate support for these systems, we will create a component for each of the systems that the help desk team supports. We will also assign a lead for each of the components. This setup allows us to establish a structure where the **Help Desk** project is led by the support team lead, and each component is led by their respective system expert (who may or may not be the same as the team lead). As we will see in later chapters, this allows for a very flexible management process when we start wiring in other JIRA features, such as notification schemes:

1. From the Project Administration interface, select the **Components** tab.
2. Type `Internal Phone System` for the new component's name.
3. Provide a short description for the new component.
4. Select a user to be the lead of the component.
5. Click on **Add** to create the new component.
6. Add a few more components.

Putting it together

Now that you have fully prepared your project, let's see how everything comes together by creating an issue. If everything is done correctly, you should see a dialog box similar to the next screenshot, where you can choose your new project to create the issue in and also the new components that are available for selection:

1. Click on the **Create** button from the top navigation bar. This will bring up the **Create Issue** dialog box.

2. Select **Global Help Desk** for **Project**.

3. Select **Task** for **Issue Type**, and click on the **Next** button.

4. Fill in the fields with some dummy data. Note that the Component/s field should display the components we just created.

5. Click on the **Create** button to create the issue.

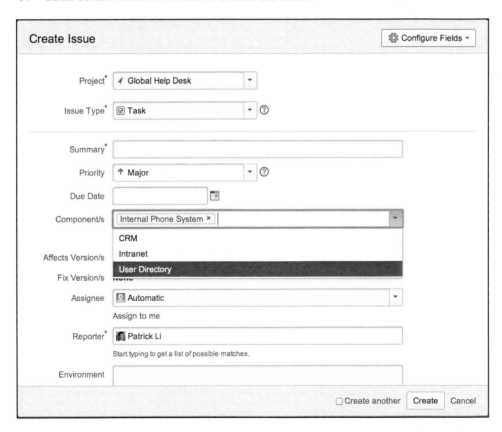

You can test out the default assignee feature by leaving the Assignee field as Automatic, select a component, and JIRA will automatically assign the issue to the default assignee defined for the component.

If everything goes well, the issue will be created in the new project.

Summary

In this chapter, we looked at one of the most important concepts in JIRA, projects, and how to create and manage them. Permissions were introduced for the first time, and we looked at three permissions that are related to creating and deleting, administering, and browsing projects.

We were introduced to the two interfaces JIRA provides for project administrators and everyday users, the Project Administration interface and Project Browser interface, respectively. In the next chapter, you will be introduced to another important concept in JIRA, **issues**.

3
Issue Management

In the previous chapter, you saw that JIRA is a very flexible and versatile tool that can be used in different organizations for different purposes. A software development organization will use JIRA to manage its software development lifecycle and bug tracking, while a customer services organization may choose to use JIRA to track and log customer complaints and suggestions. For these reasons, issues in JIRA can represent anything that is applicable to the real-world scenario. Generally speaking, an issue in JIRA often represents a unit of work that can be acted upon by one or more people.

In this chapter, we will explore the basic and advanced features offered by JIRA for you to manage issues. By the end of this chapter, you will have learned the following:

- Issues and what they are in JIRA
- Creating, editing, and deleting issues
- Moving issues between projects
- Expressing your interest in issues through voting and watching
- Advanced issue operations, including uploading attachments and linking issues

Understanding issues

In JIRA, an issue can represent any number of things. In fact, an issue in a given project may mean something that is very different in another project. So what an issue really is depends on the context of what project it is in, and how you choose to define and use JIRA. For example, an issue in a normal software development project would often represent a software bug, while in a help desk project it can represent a support request.

Despite all the different objects an issue can represent, there are a number of key aspects that are common for all issues in JIRA, as follows:

- An issue must belong to a project.
- It must have a type, otherwise known as an issue type, which indicates what the issue is representing.
- It must have a summary. The summary acts like a one-line description of what the issue is about.
- It must have a status. A status indicates where along the workflow the issue is at a given time. We will discuss workflows in *Chapter 6, Workflows and Business Processes*.

JIRA issue summary

As we have discussed, an issue in JIRA can be anything in the real world to represent a unit of work or a task to be completed. It can be a software bug, a help desk ticket, or a customer request. However, what does an issue look like in JIRA? How does JIRA achieve this level of flexibility and still present it in a consistent manner?

Let's first take a look at an issue in JIRA. The following screenshot shows a typical example of an issue and breaks it down into more digestible sections, followed by an explanation of each of the highlighted sections in a table. This view is often called the **Issue Summary** or the **View Issue** page.

These sections are described in the following table:

Section	Description
Project / Issue Key	It shows the project the issue belongs to. The issue key is the unique identifier of the current issue. This section acts as a breadcrumb for easy navigation.
Issue Summary	It is a brief summary of the issue.
Issue View Options	These are the various view options for the issue. The options include XML, Excel, and Word.
Issue Operations	These are the operations that users can perform on the issue, such as edit, assign, and comment. These are covered in the later sections of this chapter.
Workflow Options	These are the workflow transitions available. Workflow will be covered in *Chapter 6, Workflows and Business Processes.*
Issue Details / Fields	This section lists the issue fields such as issue type and priority. Custom fields are also displayed in this section. Fields will be covered in *Chapter 4, Field Management.*
User Fields	This section is specific for user-type fields such as assignee and reporter. Fields will be covered in *Chapter 4, Field Management.*
Date Fields	This section is specific for date-type fields such as create and due date. Fields will be covered in *Chapter 4, Field Management.*
Vote / Watch Issue	These are the options that allow users to vote and watch an issue.
Attachments	These list all the attachments in an issue.
Comments	These list all the comments that are visible to the current user.

Working with issues

As we have seen, issues are the center of JIRA. In the following sections, we will look at what you, as a user, can do with issues. Note that each of the actions will require you to have specific permissions, which we will cover in *Chapter 8, Securing JIRA.*

Creating an issue

When creating a new issue, you will need to fill in a number of fields. Some fields are mandatory, such as the issue's summary and type, while others are optional, such as the issue's description. We will discuss fields in more details in the next chapter.

There are several ways in which you can create a new issue in JIRA. You can choose any of the following options:

- Click on the **Create** button at the top of the screen.

- Press *C* on your keyboard.

This will bring up the **Create Issue** dialog box, as shown in the preceding screenshot. As you can see, there are quite a few fields, and the required fields will have a red asterisk (*) mark next to their names.

The administrator configures what fields will be part of the create dialog, but as a user, you can customize and make your own create screen by hiding the optional fields, by performing the following steps:

1. Click on the **Configure Fields** option at the top-right corner.
2. Select the **Custom** option.

3. Uncheck all the fields you want to hide, and check the fields that you want to show.

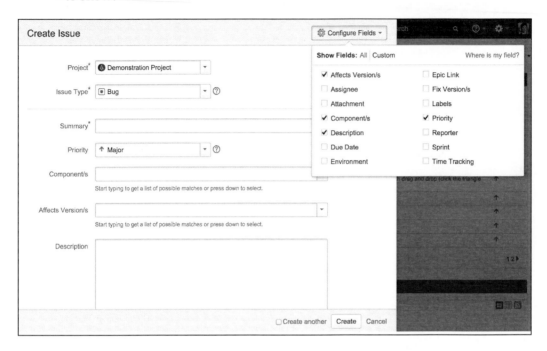

 You are only hiding or showing these fields for yourself. Only the JIRA administrator can actually hide and show fields globally for all users.

There is a **Create another** option beside the **Create** button. By ticking this option and then clicking on the **Create** button, the **Create Issue** dialog box will stay on the screen and remember the values you have previously entered, such as priority, components, and due dates. This way, you can avoid having to fill in the whole dialog box again and will only have to update some of the fields that actually are different, such as **Summary**. With this feature, you can rapidly create many issues in a much shorter time frame.

Editing an issue

There are two ways in which you can edit an issue in JIRA. The first and more traditional way is by clicking the **Edit** button or pressing *E* on your keyboard. This will bring up the Edit Issue dialog with all the editable fields for the current issue. This allows you to make changes to multiple fields at once.

The second option is called **in-line editing**. With this feature, you will be able to view the issue and edit the field you want on the spot, without having to wait for the edit dialog to load. Scroll down to find the field. To edit a field in-line, all you have to do is hover your mouse over the value for the field you want to update, wait for the **Edit** icon to show up, click the icon, and start editing.

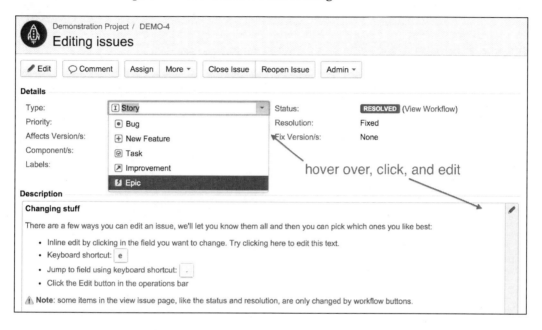

Deleting an issue

You can delete issues from JIRA. You might need to delete issues that have been created by mistake or if the issue is redundant, although normally, it is better to close and mark the issue as a duplicate. We will discuss closing an issue in *Chapter 6, Workflows and Business Processes*.

Issue deletion is permanent in JIRA. Unlike some other applications that may put deleted records in a trash bin, which you can retrieve later, JIRA completely deletes the issue from the system. The only way to retrieve the deleted issue is by restoring JIRA with a previous backup.

Perform the following steps to delete an issue:

1. Browse to the issue you wish to delete.

2. Click on the **Delete** option from the **More** menu. This will bring up the **Delete Issue** dialog box.

3. Click on the **Delete** button to remove the issue permanently from JIRA.

Deleting an issue permanently removes it from JIRA, along with all of its data including attachments and comments.

Moving an issue between projects

Once an issue has been created, the issue is associated with a project. You can, however, move the issue around from one project to another. This may sound like a very simple process, but there are many steps involved and things to be considered.

First, you need to decide on a new issue type for the issue, if the current issue type does not exist in the new project. Second, you will need to map a status of the issue. Third, you will need to decide on the values for the fields that exist in the new project but which do not exist in the current project if those fields are set to mandatory in the new project. Sounds like a lot? Luckily, JIRA comes with a wizard that is designed to help you address all those items.

Perform the following steps to start moving an issue:

1. Browse to the issue you wish to move.

2. Click on the **Move** option in the **More** menu. This will bring up the **Move Issue** wizard.

There are essentially four steps in the **Move Issue** wizard.

The first step is to select which project you wish to move the issue to. You will also need to select the new issue type. If the same issue type exists in the new project, you can usually continue to use the same issue type.

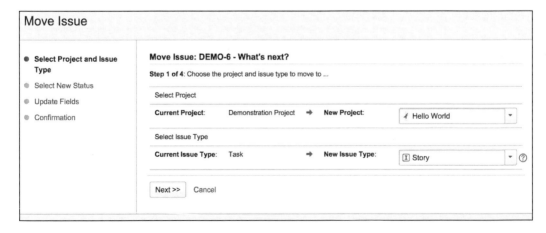

The second step allows you to map the current issue to the new project's workflow. If the issue's status exists in the target project, the wizard will skip this step.

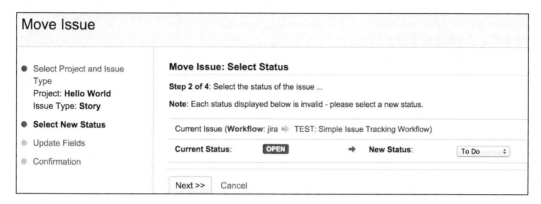

The third step shows all the fields that exist in the new project but not the current project and which require a value. Again, if there are no missing fields, this step will be skipped.

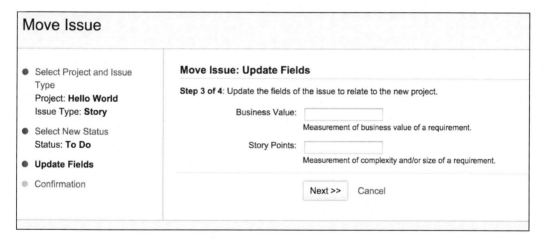

The fourth and last step shows you the summary of the changes that will be applied, by moving the issue from project A to project B. This is your last chance to make sure that all the information is correct. If there are any mistakes, you can go back to step one and start over again. If you are happy with the changes, confirm the move by clicking on **Move**.

Once the issue is moved, it will be given a new issue key based on the new project. However, JIRA is still able to redirect you if you access the issue with its old issue key.

Casting a vote on an issue

The most straightforward way to express your interest in a JIRA issue is to vote for it. For organizations or teams that manage their priorities based on popularity, voting is a great mechanism to collect this information. The Popular Issues project tab mentioned in *Chapter 2, Project Management* will display all the voted issues.

An example of this is how Atlassian uses JIRA (for example, `https://jira.atlassian.com/browse/JRA-9`) as a way to let its customers choose and vote for the features they want to be implemented or bugs to be fixed, by voting on issues based on their needs. This allows the product management and marketing team to have an insight on the market needs and how to best evolve their offerings.

One thing to keep in mind is when voting, you can only vote ONCE per issue. You can vote many times for many different issues, but for any given issue, you have only one vote. This helps prevent a single user from continuously voting on the same issue, which may blow the final statistics out of proportion. You can, however, unvote a vote you have already cast on an issue, and vote for it again later; if you choose to do this, it will still only count as one vote.

To vote for an issue, simply click on the **Vote for this issue** link next to **Votes**. When you have voted for an issue, the icon will appear as colored. When you have not yet voted for an issue, the icon will appear gray. Note that you cannot vote for issues you have created.

Receiving notifications on an issue

JIRA is able to send automated e-mail notifications about updates on issues to users. Normally, notification e-mails will only be sent out to the issue's reporter, assignee, and people who have registered interest in the issue. This behavior can be changed through **Notification Schemes**, which we will discuss in *Chapter 7, E-mails and Notifications*.

You can register your interest in the issue by choosing to watch the issue. By watching an issue, you will receive e-mail notifications on activity updates. Users watching the issue can also choose to stop watching, thus stop receiving e-mail updates from JIRA. You can also add other users as watchers by adding them to the watcher's list.

To watch an issue, simply click on the **Start watching this issue** link. When you are already watching the issue, the text will be **Stop watching this issue**. If you click on the link again, you will stop watching the issue, as shown in the following screenshot:

 JIRA will automatically add you as a watcher for issues created by you.

JIRA also shows how many people are actively watching the issue by displaying the total watchers next to the watch icon. You can click on the number next to **Watchers** to see the full list of watchers.

Assigning issues to users

Once an issue has been created, the user normally assigned to the issue will start working on it. Afterwards, the user can assign the issue further, for example, to QA staff for further verification.

There are many instances where an issue needs to be reassigned to a different user. For example, the current assignee may be unavailable, or if issues are created with no specific assignees. Another example will be that issues are assigned to different people at different stages of the workflow. For this reason, JIRA allows users to reassign issues once they have been created.

Perform the following steps to assign an issue:

1. Browse to the issue you wish to assign.
2. Click on the **Assign** button in the **Issue** menu bar or press *A* on your keyboard (you can also use the in-line edit feature here). This will bring up the **Assign** dialog.
3. Select the new assignee for the issue, and optionally add a comment to provide some information to the new assignee.
4. Click on the **Assign** button.

Once this issue has been reassigned, its assignee value will be updated to the new user. The new assignee will also receive a notification e-mail, alerting him/her of the assignment. You can also un-assign an issue this way by simply selecting the **Unassigned** option. Unassigned issues do not have an assignee and will not show up on anyone's list of active issues.

> You can press *I* on your keyboard to quickly assign the issue to yourself.

Sharing issues with other users

If you want to e-mail an issue to other users in JIRA, instead of having to manually copy and paste the issue's URL in an e-mail, you can use the built-in share feature in JIRA. All you have to do is go to the issue you want to share, click on the share icon or press *S* on your keyboard as shown in the following screenshot. Then select the users you want to share the issue with and click the **Share** button.

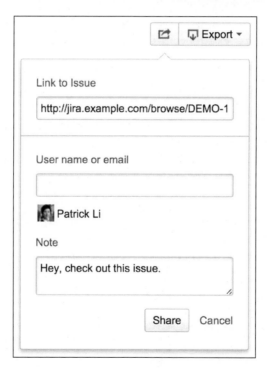

> If the user you are sharing the issue with does not have access to the issue, he/she will not be able to see the issue's details.

Issue linking

JIRA allows you to create custom hyper-links for issues. This allows you to provide more information to the issue. For example, for a support-type issue, you can link it to a web page that contains information on how to resolve similar types of problems. Another example will be to link the issue to other related issues.

Enabling issue linking

Issue linking is enabled by default when you first install JIRA. Issue linking is configured globally, so once it is enabled, it will become available for all projects in JIRA.

If issue linking is disabled, you can enable it by the following steps to enable issue linking. Note that you need to be a JIRA administrator:

1. Log in as a JIRA administrator user.
2. Browse to the JIRA administration console.
3. Select the **System** tab and then the **Issue Linking** option. This will take you to the **Issue Link Administration** page.
4. Click on **Activate** to enable issue linking in JIRA.

From this page, you will be able to see a list of **Link Types** available. A link type defines the nature of the link between issues. As shown in the screenshot in the next section, the default Blocks link type defines that issue A blocks issue B. This means that issue B cannot be completed until issue A is resolved. It is important to note that issue linking does not place any restrictions on issues. So in our example, although the link states that issue B cannot be completed until issue A is done, this is not enforced and users can close issue A while issue B remains open.

All the link types shown here are for standard issue links. There are no remote issue link types. However, you do need to enable issue linking to make use of remote issue links.

Creating link types

JIRA comes with four link types by default: Blocks, Clones, Duplicate, and Relates. As we have discussed earlier, a link type is simply a type of association or a label on the association, which describes the relationships between two issues. Therefore, you can define your own link types in JIRA. For example, one issue can support another issue, and we can create a link type called Supports.

Perform the following steps to create a new link type:

1. Browse to the **Issue Linking Administration** page.

2. Make sure issue linking is enabled.

3. Fill in the **Add New Link Type** form. Do the following for the **Support** link type:

   1. Enter Supports for the **Name** field.

   2. Enter supports for the **Outward Link Description** field.

   3. Enter is supported by for the **Inward Link Description** field.

4. Click on the **Add** button.

Outward and inward link descriptions define what is shown when users select the type of link to use when linking two issues together. We will see an example of this in a later section. Once a new link type is added, it will be displayed in the table on the **Issue Linking Administration** page.

Linking issues with other issues

Issues are often related to other issues in some way. For example, issue A might be blocking issue B, or issue C might be a duplicate of issue D. You can add descriptions to the issue to capture this information, or delete one of the issues in the duplication case, but with this approach, it is hard to keep a track of all these relationships. Luckily, JIRA provides an elegant solution for this, with the standard issue link feature.

The **standard issue link** lets you link an issue with one or more other issues in the same JIRA instance. So, you can link two issues from different projects together (if you have access to both the projects). Linking issues in this way is very simple; all you need to know is the target issues to link to:

1. Browse to the **View Issue** page for the issue you wish to create a link for.

2. Select **Link** from the **More Actions** menu. This will bring up the **Link Issue** dialog box.

3. Select the **JIRA Issue** option from the left panel.

4. Select the type of issue linking.

5. Select the issues to link to. You can use the search facility to help you locate the issues you want.

6. Click on the **Link** button.

After you have linked your issues, they will be displayed in the **Issue Links** section on the **View Issue** page. JIRA will display the target issue's key, description, priority, and status.

Linking issues with remote contents

The standard JIRA issue link allows you to link multiple issues in the same JIRA instance. JIRA also lets you link issues to resources such as a web page on the Internet.

Using remote issue links is very similar to the standard issue link; the difference is that instead of selecting another issue, the URL address of the target resource is specified:

1. Open up the **Link Issue** dialog box.
2. Select the **Web Link** option from the left panel.
3. Specify the URL address for the target resource. JIRA will automatically try to find and load the appropriate icon for the resource.
4. Provide the name for the link in **Link Text** field. The name you provide here will be what is shown for the link when viewing the issue.
5. Click on the **Link** button.

Issue cloning

When you need to create a new issue and you already have a baseline issue, JIRA allows you to quickly create it with the data based on your existing issues, by cloning the original one. Cloning an issue allows you to quickly create a new one with most of its fields populated. For example, you might have two software products with the same bug. After creating a bug report in one project, you can simply clone it for the other project.

A cloned issue will have all the fields copied from the original issue; however, it is a separate entity nonetheless. Further actions performed on either of the two issues will not affect the other.

When an issue is being cloned, a **Clone** link is automatically created between the two issues, establishing a relationship.

Cloning an issue in JIRA is simple and straightforward. All you have to do is specify a new summary (or accept the default summary with CLONE—text at the front) for the cloned issue:

1. Browse to the issue you wish to clone.
2. Select **Clone** from the **More Actions** menu. This will bring up the **Clone Issue** page.
3. Type in a new summary for the new cloned issue.
4. Check the **Clone Attachments** checkbox if you also want to copy over all the attachments.
5. Click on the **Create** button.

Once the issue is successfully cloned, you will be taken to the issue summary page for the newly cloned issue.

Time tracking

Since issues often represent a single unit of work that can be worked on, it is logical for users to log the time they have spent working on it. You can specify an estimated effort required to complete an issue, and JIRA will be able to help you track the progress. JIRA displays the time tracking information of an issue in the **Time Tracking** panel at the right-hand side, as shown in the following screenshot with its description:

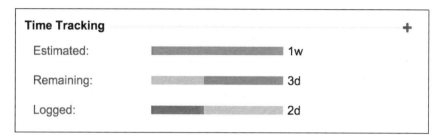

- **Estimated**: This represents the original estimated effort required to complete the issue. For example, the estimated time required for fixing a bug by a developer.

- **Remaining**: This represents the remaining time for the issue to be completed. It is calculated automatically by JIRA based on the original estimate and total time logged by users. However, the user logging work on the issue, as described in the following section, can also override this value.

- **Logged**: This represents the total time spent on the issue so far.

Configuring time tracking

Time tracking is enabled by default when you install JIRA. To change your time tracking settings, you will first need to deactivate it, and then activate it again with the new settings:

1. Log in as a JIRA administrator user.

2. Browse to the JIRA administration console.

3. Select the **System** tab, and then select the **Time Tracking** option. This will take you to the **Time Tracking** page.

4. Click on the **Deactivate** button.

5. Configure the time tracking parameters.

6. Click on **Activate** to enable time tracking in JIRA.

Time Tracking is currently OFF. ⑦

Activate Time Tracking below.

Hours per day `8`
Please specify the number of hours per working day. The default for this value is 8 hours.

Days per week `5`
Please specify the number of working days per week. The default for this value is 5 days.

Time format ⦿ pretty (e.g. 4 days, 4 hours, 30 minutes)
○ days (e.g. 4d 4.5h)
○ hours (e.g. 36.5h)

Default Unit `minute ⁞`
Time unit used for input that doesn't explicitly specify one. The default for this value is "minute".

Legacy Mode ☐
In legacy mode, the original estimate and remaining estimate are linked and only one value can be updated at a time. This is no longer the default for new installations of JIRA version 4.2 and later.

Copy Comment To Work ☑
Description When this option is enabled, any comment entered as part of a workflow transition on an issue will be copied to the work log description *if* work is logged as part of that transition.

[Activate]

You can set several parameters on the **Time Tracking** page. As we will see in later sections, these parameters will determine the time tracking behavior for JIRA, as shown in the following table:

Parameter	Description
Hours per day	This is the number of working hours per day in JIRA. For example, if this is set to 8 hours per day, when the user puts in 16 hours, JIRA will automatically convert it to 2 days.
Days per week	This is the number of working days per week in JIRA. For example, if this is set to 5 days per week, when the user puts in 10 days, JIRA will automatically convert it to 2 weeks.
Time format	This is the format in which JIRA will display time in the Time Spent field.
Default Unit	This is the default time tracking unit if the user does not supply one.
Legacy Mode	This will make JIRA use the old time tracking behavior.
Copy Comment To Work Description	This is a very handy feature, where JIRA will automatically copy comments made during a workflow transition (workflow will be discussed in *Chapter 6, Workflows and Business Processes*) that allows time logging.

Specifying original estimates

Original estimate represents the anticipated time required to complete the work represented by the issue. It is shown as the blue bar under the **Time Tracking** section.

In order for you to specify an original estimate value, you need to make sure that time tracking is enabled and the **Time Tracking** field is added to the issue's create and/or edit screen. We will discuss fields and screens in *Chapter 4, Field Management* and *Chapter 5, Screen Management*, respectively.

To specify an original estimate value, provide a value for the **Original Estimate** field on the create issue and/or edit issue screen.

Logging work

Logging work in JIRA allows you to specify the amount of time (work) you have spent working on an issue. You can log work against any of the issues, provided that **Time Tracking** is enabled and you have the permission to do so. We will cover permissions in *Chapter 9, Searching, Reporting, and Analysis*.

Perform the following steps to log work against an issue:

1. Browse to the issue you wish to log work against.
2. Select **Log Work** from the **More Actions** menu. This will bring up the **Log Work** page.
3. Enter the amount of time you wish to log. Use w, d, h, and m to specify week, day, hour, and minute, respectively.
4. Select the date you wish to log your work against.
5. Optionally, select how the remaining estimate should be adjusted.
6. Add a description to the work you have done.
7. Optionally, select who can view the work log entry.

8. Click on the **Log** button.

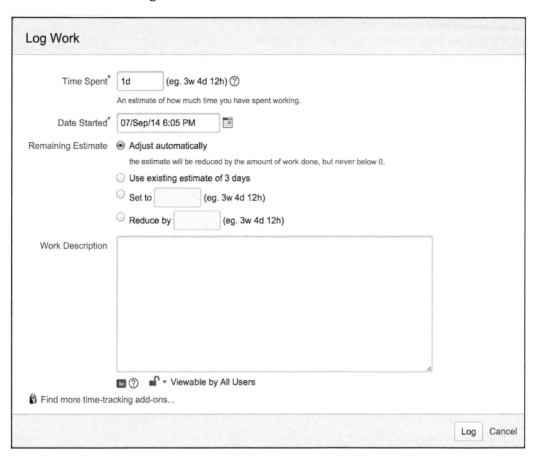

When you log work on an issue, you have the option to choose how the **Remaining Estimate** value will be affected. By default, this value will be automatically calculated by subtracting the amount logged from the original estimate. You can, however, choose other options available, such as setting the remaining estimate to a specific value or reducing it by an amount that is different from the amount of work being logged.

 You can also click on the + sign in the **Time Tracking** section to log time.

Issues and comments

JIRA lets users create comments on issues. As we have already seen, you will be able to create comments when assigning an issue to a different user. This is a very useful feature that allows multiple users to collaborate to work on the same issue and share information. For example, the support staff (issue assignee) may request more clarification from the business user (issue reporter) by adding a comment to the issue. When combined with JIRA's built-in notification system, automatic e-mail notifications will be sent to the issue's reporter, assignee, and any of the other users watching the issue. Notifications will be covered in *Chapter 7, E-mails and Notifications*.

Adding comments

By default, all logged-in users will be able to add comments to issues they can access. Perform the following steps to add a comment to an issue:

1. Browse to the issue you wish to add a comment to.

2. Click on the **Comment** option in the **Issue** menu bar or press *M* on your keyboard. This will bring up the **Comment input** section.

3. Type a comment into the text box. The text box will adjust its size as you type.

4. Click on the **Add** button to add the comment.

Once a comment has been added, the comment will be visible in the **Comments** tab in the **Activity** section. When you are creating comments, you can select who can view your comment using the comment access control. This is very useful if you have external users viewing the issue and you only want to share your comments with internal users.

Managing your comments

After you have added your comment to an issue, you can edit its contents and security settings or delete it altogether. To edit or delete a comment, simply hover over the comment, and the comment management option will appear to the right-hand side.

Permalinking a comment

From time to time, you will want to refer other people to a comment you made previously. While you can tell them the issue and let them scroll down to the bottom until they find your comment amongst hundreds of others, JIRA allows you to create a quick permalink to your comment that will take you directly to the comment of interest.

Perform the following steps to create a permalink for a comment:

1. Browse to the comment you wish to permalink.
2. Hover over the comment to bring up the comment management options.
3. Click on the permalink icon. This will highlight the comment in pale blue.

You will now notice that your browser's URL bar will look something similar to `http://sample.jira.com/browse/DEMO-1?focusedCommentId=10100 &page=com.atlassian.jira.plugin.system.issuetabpanels:comment-tabpanel#comment-10100` as a sample link (notice the `focusedCommendId` section after the issue key). Copy and paste that URL and give it to your colleagues; once they click on this link, they will be taken directly to the highlighted comment.

Attachments

As we have seen so far, JIRA uses fields such as summary and description to capture data. This works for most cases, but when you have complex data such as application log files or screenshots, fields become insufficient. This is where attachments come in. JIRA allows you to attach files to issues as support documents.

Enabling attachments in JIRA

Attachments are saved as files on the JIRA file server and not in the database, so you need to ensure that there is sufficient disk space to accommodate the volume of attachments for now and future growth. As attachments are not stored in the database, JIRA will not backup the files as a part of its backup process. Attachments need to be backed up separately.

Attachments are enabled by default in JIRA, so users will be able to attach files to issues as soon as JIRA is installed. However, if it is disabled for some reason, you can re-enable it. Perform the following steps to enable attachments for JIRA:

1. Log in to JIRA as a JIRA administrator.
2. Browse to the JIRA administration console.
3. Select the **System** tab and then the **Attachments** option. This will take you to the **Attachment Settings** page.
4. Click on the **Edit Settings** button. This will bring up the **Edit Attachment Settings** page.
5. Select **Use Default Directory** for the **Attachment Path** option.
6. Click on the **Update** button to enable attachments in JIRA.

On the **Attachment Settings** page, as shown in the following screenshot, there are a few options that you will need to configure while enabling attachments in JIRA:

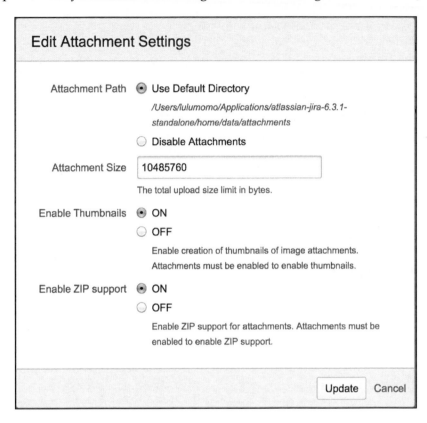

The following table summarizes the configuration options:

Options	Description
Attachment Path	This specifies the location where attachments will be stored on the filesystem. The only options are the default directory, which is inside your JIRA_HOME directory, or disabled attachments in JIRA.
Attachment Size	This specifies the maximum size of the attachment that users can upload. Default is 10 MB.
Enable Thumbnails	This specifies whether or not to enable thumbnail generation when the attachment is an image.
Enable ZIP support	This specifies whether or not to enable ZIP support, which allows users to download multiple attachments as a single ZIP file, and also view the contents of the ZIP attachment files.

Attachments are enabled and disabled globally across JIRA. You cannot selectively enable or disable attachment functions on a per project basis. You can, however, achieve a similar result by controlling the permission around who can attach files. Permissions are discussed in *Chapter 8, Securing JIRA*.

Attaching files

JIRA allows you to attach any arbitrary file to issues. These can be image files, Microsoft Office documents, and other binary files. Perform the following steps to attach a file to an issue:

1. Browse to the issue you wish to attach a file.
2. Select **Attach File** from the **More** menu. This will bring up the **Attach Files** dialog.
3. Click on the **Browse** button to select the file you wish to attach. You can repeat this step to attach more than one file.
4. Optionally, provide a comment for the attached file. The comment will be added as a normal comment to the issue.
5. Click on the **Attach** button.

Attaching screenshots

Apart from letting you attach any file to an issue, JIRA also allows you to directly attach a screenshot from your system clipboard to issues. This saves you from having to take a screenshot, save it as a physical file on the disk, and finally attach it to JIRA.

Perform the following steps to attach a screenshot:

1. Take a screenshot with your operating system. For example, if you are on Windows, press the *Print Screen* key.
2. Browse to the issue you wish to attach a screenshot.
3. Select **Attach screenshot** from the **More** menu. This will bring up the **Attach screenshot** dialog.
4. Press the *Ctrl + V* keys on your keyboard, and the screenshot will be pasted into the panel above.
5. Enter a filename for the screenshot or accept the default name.
6. Click on the **Upload** button.

Issue types and subtasks

As seen earlier, issues in JIRA can represent many things ranging from software development tasks to project management milestones. Issue type is what differentiates one kind of issue from another.

Each issue has a type (therefore, the name issue type), which is represented by the issue type field. This lets you know what type of issue it is, and also helps you determine many other aspects of it, such as what fields will be displayed for this issue.

JIRA comes with a set of default issue types, as shown in the following table:

Issue type	Description
Bug	A problem that impairs or prevents the functions of the product
Improvement	An enhancement to an existing feature
New feature	A new feature of the product
Task	A task that needs to be done

The default issue types are great for simple software development projects, but they do not necessarily meet the needs of others. Since it is impossible to create a system that can address everyone's needs, JIRA lets you create your own issue types and assigns them to projects. For example, for a help desk project, you might want to create a custom issue type called `ticket`. You can create this custom issue type and assign it to the Help Desk project, and users will be able to log tickets, instead of bugs in the system.

Issue types are managed through the **Manage Issue Types** page. Perform the following steps to access this page:

1. Log in to JIRA as a JIRA administrator.
2. Browse to the JIRA administration console.
3. Select the **Issues** tab and then the **Issue Types** option. This will take you to the **Issue Types Administration** page.

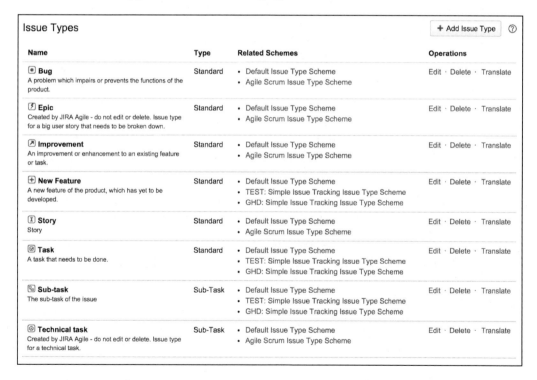

The preceding screenshot shows a list of default issue types along with custom issue types created by the administrator.

Creating issue types

You can create any number of issue types. Perform the following steps to create a new issue type:

1. Browse to the **Manage Issue Types** page.
2. Click on the **Add Issue Type** button.
3. Type a unique name for the new issue type.
4. Type in a general description for the issue type.
5. Select whether the new issue type will be a standard issue type or a subtask issue type.
6. Click on **Add** to create the new issue type.

Once the new issue type is created, it will be assigned a default icon. If you want to change the icon, you will need to click on the **Edit** link for the issue type, and then select a new image as its icon.

Deleting issue types

When deleting an issue type, you have to keep in mind that the issue type might already be in use; meaning there are issues created with that issue type. So, if you delete an issue type, you will need to select a new one for those issues. The good news is that JIRA takes care of this for you. As shown in the following screenshot, we delete the **Bug** issue type and JIRA informs us of the already existing 19 issues of type **Bug**. You will need to assign them to a new issue type, such as **Improvement**.

Delete Issue Type: Bug   click to view the 19 issues using this issue type

Note: This issue type cannot be deleted - there are currently 19 matching issues with no suitable alternative issue types (only issues you have permission to see will be displayed, which may be different from the total count shown on this page).

In order for an issue type to be deleted, it needs to be associated with one workflow, field configuration and field screen scheme across all projects. If this is not the case, JIRA can not provide a list of valid replacement issue types.

Cancel

Perform the following steps to delete an existing issue type:

1. Browse to the **Manage Issue Types** page.

2. Click on the **Delete** link for the issue type you wish to delete. This will bring up the **Delete Issue Type** page. If there are existing issues with the issue type you are trying to delete, you will be asked to select a new issue type.

3. Select the new issue type for the existing issues. Once deleted, those issues will be automatically updated to the new issue type.

4. Click on the **Delete** button to delete the issue type.

Subtasks

JIRA allows only one person (assignee) to work on one issue at a time. This design ensures that an issue is a single unit of work that can be tracked against one person. However, in the real world, we often find ourselves in situations where we need to have multiple people working on the same issue. This may be caused by a poor breakdown of tasks or simply because of the nature of the task at hand. Whatever the reason, JIRA provides a mechanism to address this problem through subtasks.

Subtasks are similar to issues in many ways, and as a matter of fact, they are a special kind of issue. They must have a parent issue, and their issue types are flagged as subtask issue types. You can say that all subtasks are issues, but not all issues are subtasks.

For every issue, you can have one or more subtasks that can be assigned and tracked separately from another. Subtasks cannot have other subtasks. JIRA allows only one level of subtasks.

Enabling subtasks

Subtasks are enabled by default. If you have subtasks disabled for some reason, you will need to enable this feature.

Perform the following steps to enable subtasks in JIRA:

1. Browse to the JIRA administration console.

2. Select the **Issues** tab and then the **Sub-Tasks** option. This will take you to the **Sub-Tasks Administration** page.

3. Click on **Enable** to enable subtasks in JIRA.

Creating subtasks

Since subtasks belong to an issue, you need to browse to the issue first before you can create a new subtask:

1. Browse to the issue you wish to create subtasks for.

2. Select **Create Sub-Task** from the **More Actions** menu.

You will see a familiar **Create Issue** dialog box. However, one thing you will notice is that, unlike when you are creating an issue, you do not select which project to create the subtask in. This is because JIRA can determine the project value based on the parent issue. You will also notice that you can only select issue types that are subtasks.

Other than these differences, creating a subtask is no different than creating a normal issue. You can customize the fields shown in the dialog box and choose to rapidly create multiple subtasks by selecting the **Create another** option.

Once the subtask has been created, it will be added to the **Sub-Tasks** section of the parent issue. You will see all the subtasks that belong to the issue and their status. If a subtask has been completed, it will have a green tick next to it.

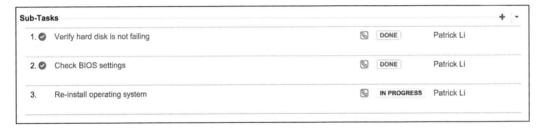

Issue type schemes

Issue type schemes are templates or collections of issue types that can be applied to projects. As shown in the following screenshot, JIRA comes with **Default Issue Type Scheme**, which is applied to all projects that do not have specific issue type schemes applied.

When a new issue type is created in JIRA, it is added to **Default Issue Type Scheme**. This means that the new issue type will be available to all the projects by default. This will become a problem when you start to have specialized projects such as help desk, and issue types such as **Bug** become inappropriate.

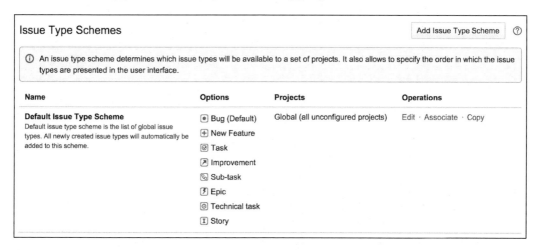

To overcome this problem, JIRA lets us group a collection of issue types together. We can also rearrange the order of the issue types within the collection so that they appear in the drop-down list in a logical manner to the users. In effect, we create an issue type scheme, a template for issue types, and their order, which can be reused and applied to one or more projects.

We will create a new issue type scheme for our example of JIRA implementation later in this chapter.

Creating issue type schemes

Perform the following steps to create a new issue type scheme:

1. Browse to the administration console.
2. Select the **Issues** tab and then the **Issue Type Schemes** option. This will bring you to the **Issue Type Schemes** page.
3. Click on the **Add Issue Type Scheme** button.
4. Provide a name for the new issue type scheme in **Scheme Name**.
5. Drag the issue types you want to be part of the scheme from the **Available Issue Types** list and drop them into the **Issue Types for Current Scheme** list.

6. Select a **Default Issue Type** value. Note that this is optional, and you can only select a default issue type after you have selected at least one issue type for the new scheme.

7. Click on the **Save** button.

After the issue type scheme has been created, you will need to associate it with the projects you want to apply the scheme to. The simplest way to do this is to click on the **Associate** link for the issue type scheme, and then select the projects you want. This allows you to apply the scheme to multiple projects at once. If there are already issues of issue type that does not belong to the new issue type scheme, JIRA will prompt you and walk you through to change the issue type value for all the affected issues.

Issue priorities

Priorities help users to set the importance of issues. Users can first assign priority values to issues and later use it to sort the list of issues they have to work on. Thus, helping the team decide which issues to focus on first. JIRA comes with five levels of priorities out of the box, as shown in the following screenshot:

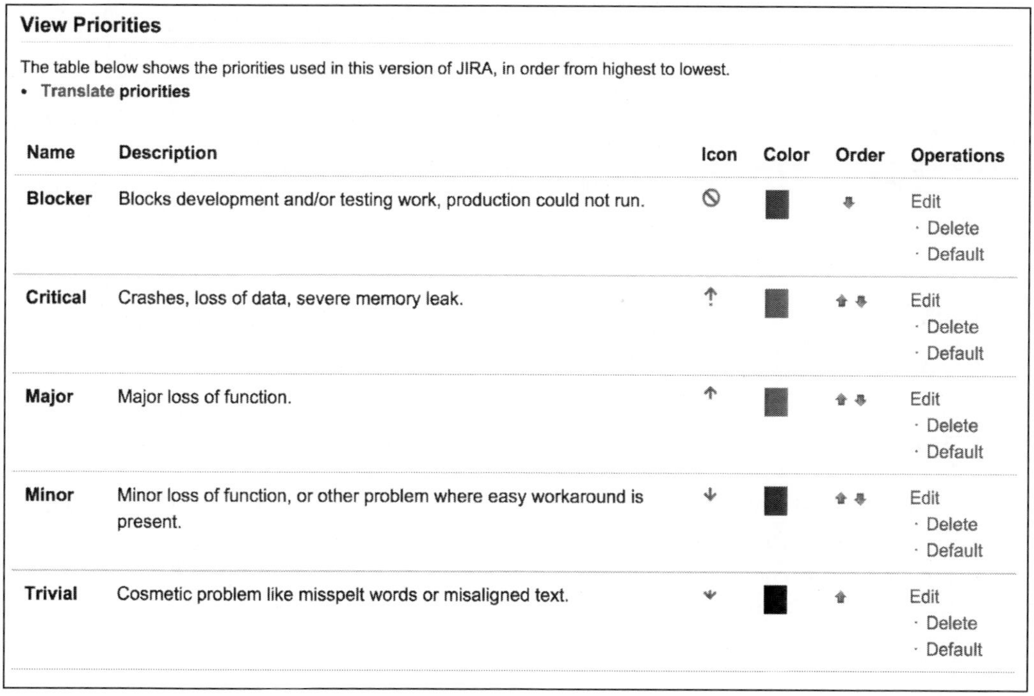

View Priorities

The table below shows the priorities used in this version of JIRA, in order from highest to lowest.
* Translate **priorities**

Name	Description	Icon	Color	Order	Operations
Blocker	Blocks development and/or testing work, production could not run.	⊘	■	⬇	Edit · Delete · Default
Critical	Crashes, loss of data, severe memory leak.	↑	■	⬆ ⬇	Edit · Delete · Default
Major	Major loss of function.	↑	■	⬆ ⬇	Edit · Delete · Default
Minor	Minor loss of function, or other problem where easy workaround is present.	↓	■	⬆ ⬇	Edit · Delete · Default
Trivial	Cosmetic problem like misspelt words or misaligned text.	↓	■	⬆	Edit · Delete · Default

You can customize this list by creating your own priorities. To create new priorities, follow these steps:

1. Browse to the administration console.
2. Select the **Issues** tab and then the **Priorities** option.
3. Specify the name of the new priority.
4. Click the **select image** link to choose an icon for the priority.

5. Specify a color for the priority. You can either type in HTML color hex code directly or use the color picker to help you select the color you want. The color chosen here will be used when icon images cannot be displayed, such as when you export issues to a spreadsheet.

6. Click on the **Add** button.

 Priorities are global. This means that all projects will share the same set of priorities.

The help desk project

In this exercise, we will continue our setup for the project we have created in the previous chapter. We will add the following configurations to our project:

* A set of new issue types that are specific to our help desk project
* A new scheme to limit the selection of issue types

Adding new issue types

Since our project is for a help desk support team, the default issue types that come with JIRA are not appropriate for this purpose. For this reason, let's create our own issue types and associate them with the project. For this exercise, we will create two new issue types, **incident** and **ticket**.

The first step to set up an issue type association is to create the two issue types we need, incident and ticket:

1. Browse to the **Issue Types** page.
2. Click on the **Add Issue Type** button.
3. Type in Incident for the **Name** field.
4. Click on **Add** to create the new Incident issue type.

You should now see the new Incident issue type in the table. Now, let's add the Ticket issue type:

1. Type in Ticket for the **Name** field.
2. Click on **Add** to create the new Ticket issue type.

You should see both the `Incident` and `Ticket` issue types. However, this will only make our new issue types available, but will not make them the only options when creating a new issue for our project. Default issue types, such as Bug and New Feature, which are not applicable for a help desk, are still available. By leaving them there, we are running the risk of confusing the users and allowing mistakes to be made.

If you remember from previous discussions, we can address this problem with a new issue type scheme. Let's go ahead and create one.

Creating an issue type scheme

We want to limit the issue types to be only `Incident` and `Ticket` for our `Global Help Desk` project, but we do not want to affect the other projects that still need to have Bug and other default issue types. So, we need to create a new issue type scheme specifically for support projects, which can be used by us and other teams:

1. Browse to the **Issue Type Schemes** page.
2. Click on the **Add Issue Type Scheme** button.
3. Name our new issue type scheme `Support Desk Issue Type Scheme`.
4. Drag the `Incident` and `Ticket` issue types from the **Available Issue Types** panel to the **Issue Types for Current Scheme** panel.
5. Select **Incident** as the **Default Issue Type** value.
6. Click on the **Save** button.

With the issue type scheme in place, the last step is to apply it to our `Support Desk` project:

1. Click on the **Associate** link for the **Help Desk Issue Type Scheme** option.
2. Select your **Global Help Desk** project.
3. Click on the **Associate** button to apply this issue type scheme to the project.

If you have issues in the Global Helpdesk project with issue types that do not exist in our new issue type scheme, follow the issue type change wizard and change those issues to either Incident or Ticket.

Putting it together

With everything created and set up, you can go back and create a new issue to see how it all looks. If everything works out, you should see something similar to the following screenshot:

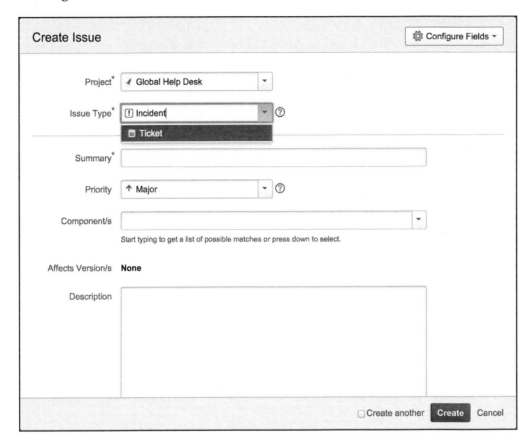

As you can see, `Incident` and `Ticket` are the only issue types that can be selected when creating a new issue for the `Global Help Desk` project.

Summary

In this chapter, we looked at what issues are in JIRA and explored the basic operations of creating, editing, and deleting issues. We also looked at the advanced operations offered by JIRA to enhance how you can manipulate and use issues, such as adding attachments, creating subtasks, linking multiple issues, and so on.

In the next chapter, we will look at fields and what we can do with them.

4

Field Management

Projects are collections of issues, and issues are collections of fields. As we have seen in the earlier chapters, fields are what capture data that can be then displayed to users. There are many different types of fields in JIRA, ranging from simple text fields that let you input alphanumeric texts, to more complicated fields with pickers to assist you in choosing dates and users.

An information system is only as useful as the data that goes into it. By understanding how to effectively use fields, you can turn JIRA into a powerful information system for data collection, processing, and reporting.

In this chapter, we will expand our Help Desk project with these customized fields and configurations, by exploring fields in detail and learning how they relate to other aspects of JIRA. By the end of this chapter, you will have learned the following:

- Understanding built-in and custom fields
- Collecting custom data through custom fields
- Adding behaviors to fields with field configurations
- Understanding field configuration schemes and how to apply them to projects

Built-in fields

JIRA comes with a number of built-in fields. You have already seen a few of them in the previous chapters. Fields such as summary, priority, and assignee are all built-in. They make up the backbone of an issue, and you cannot remove them from the system. For this reason, they are referred to as **system fields**. The following table lists the most important built-in fields in JIRA:

System field	Description
Assignee	Specifies the user who is currently assigned to work on the issue.
Summary	Specifies a one-line summary of the issue.
Description	Provides a detailed description of the issue.
Reporter	Specifies the user who has reported this issue (although most of the time it is also the person who has created the issue, but not always).
Component/s	Specifies the project components the issue belongs to.
Effects Version/s	Specifies the versions the issue effects are found in.
Fix Version/s	Specifies the versions the issue will be fixed in.
Due Date	Specifies the date this issue is due.
Issue Type	Specifies the type of the issue (for example, **Bug** and **New Feature**).
Priority	Specifies how important the issue is compared to other issues.
Resolution	Specifies the current resolution value of the issue (for example, **Unresolved** or **Fixed**).
Time Tracking	Lets users estimate how long the issue will take to be complete.

Custom fields

While JIRA's built-in fields are quite comprehensive for basic general uses, most organizations soon find they have special requirements that cannot be addressed simply with the default fields available. To help you tailor JIRA to your organization's needs, JIRA lets you create and add your own fields to the system, called **custom fields**.

Custom field types

Every custom field belongs to a custom type, which dictates its behavior, appearance, and functionality. Therefore, when you add a custom field to JIRA, you really add another instance of a custom field type.

JIRA comes with over 20 custom field types that you can use straight out of the box. Many of the custom field types are identical to the built-in fields, such as date picker, which is like the due date field. They provide you with simplicity and flexibility that are not available with their built-in counterparts. The following tables break down and list all the JIRA standard custom field types and their characteristics.

Standard fields

These fields are the most basic field types in JIRA. They are usually simple and straightforward to use, such as text field, which allows users to input any text:

Custom field type	Description
Date Picker	These are input fields that allow input with a date picker and enforce valid dates.
Date Time Picker	These are input fields that allow input with a date and time picker and enforce valid date timestamps.
Labels	These are input fields that allow tags to be added to an issue.
Number Field	These are input fields that store and validate numeric values.
Radio Buttons	These are radio buttons that ensure only one value can be selected.
Select List (cascading)	These are multiple select lists where the options for the second select list is dynamically updated based on the value of the first.
Select List (multiple choice)	These are multiple select lists with a configurable list of options.
Select List (single choice)	These are single select lists with a configurable list of options.
Text Field (multi-line)	These are multiple line text-areas enabling entry for large text contents.
Text Field (single-line)	These are basic single link input fields that allow simple text inputs of less than 255 characters.
URL Field	These are input fields that validate a valid URL.
User Picker (single user)	These choose a user from the JIRA user base through either a pop-up user picker window or auto completion.

Advanced fields

These fields provide specialized functions. For example, the **Version Picker** field lets you select a version from the current project. If you have any custom fields from third-party add-ons (see the following section), they will also be listed here:

Custom field type	Description
Group Picker (multiple group)	This chooses one or more user groups using a pop-up picker window.
Group Picker (single group)	This chooses a user group using a pop-up picker window.
Hidden Job Switch	This field type is used for Perforce integration with JIRA.
Job Checkbox	This field type is used for Perforce integration with JIRA.
Project Picker (single project)	This selects lists displaying the projects that are viewable to the user in the system.
Text Field (read only)	This is a read-only text field that does not allow users to set their data. It's only possible to programmatically set the data.
User Picker (multiple users)	This chooses one or more users from the user base through a pop-up picker window.
Version Picker (multiple versions)	This chooses one or more versions from the available versions in the current project.
Version Picker (single version)	This chooses a single version from the available versions in the project.

As you can see, JIRA provides you with a comprehensive list of custom field types. In addition, there are many custom field types developed by third-party vendors (available as **plugins** or **add-ons**) that you can add to your JIRA to enhance its functionality. These custom fields provide many specialized functionalities such as automatically calculating values and retrieving data from databases directly or connecting to an external system. Once you install the plugin, the process of adding custom fields from other vendors is mostly the same as adding custom fields shipped with JIRA. The following list shows some examples of plugins that provide additional useful custom fields:

- **JIRA Enhancer Plugin**: This includes a number of custom fields that will automatically display dates when key events occur for an issue. For example, when the issue was last closed.

- **JIRA Toolkit Plugin**: This provides a number of useful custom fields such as showing the statistics on the users that participate in a given issue and the date when the issue was last commented on.

- **nFeed**: This provides a suite of custom fields that let you connect to databases, remote files, and web services to retrieve data and display them in JIRA.

- **21 CFR Part 11 E-Signature**: This lets users electronically sign issues in JIRA as they work on them, for example, approving an issue to be closed.

- **SuggestiMate for JIRA**: This provides a specialized custom field that shows similar and potentially duplicated issues when creating new issues or browsing through existing ones.

Searchers

For any information system, capturing data is only half of the equation. Users will need to be able to retrieve the data at a later stage, usually through searching, and JIRA is no different. While fields in JIRA are responsible for capturing and displaying data, it is their corresponding searchers that provide the search functionality.

In JIRA, all the built-in fields have searchers associated by default, so you will be able to search issues by their summary or assignee, without any further configuration. For custom fields, however, you will need to specify a searcher for each custom field you add. If you do not specify a searcher, you will not be able to search data based on that field.

For all custom field types that come with JIRA, one or more searchers are available for you to choose from. For example, the Date Picker custom field has a date range searcher, and the User Picker custom field has a user and group searcher. You can select/change the searcher after you create the custom field, as we will see when we cover how to manage custom fields.

Custom field context

Built-in fields, such as priority and resolution, are global across JIRA. What this means is that these fields will have the same set of selections for all projects. Custom fields, on the other hand, are a lot more flexible.

Custom field types, such as select list and radio buttons, can have different sets of options for different projects or different issue types within the same project. This is achieved through what is called **custom field context**.

A custom field context is made up of a combination of applicable projects and applicable issue types. When you are working with an issue, JIRA will check the project and issue type of the current issue to determine if there is a specific context that matches the combination. If one is found, JIRA will load the custom field with any specific settings such as selection options. However, if no context is found, the custom field will not be loaded.

> In JIRA, if no context can be found that matches the project and issue type combination, a custom field does not exist for the said issue.

We will look at how to set custom field contexts in a later section. What you need to remember now is when adding a custom field, you need to make sure that it has the correct context setting.

Managing custom fields

Custom fields are used globally across JIRA, so you will need to have the JIRA Administrator global permission to carry out management operations such as creation and configuration.

JIRA maintains all the custom fields in a centralized location for easy management. Perform the following steps to access the custom field management page:

1. Log in as a JIRA administrator user.

2. Browse to the JIRA administration console.

3. Select the **Issues** tab and then the **Custom Fields** option:

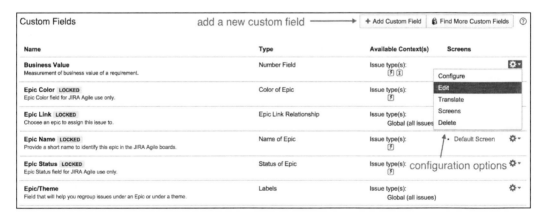

On the **Custom Fields** page, all existing custom fields will be listed. From here, you can see the name of each custom field, their type, the context they belong to, and the screens they are displayed on.

Adding a custom field

Creating a new custom field is a multistep process, and JIRA provides a wizard to help you through it. There are two required steps and an optional step when adding a new custom field. You need to first select the type of custom field, then its name, followed by options if you are adding a select list custom field type. The last optional step is to decide what screens to add the field onto. We will walk you through the following process:

1. Browse the **Custom Fields** page.

2. Click on the **Add Custom Field** button. This will bring you to step 1 of the process, where you can select the custom field type.

3. Search and select the custom field type you wish to add, and click on **Next**. This will bring you to step 2 of the process, where you can specify the custom field's name and options:

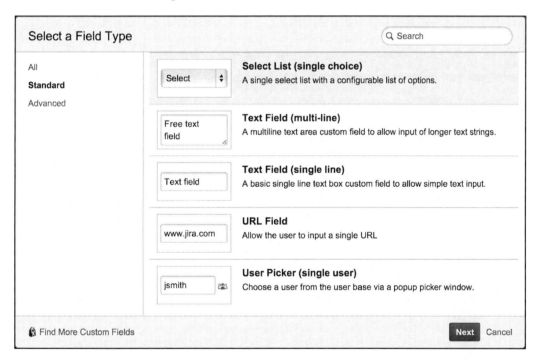

If you do not see the field type you are looking for, select the **All** option from the left-hand side and then search again.

4. Enter values for the **Name** and **Description** fields. If you are creating a selection-based custom field, such as a select list, you will need to add its select options, too (you can update this list later):

5. Click on the **Create** button. This will bring you to the last step of the process, where you can specify which screen you would like to add the field onto. This step is optional as the custom field has already been added in JIRA. You do not have to add the field onto a screen. We will discuss fields and screens in *Chapter 5, Screen Management*.

6. Select the screens and click on **Update**. The following screenshot shows that the newly created field is added to the **Default Screen**:

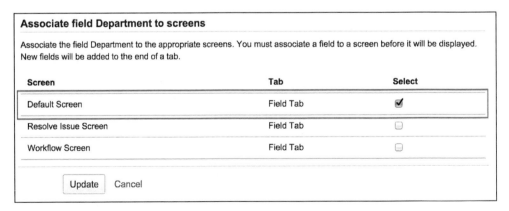

Once a custom field has been created, you will be able to manage its configurations and settings.

Editing/deleting a custom field

Once a custom field has been created, you can edit its details at any time. You may already notice that there is a **Configure** option and an **Edit** option for each custom field. It can be confusing in the beginning to differentiate between the two. Configure specifies options related to the custom field context, which we will discuss in the following sections. Edit specifies options that are global across JIRA for the custom field; these include its name, description, and search templates:

1. Browse to the **Custom Fields** page.

2. Select the **Edit** option by clicking on the cog icon for the custom field you wish to edit from the list of custom fields.

3. Change the custom field details.

4. Click on the **Update** button to apply the changes:

When making changes to the search templates for your custom fields, it is important to note that while the change will take effect immediately, you need to perform a full system re-index in order for JIRA to return the correct search results. This is because for each search template, the underlying search data structure may be different, and JIRA will need to update its search index for the newly applied search template.

For example, if you have a custom field that did not have a searcher and you just applied a searcher to it, no results will be returned until you re-index JIRA. When you make changes to the search template, JIRA will alert you with a message that a re-index will be required, as shown in the following screenshot:

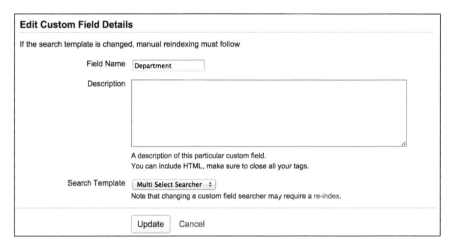

 You can select the background re-index option to avoid any downtime.

We will discuss searching and indexing in more detail in *Chapter 9, Searching, Reporting, and Analysis.*

You can also delete the existing custom fields, as follows:

1. Browse to the **Custom Fields** page.
2. Select the **Delete** option by clicking on the tools icon for the custom field you wish to delete.
3. Click on the **Delete** button to delete the custom field.

Once deleted, you cannot get the custom field back, and you will not be able to retrieve and search the data held by those fields. If you try to create another custom field of the same type and name, it will not inherit the data from the previous custom field, as JIRA assigns unique identifiers to each of them. It is highly recommended to back up your JIRA project before you delete the field.

Configuring a custom field

Now that we have seen how to create and manage custom fields, we can start looking at more advanced configuration options. Different custom field types will have different configuration options available to them. For example, while all the custom fields will have the option to specify one or more contexts, the selection list-based custom fields will also allow you to specify a list of options. We will look at each of the configuration options in the following sections.

To configure a custom field, you need to access the **Configure Custom Field** page, as follows:

1. Browse to the **Custom Fields** page.
2. Select the **Configure** option by clicking on the cog icon for the custom field you wish to configure from the list of custom fields. This will bring you to the **Configure Custom Field** page.

The following screenshot shows that the **Department** custom field has two available contexts, the default context (**Default Configuration Scheme** for **Department**) and **Help Desk Context**, which is applied only to the **Help Desk** project:

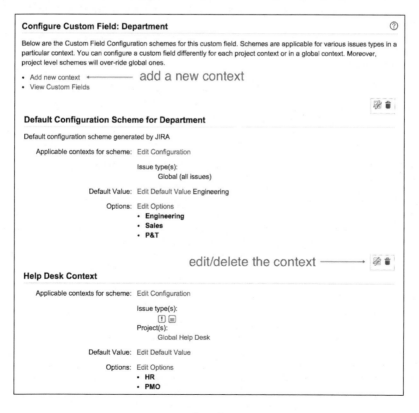

Adding custom field contexts

From time to time, you may need your custom fields to have different behaviors depending on what project the issue is in. For example, if we have a select list custom field called **Department**, we may want it to have a different set of options based on which project the issue is being created in, or even a different default value.

To achieve this level of customization, JIRA allows you to create multiple custom field contexts for a custom field. As we have seen already, a custom field context is a combination of issue types and projects. Therefore, in our example, we can create a context for issue type **Bug** and project **Support** and set the default department to **Engineering**.

 JIRA allows you to configure custom fields based on issue types and projects through contexts. Each project can have only one configuration context per custom field.

Creating a new custom field context is simple. All you need to do is decide the issue type and project combination that will define the context:

1. Browse to the **Configure Custom Field** page for the custom field you wish to create a new context for.

2. Click on the **Add new context** link. This will take you to the **Add configuration scheme context** page.

3. Give a name to the new custom field context in the **Configuration scheme** label field.

4. Select the issue types for the new context under the **Choose applicable issue types** section.

5. Select the projects for the new context under the **Choose applicable context** section.

6. Click on the **Add** button to create the new custom field context.

Each project can only belong to one custom field context per custom field (global context is not counted for this). Once you select a project for context, it will not be available the next time you create a new context. For example, if you create a new context for **Project A**, it will not be listed as an option when you create another context for the same custom field. This is to prevent you from accidentally creating two contexts for the same project.

After a new custom field context has been created, it will not "inherit" any configuration values as the default context such as **Default Value** and **Select Options** from other contexts. You will need to repopulate and maintain the configuration options for each newly created context.

Configuring select options

For custom field types, select the list, checkboxes, radio buttons, and their multiversions. You need to configure their select options before they can become useful to the users. The select options are configured and set on a per custom field context basis. This provides the custom field with the flexibility of having different select options for different projects.

To configure the select options, you need to first select the custom field and then the context that the options will be applied to, as follows:

1. Browse to the **Custom Fields** page.

2. Click on the **Configure** option for the custom field you wish to configure the select options for.

3. Click on the **Edit Options** link for the custom field context to apply the options to.

4. Enter the option values in the **Add New Custom Field Option** section, and click on the **Add** button to add the value. The options will be added in the order in which they are entered into the system. You can manually move the option values up and down or click on **Sort options alphabetically** to let JIRA perform the sorting for you.

5. Click on the **Done** button once you finish configuring the select options:

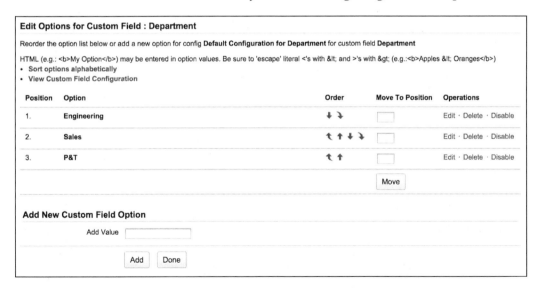

Setting default values

For most custom fields, you can set a default value so your users will not need to fill them unless they have special needs. For text-based custom fields, the default values will be displayed as text by default, when the users create or edit an issue. For selection-based custom fields, the default values will be preselected options for the users.

Just like setting selection options, default options are also set on a per custom field context basis:

1. Browse to the **Custom Fields** page.
2. Click on the **Configure** option for the custom field you wish to configure the select options for.
3. Click on the **Edit Default Value** link for the custom field context to apply the default values to.
4. Set the default value for the custom field.
5. Click on the **Set Default** button to set the default value.

Setting the default value will be different for different custom field types. For text-based custom fields, you will be able to type any text string. For select-based custom fields, you will be able to select from the options you add. For picker-based custom fields, such as User Picker, you will be able to select a user directly from the user base:

Field configuration

As you have already seen, fields are used to capture and display data in JIRA. Fields can also have behaviors, which are defined by field configuration. For each field in JIRA, you can configure its behaviors listed as follows:

- **Field description**: This is the description text that appears under the field when an issue is edited. With field configuration, you can have different description texts for different projects and issue types.

- **Visibility**: This determines if a field should be visible or hidden.

- **Required**: This specifies if a field will be optional or required to have a value when an issue is being created/updated. When applied to a select, checkbox, and radio button custom fields, this will remove the **None** option from the list.

- **Rendering**: This specifies how the content is to be rendered for text-based fields (for example, wiki renderer or simple text renderer for text fields).

A field configuration provides you with control over each individual field in your JIRA, including both built-in and custom fields. Since it is usually a good practice to reuse the same set of fields instead of creating new ones for every project, JIRA allows you to create multiple field configurations, with which we can specify different behaviors on the same set of fields and apply them to different projects.

We will be looking at how to manage and apply multiple field configurations in the later sections of this chapter. But first, let's take a close look at how to create new field configurations and what we can do with them.

You can access the field configuration management page through the JIRA administration console:

1. Browse to the JIRA administration console.

2. Select the **Issues** tab and then the **Field Configurations** option. This will bring you to the **View Field Configurations** page:

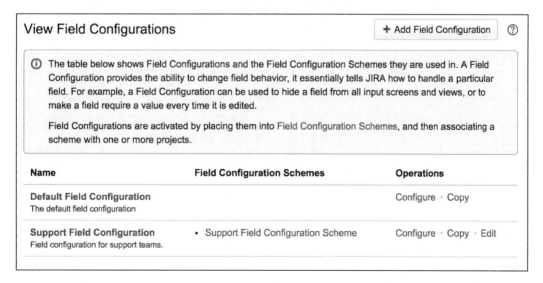

Adding a field configuration

Creating new field configurations is simple. All you need to do is specify the name and the short description for the new configuration:

1. Browse to the **View Field Configurations** page.

2. Specify the name for the new field configuration in the **Add Field Configuration** section.

3. Provide a short description for the field configuration.

4. Click on the **Add** button to create a field configuration.

As we will see later in the *Field Configuration Scheme* section, field configurations are linked to issue types, so it is recommended to name them based on the issue type they will be applied to and with a version number at the end, for example, Bugs Field Configuration 1.0. This way, when you need to make changes to the field configuration, you can increment the version number, leaving a history of changes you can revert back to.

After a field configuration is created, it is put into what we call the inactive state. This means the configuration is not being used anywhere in JIRA and you are free to edit and delete it. In order to activate the field configuration, we need to associate it with a field configuration scheme. We will look at how to do this in later sections.

Editing/deleting a field configuration

You can update existing field configuration details and delete them all together. The details you can edit are the configuration's name and description:

1. Browse to the **View Field Configurations** page.

2. Click on the **Edit** link for the field configuration you wish to edit. This will take you to the **Edit Field Configuration** page.

3. Update the **Name** and **Description** fields with new values.

4. Click on the **Update** button to apply the changes.

You will be able to edit field configuration details at anytime. However, for deletion, you can only delete the configuration when it is inactive. Once you associate the configuration with a scheme, which will put the configuration into an active state, you cannot delete it until it is back to the inactive state. For you to put the field configuration back into the inactive state, you need to unassociate it from the field configuration scheme:

1. Browse to the **View Field Configurations** page.

2. Click on the **Delete** link for the field configuration you wish to delete. This will take you to the **Delete Field Configuration** page for confirmation.

3. Click on the **Delete** button to delete the field configuration.

Copying a field configuration

A field configuration contains configuration details for all fields in JIRA. For a moderately complicated instance, you are likely to have over 20 fields. It will be very unproductive if you have to reconfigure every single field again, whenever you need to create a new set of field configurations, usually with only minor differences for a few fields.

To simplify your task, JIRA allows you to copy an existing field configuration and use that as a base for you to make only the necessary changes. This greatly reduces the amount of effort required as you will not have to reconfigure all the fields that are common across all the use cases:

1. Browse to the **View Field Configurations** page.

2. Click on the **Copy** link for the field configuration you wish to copy. This will take you to the **Copy Field Configuration** page.

3. Enter a new name and description for the field configuration.

4. Click on the **Copy** button to copy the field configuration.

Managing field configurations

Now that we have seen how to create, edit, delete, and copy field configurations, it is time for us to take a closer look at the different configuration options. Just a quick recap—each field configuration includes all fields available in JIRA, and its behavior is defined specifically to each field configuration. We will then set a context for the field configurations through the use of the field configuration scheme, which will determine when a field configuration will become active for a given issue.

Perform the following steps to access the field configuration options:

1. Browse to the **View Field Configurations** page.

2. Click on the **Configure** link for the field configuration you wish to configure. This will take you to the **View Field Configuration** page.

On this page, all the fields and their current configuration options that are currently set for the selected field configuration are listed:

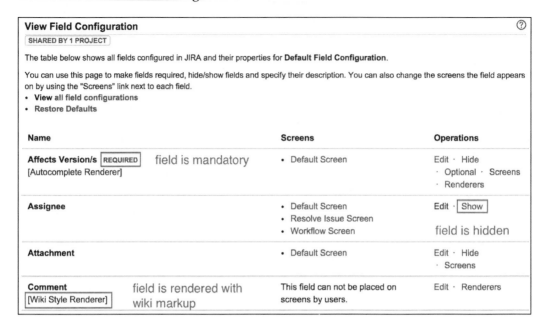

As you can see, there are several options you can configure for each field, and depending on the field type, the options may vary. While we will be looking at each of the options, it is important to note that some of the options will override each other. This is JIRA trying to protect you from accidentally creating a configuration combination that will break your production system. For example, if a field is set to both hidden and required, your users will not be able to create or edit issues, so JIRA will not allow you to set a field to required if you have already set it to hidden.

Field description

While having a meaningful name for your fields will help your users understand what the fields are for, providing a short description will provide more context and meaning. Field descriptions are displayed under the fields when you create or edit an issue. To add a description for a field, do the following:

1. Browse to the **View Field Configuration** page for the field configuration you wish to use.

2. Click on the **Edit** link for the field you wish to set a description for.

3. Add a description for the field, and click on **Update**.

For custom fields, the description you enter here will override the description you provide when you first create them.

Field requirement

You can set certain fields as required or mandatory for issues. This is a very useful feature as it ensures that critical information can be captured when users create issues. For example, for our support system, it makes sense to have our users enter in the system that is misbehaving in a field and make that field compulsory to help our support engineers.

You have already seen required fields in action. System fields, such as **Summary** and **Issue Type**, are compulsory in JIRA (and you cannot change that). When you do not specify a value for a required field, JIRA will display an error message underneath the field, telling you that the value is required.

When you add a new field into JIRA, such as custom fields, it is optional by default, meaning users do not need to specify a value. You can then change the setting to make those fields required:

1. Browse to the **View Field Configuration** page for the field configuration you wish to use.
2. Click on the **Required/Optional** link for the field you wish to set as the mandatory requirement.

You will notice that once a field is set to required, there will be a small required text label in red next to the field name. When you create or edit an issue, the field will have a red * character next to its name. This is JIRA's way of indicating that a field is mandatory.

Field visibility

Most fields in JIRA can be hidden from user's view. When a field is set to hidden, users will not see the fields on any screens including issues such as create, update, and view. Perform the following steps to show or hide a field:

1. Browse to the **View Field Configuration** page for the field configuration you wish to use.
2. Click on the **Show/Hide** link for the field you wish to show or hide, respectively.

Once a field has been set to hidden, it will not appear on screen and you will not be able to search in it. However, you can still use tools such as scripts to set values for hidden fields. For this reason, hidden fields are used to store data that is used by automated processes.

Not all fields can be hidden. Built-in fields, such as Summary and Issue Type, cannot be hidden. When you set a field to hidden, you will notice that you can no longer set the field as required. As stated earlier, setting a field to required will make JIRA enforce a value to be entered into the field when you create or edit an issue. If the field is hidden, there will be no way for you to set a value and you will be stuck. This is why JIRA will automatically disable the required option, especially if you have already hidden a field. On the other hand, if you marked a field as required, when you hide the same field, you will notice that the field is no longer required. The rule of thumb is that field visibility will override field requirement.

 A field cannot be both hidden and required.

Field rendering

Renderers control how a field will be displayed when it is being viewed or edited. Some built-in and custom fields have more than one renderer, and for these fields, you can choose which one to use. For example, for text-based fields, such as **Description**, you can choose to use the default simple text renderer or the more sophisticated wiki style renderer that will allow you to use wiki markup to add more styling.

JIRA ships with four different renderers:

- **Default text renderer**: This is the default renderer for text-based fields. Contents are rendered as plain text. If the text resolves a JIRA issue key, the renderer will automatically turn that into an HTML link.

- **Wiki style renderer**: This is an enhanced renderer for text-based fields. It allows you to use wiki markup to decorate your text content.

- **Select list renderer**: This is the default renderer for selection-based fields. It is rendered as a standard HTML select list.

- **Autocomplete renderer**: This is an enhanced renderer for selection-based fields, and it provides an autocomplete feature to assist users as they start typing into the fields.

The following table lists all the fields that can have special renders configured and their available options:

Field	Available renderers
Description	Wiki style renderer and default text renderer.
Comment	Wiki style renderer and default text renderer.
Environment	Wiki style renderer and default text renderer.
Component	Autocomplete renderer and select list renderer.
Affects version	Autocomplete renderer and select list renderer.
Fix versions	Autocomplete renderer and select list renderer.
Custom field of type "Free Text Field (unlimited text)"	Wiki style renderer and default text renderer.
Custom field of type "Text Field"	Wiki style renderer and default text renderer.
Custom field of type "Multi Select"	Autocomplete renderer and select list renderer.
Custom field of type "Version Picker"	Autocomplete renderer and select list renderer.

Perform the following steps to set the renderer for a field:

1. Browse the **View Field Configuration** page for the field configuration you wish to use.

2. Click on the **Renderer** link for the field you wish to set a renderer for (if it is available). You will be taken to the **Edit Field Renderer** page.

3. Select the renderer from the available drop-down list.

4. Click on the **Update** button to set the renderer:

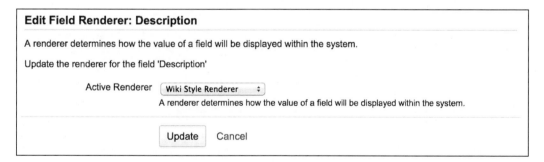

There are other custom renderers developed by third-party vendors. Just like custom fields, these are packaged as add-ons that you can install in JIRA. Once installed, these custom renderers will be available for the selection of the appropriate field types.

A good example is the **JEditor** plugin, which provides a rich-text editor for all text-based fields such as **Description**.

Screens

In order for a field to appear, it needs to be placed onto a screen. You have already seen this when creating new custom fields. One of the steps in the creation process is to select what screens to add the custom field to. Screens will be discussed further in *Chapter 5, Screen Management,* so we will not spend too much time understanding them right now.

What you need to know for now is that after a field has been added to a screen, you can add it to additional screens or take it off completely. If you are working with just one field, you can configure it here from the field configurations. If you have multiple fields to update, a better approach will be to work directly with screens, as we will see in *Chapter 5, Screen Management.*

Field configuration scheme

With multiple field configurations, JIRA determines when to apply each of the configurations through the field configuration scheme. A field configuration scheme maps field configurations to issue types. This scheme can then be associated with one or more projects.

This allows you to group multiple field configurations mapped to issue types and apply them to a project in one go. The project will then be able to determine which field configuration to apply, based on the type of the issue. For example, for a given project, you can have different field configurations for bugs and tasks.

This grouping of configurations into schemes also provides you with the option to reuse existing configurations without duplicating work, as each scheme can be reused and associated with multiple projects.

Managing field configuration schemes

You can manage all your field configuration schemes from the **View Field Configuration Schemes** page. From there, you will be able to add, configure, edit, delete, and copy schemes:

1. Browse to the JIRA administration console.

2. Select the **Issues** tab and then the **Field Configuration Schemes** option. This will bring you to the **View Field Configuration Schemes** page:

Adding a field configuration scheme

The first step to group your field configurations is to create a new field configuration scheme. By default, JIRA does not come with any field configuration schemes. All the projects will use the system default field configuration. The new field configuration scheme will hold all the mappings between our field configurations and issue types.

To create a new field configuration scheme, all you need to do is specify the name and an optional description for the scheme:

1. Browse to the **View Field Configuration Schemes** page.
2. Enter in a name for the new field configuration scheme in the **Add Field Configuration Scheme** section.
3. Optionally, enter a short description for the scheme.
4. Click on the **Add** button to create the scheme.

Since field configuration schemes are applied to projects, it is a good practice to name them according to the projects. For example, the scheme for the sales project can be named **Sales Field Configuration Scheme**. You can add a version number after the name to help you maintain changes.

Once the new field configuration scheme is created, it will be displayed in the table that lists all the existing schemes. At this time, the scheme is in an inactive state as it does not contain any configuration mappings and is not active in JIRA yet.

Editing/deleting a field configuration scheme

You can update existing field configuration scheme details and delete them altogether. The details you can edit are the scheme's name and description. You can also update its field configurations mapping, which will be covered in later sections:

1. Browse to the **View Field Configuration Schemes** page.

2. Click on the **Edit** link for the field configuration scheme you wish to edit. This will take you to the **Edit Field Configuration Scheme** page.

3. Update the **Name** and **Description** fields with new values.

4. Click on the **Update** button to apply the changes.

Just like field configurations, you can only delete a field configuration scheme if it is not being used by a project. To delete the scheme, you will have to first unassociate the scheme from all the projects you applied it to and then:

1. Browse to the **View Field Configuration Schemes** page.

2. Click on the **Delete** link for the field configuration scheme you wish to delete. This will take you to the **Delete Field Configuration Scheme** page for confirmation.

3. Click on the **Delete** button to delete the scheme.

Copying a field configuration scheme

There will be times when you need a new field configuration scheme and the requirements are very similar to a scheme that you already have. Instead of creating a new scheme from scratch, you can choose to copy the existing scheme as a base and simply make some quick modifications. JIRA allows you to achieve this by letting you copy the existing schemes:

1. Browse to the **View Field Configuration Schemes** page.

2. Click on the **Copy** link for the field configuration scheme you wish to copy. This will take you to the **Copy Field Layout Configuration** page.

3. Specify the name and description of the new scheme.

4. Click on the **Copy** button to create a copy.

Once the newly copied scheme is created, you will be able to modify its field configuration and issue type mappings as per your requirements, which we will look at in the next section.

Configuring a field configuration scheme

Once you have a new field configuration scheme set up, you will be able to add mapping between field configurations and issue types. For each field configuration scheme, one issue type can be mapped to only one field configuration, while each field configuration can be mapped to multiple issue types. The following screenshot shows how **Development Field Configuration** is applied to both the **Technical Task** and **Improvement** issue types, and also how **Bug Field Configuration** is applied to the **Bug** issue type:

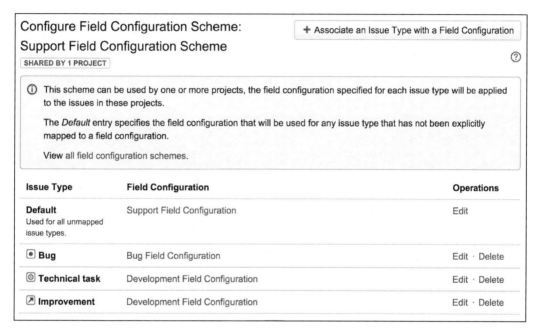

 One issue type can only be mapped to one field configuration.

When a field configuration scheme is first created, JIRA creates a default mapping, which maps all unmapped issue types to the default field configuration. You cannot delete this default mapping as it acts as a "catch all" condition for mappings that you do not specify in your scheme. What you need to do is add more specific mappings that will take precedence over this default mapping:

1. Browse to the **View Field Configuration Schemes** page.

2. Click on the **Configure** link for the field configuration scheme you wish to configure.

3. Click on the **Associate an Issue Type with a Field configuration** button.

4. Select the issue type and field configuration from the dialog.

5. Click on the **Add** button to add the mapping.

You can repeat these steps to add more mapping for other issue types. All unmapped issue types will use the **Default** mapping.

Associating a field configuration scheme with a project

After you create a new field configuration scheme and establish the mappings, the configurations will not take effect immediately. The scheme is still in the inactive state. In order to activate the scheme, you need to associate the scheme with a project for the configurations to take effect.

It is important to note that once you associate the field configuration scheme with a project, you cannot delete it until you remove all the associations so the scheme becomes inactive again.

To activate a field configuration scheme, you need to establish the association on a per project level. This means you need to go to each individual project and set the field configuration scheme option for them:

1. Browse to the project you wish to associate the field configuration scheme to.

2. Click on the **Administration** tab to go to the project's administration page.

3. Click on the **Fields** option from the left panel.

4. Select the **Use a different scheme** option from the **Actions** menu.

5. Select the new field configuration scheme and click on the **Associate** button.

As shown in the following screenshot, the project is using the **Support Field Configuration Scheme**, which has three configurations:

- The Bug issue type is using **Bug Field Configuration**.

- **Improvement** and **Technical Task** are using **Development Field Configuration**.

- All other issue types are using the default **Support Field Configuration**.

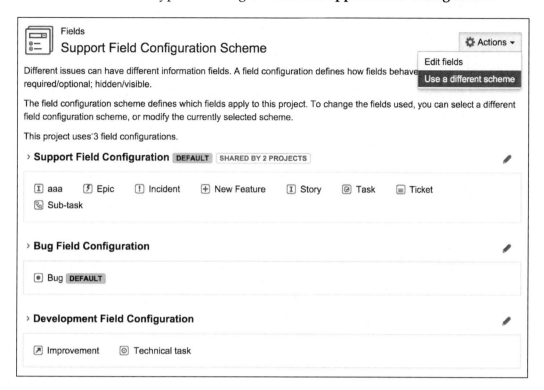

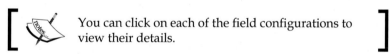

You can click on each of the field configurations to view their details.

You can repeat steps 3 to 6 to associate the field configuration scheme with more projects.

The Help Desk project

Now that you have seen how to manage fields in JIRA, it is time to expand on your Help Desk project to include some customized fields and configurations to help your support staff.

What we will do this time is add a few new custom fields to help capture some additional useful data from the business users when they log an incident. We will also create a customized field configuration specially designed for our support team. Lastly, we will tie everything together by associating our fields, configurations, and projects through the field configuration schemes.

Setting up a custom field

Since you are implementing a support system, one common feature is to be able to escalate the incident, and for every escalation, a group of users will be notified automatically. The automatic escalation and notification aspects of this feature will be covered and implemented in later chapters, but what we do need right now is a way to capture the information, such as the following:

- Does the issue require escalation?
- What is the current escalation level?
- Who should be notified when the issue is escalated?

To address these requirements, we will add three custom fields, one per data requirement.

The first custom field we will add is `Is Escalation Required`. We want to have this as an option so that not all tickets raised will require escalation. Some tickets may not be urgent or are simply for investigation purposes. We will also mark this field as required, so the users will need to indicate if they require an escalation. To help our users, we will provide a default value of `Yes`, so tickets by default will require escalation. Since this is a single selection field, we will be using radio buttons:

1. Browse to the **View Custom Fields** page.
2. Click on the **Add Custom Field** link.
3. Select the **Radio Buttons** custom field type.
4. Give the custom field the name `Is Escalation Required`.
5. Add two options, `Yes` and `No`, and click on **Create**.
6. Select **Default Screen** and click on **Update**.

The second custom field is a simple text-based field, which will indicate what level of escalation the ticket is currently at. We do not want users (support or business) to be able to change the values as this should be determined by the system automatically, so we will be using a read-only text field. We will make use of this field in later chapters:

1. Browse to the **View Custom Fields** page.
2. Click on the **Add Custom Field** link.
3. Select the **Read-only Text Field** custom field type.
4. Give the custom field the name as `Escalation Level`.
5. Select **Default Screen** and click on **Update**.

Finally, the third custom field will contain a list of users from JIRA's user base who will receive notifications when the ticket is being escalated:

1. Browse to the **View Custom Fields** page.

2. Click on the **Add Custom Field** link.

3. Select **User Picker (multiple users)** custom field type and click on **Next**.

4. Name the custom field `Escalation List` and click on **Create**.

5. Select **Default Screen** and click on **Update**.

Setting up the field configuration

Now that we have our custom fields ready, the next step is to create a new field configuration so that we can specify the behaviors of our custom fields. Previously, we decided to make the **Is Escalation Required** field required, so there will be no ambiguity when it comes to determining if a ticket needs to be escalated. Let's now start with creating a new field configuration first:

1. Browse to the **View Field Configurations** page.

2. Click on the **Add Field Configuration** button.

3. Name the new field configuration `Help Desk Field Configuration`.

4. Provide a helpful description **Field configuration** for the Help Desk team.

5. Click on the **Add** button to create a new field configuration. Now that we have our new field configuration, we can start adding configurations to our new custom fields.

6. Click on the **Required** link for the **Is Escalation Required** custom field. (If you do not see the **Is Escalation Required** field in the list of fields, please go back to the **View Custom Fields** page to check whether the field has been created successfully.)

Setting up a field configuration scheme

We have our custom fields, have configured the relevant options, created a new field configuration, and set the behavior of our fields. It is time to add them to a scheme:

1. Browse to the **View Field Configuration Schemes** page.

2. Click on the **Add Field Configuration Scheme** button.

3. Name the new field configuration scheme `Help Desk Field Configuration Scheme`, as we will be applying this to our Help Desk project.

4. Provide a helpful description such as Field configuration scheme for the Help Desk team.

5. Click on the **Add** button to create a new field configuration scheme.

With the field configuration scheme in place, we can now activate our configurations. Since this is designed for our Help Desk team, we would want to apply the field configurations to the issue types that are applicable to the Help Desk project, that is, **Ticket** and **Incident**:

1. Click on the **Associate an Issue Type with a Field Configuration** button.

2. Select the issue type as **Ticket** and the field configuration as **Help Desk Field Configuration**.

3. Click on the **Add** button to add the association.

4. Repeat steps 1 to 3 for the **Incident** issue type.

Putting it together

OK, we have done all the hard work. We created new custom fields, a new field configuration, and a new field configuration scheme; the last step is to put everything together and see it in action:

1. Browse to the **Project Administration** page for our Help Desk project.

2. Click on the **Fields** link from the left-hand side and the **Use a different scheme** option from the **Actions** menu.

3. Select **Help Desk Field Configuration Scheme** and click on the **Associate** button.

Alright, we are all done! You can pat yourself on the back, sit back, and take a look at your hard work in action.

Create a new issue type, **Incident**, under the Help Desk project, and you will see your new custom fields at the bottom of the page (you will not see **Escalation Level**, as it is read-only, so it does not appear on the **Create/Edit** screen). As shown in the following screenshot, the **Is Escalation Required** field is mandatory and an error message is displayed if we do not select a value for it:

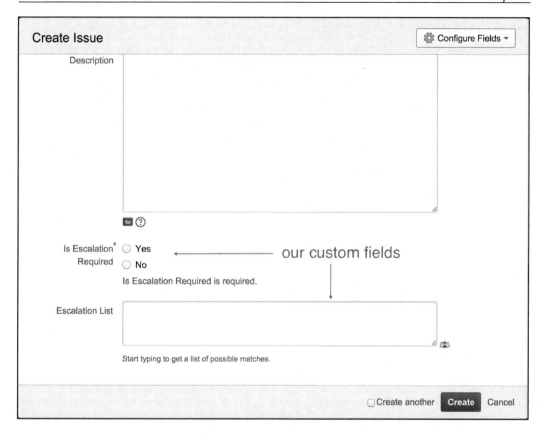

Go ahead and create the incident by filling in the fields. On the **View Issue** page, you will see your new custom fields displayed along with the values you provide:

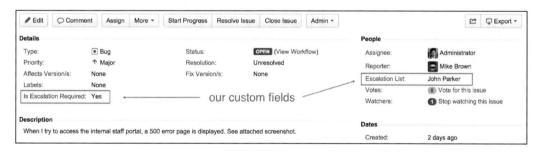

Summary

In this chapter, we looked at fields in JIRA. We also looked at how JIRA is able to extend its ability to capture user data through custom fields. We explored how we can specify different behavior for fields under different contexts through the use of field configurations and schemes.

In the next chapter, we will expand on what we learned about fields by formally introducing you to screens, and how combining fields and screens provide users with the most natural and logical forms to assist them in creating and logging issues.

5
Screen Management

Fields collect data from users, and you have seen how to create your own custom fields from a wide range of field types, to address your different requirements. Indeed, data collection is at the center of any information system, but that is only half of the story. How data is captured is just as critical. Data input forms need to be organized so that users do not feel overwhelmed, and the general flow of fields needs to be logically structured and grouped into sections. This is where screens come in.

In this chapter, we will pick up where we left off from the last chapter and explore the relationship between fields and screens. We will further discuss how you can use screens to customize your JIRA to provide users with a better user experience. By the end of the chapter, you will learn the following:

- What screens are and how to create them
- How to add fields onto screens
- How to break down your screen into logical sections with tabs
- The relationship between screens and issue operations
- How to link screens with projects and issue types

JIRA and screens

Before you can start working with screens, you need to first understand what they are and how they are used in JIRA.

Compared to a normal paper-based form, fields in JIRA are like the checkboxes and spaces that you have to fill in, and screens are like the form documents themselves. When fields are created in JIRA, they need to be added to screens in order to be presented to users. Therefore, you can say that screens are like groupings or containers for fields.

In most cases, screens need to be associated with issue operations through what are known as screen schemes. **Screen schemes** map screens to operations such as creating, viewing, and editing issues so that you can have different screens for different operations. Screen schemes are then associated with issue type screen schemes, which when applied to projects will map screen schemes to issue types. This lets each issue type in a project have its own set of screens. The only time when a screen will be used directly is when it is associated with a workflow transition. In JIRA, a workflow defines the various statuses an issue can go through, for example, an issue can go from open to closed. Transitions are the actions that take the issue from one status to the next, and JIRA lets you display a screen as part of the action if you choose to. We will cover workflows in *Chapter 6, Workflows and Business Processes*.

To help you visualize how screens are used in JIRA, Atlassian has provided the following figure that summarizes the relationship between fields, screens, and their respective schemes:

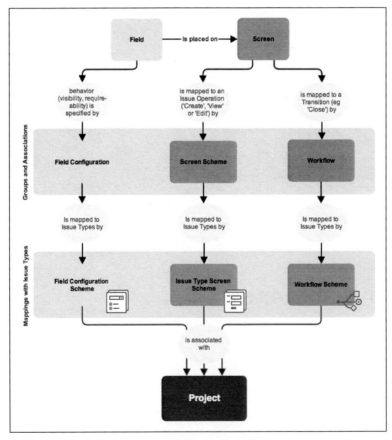

Image source: https://confluence.atlassian.com/display/JIRA/
Configuring+Fields+and+Screens

Working with screens

While many other software systems provide users with limited control over the presentation of screens, JIRA is very flexible when it comes to screen customizations. You can create your own screens and decide what fields are to be placed on them and their orders. You can also decide which screens are to be displayed for major issue operations. In JIRA, you can create and design customized screens for the following operations:

- Create an issue in the create issue dialog box
- Edit an issue when an issue is being updated
- View an issue after an issue is created and is being viewed by users
- Manage workflows during workflow transitions (workflows will be covered in *Chapter 6, Workflows and Business Processes*)

Screens are maintained centrally from the administration console, which means you need to be a JIRA administrator to create and configure screens. Perform the following steps to access the screens page:

1. Log in as a JIRA administrator user.
2. Browse to the JIRA administration console.
3. Select the **Issues** tab and then the **Screens** option, this will bring up the **View Screens** page.

The **View Screens** page lists all the screens that are currently available in your JIRA instance. You can select a screen and configure what fields will be on this screen, and decide how you can divide a screen into various tabs.

For each of the screens listed here, JIRA will also tell you what screen scheme each of the screens are a part of and the workflows that are being used. You have probably noticed that for screens that are either part of a screen scheme or workflow, there is no **Delete** option available as you cannot delete screens that are in use. You need to unassociate the screen from screen schemes and/or workflows to delete them, as shown in the following screenshot:

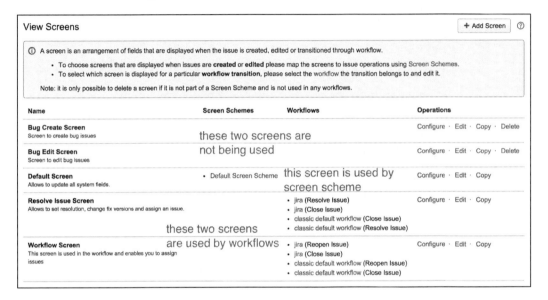

As shown in the preceding screenshot, for each screen, you can perform the following operations:

- **Configure**: This configures what fields are to be placed on the screen. Not to be confused with the **Edit** operation.

- **Edit**: This updates the screen's name and description.

- **Copy**: This makes a copy of the selected screen, including its tabs and field configurations.

- **Delete**: This deletes the screen from JIRA. Only available if it is not being used by a screen scheme or workflow.

Adding a new screen

JIRA comes with three screens by default. You have already seen them while creating a new issue, resolving an issue, and transitioning an issue through a workflow. As a matter of fact, if you have not made any customizations to screens, every issue screen you see will be one of the following:

- **Default Screen**: This screen is used for creating, editing, and viewing issues
- **Resolve Issue Screen**: This screen is used when resolving and closing issues
- **Workflow Screen**: This screen is used when transitioning issues through workflows (if configured to have a screen, such as **Reopen Issue**)

While these screens are able to cover the most basic requirements, you will soon find yourself outgrowing them, and adjustments will need to be made. For example, if you want to keep certain fields, such as priority or read-only, so that they shouldn't be changed after issue creation, you can achieve this by setting up different screens for creating and editing issues. Another example will be to have different create and edit screens for different issue types, such as bug and task. In these cases, you will need to create your own screen in JIRA using the following steps:

1. Browse to the **View Screens** page.
2. Click on the **Add Screen** button. This will bring up the **Add Screen** dialog box.
3. Enter a meaningful name for the new screen. It is a good idea to name your screen after its purpose, for example, `Bug Create Screen` to indicate that it is the screen to create new bug issues.
4. Enter an optional short description for the screen.
5. Click on the **Add** button to create the screen.

At this point, your new screen is blank with no fields in it. You will see in later sections how to add fields onto screens and put them to use.

Editing/deleting a screen

You can edit existing screens to update their details to help keep your configurations up to date and consistent. Perform the following steps to edit a screen:

1. Browse to the **View Screens** page.
2. Click on the **Edit** link for the screen you wish to update. This will take you to the **Edit Screen** page.
3. Update the name and description of the screen.
4. Click on the **Update** button to apply your changes.

To delete an existing screen, it must not be used by any screen schemes or workflows. If it is associated with a screen scheme or workflow, you will not be able to delete it. You will need to undo the association first. Perform the following steps to delete a screen:

1. Browse to the **View Screens** page.
2. Click on the **Delete** link for the screen you wish to remove. This will take you to the **Delete Screen** page for confirmation.
3. Click on the **Delete** button to remove the screen.

By deleting a screen, you do not delete the fields that are on the screen from the system.

Copying a screen

Screens can be complicated with many of fields ordered logically, so creating a new screen from scratch may not be the most efficient method if there is already a similar one available. Just like with many other entities in JIRA, you can make a copy of an existing screen, thus cutting down the time that would otherwise take you to re-add all the fields:

1. Browse to the **View Screens** page.
2. Click on the **Copy** link for the screen you wish to copy. This will take you to the **Copy Screen** page.
3. Enter a new name and description for the screen.
4. Click on the **Copy** button to copy the screen.

Configuring screens

Creating a new screen is like getting a blank piece of paper; the fun part is to add and arrange the fields on the screen. Fields in JIRA are arranged and displayed from top to bottom in a single column. You have full control of what fields can be added and in what order they can be arranged.

The only exception to this is for the View screen. When you are viewing an issue, fields are grouped together by type. For example, user fields such as reporter and assignee are displayed together on the top right-hand side of the page. Also note that for built-in fields such as **Summary** and **Issue** type, even if you take them off the screen, they will still be displayed when viewing an issue. For these fields, you cannot change their position on the screen.

JIRA also allows you to break your screens into tabs or pages within a form, and you can do all of this within a single configuration page. It is this level of flexibility combined with simplicity that makes JIRA a very powerful tool.

Perform the following steps to configure an existing screen:

1. Browse to the **View Screens** page.
2. Click on the **Configure** link for the screen you wish to configure.

On this page, you can do the following:

- Add/remove fields onto the screen
- Arrange the order of the fields
- Create/delete tabs on the screen
- Move fields from one tab to another

Adding a field to a screen

When you first create a screen, it is of little use. In order for screens to have items to present to the users, you must first add fields onto the screens:

1. Browse to the **Configure Screen** page for the screen you wish to configure.
2. Select the fields you would like to add by typing in the field's name in the **Select Field ...** drop-down list. JIRA will auto match the field as you type, as shown in the following screenshot.

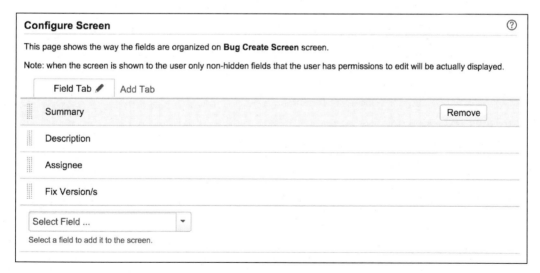

Fields are added to the bottom of the list. You can reorder the list of fields by simply dragging them up and down.

Deleting a field from a screen

Fields can be taken off from a screen completely. When a field is taken off, the field will not appear when the screen is presented to the users. There is a subtle difference between deleting a field from a screen and hiding it (discussed in the previous chapter). Although both the actions will prevent the field from showing up, by removing the field, issues will not receive a value for that field when they are created. This becomes important when a field is configured to have a default value. When the field is removed, the issue will not have the default value for the field, while if the field is simply hidden, the default value will be applied.

You will also need to pay close attention when deleting fields off a screen as there is no confirmation dialog. Make sure you do not delete required fields, such as summary, from a screen used to create new issues. As seen in *Chapter 4, Field Management*, JIRA will prevent you from hiding fields that are marked as required, but JIRA does not prevent you from taking the required fields off the screen. Therefore, it is possible for you to end up in a situation where JIRA requires a value for a field that does not exist on the screen. This can lead to very confusing error messages to the end users:

1. Browse to the **Configure Screen** page for the screen you wish to configure.

2. Hover your mouse over the field you want to delete and click on the **Remove** button.

When you delete a field from a screen, existing issues will not lose their values for the field. Once you add the field back, the values will be displayed again.

Using screen tabs

For most cases, you will be sequentially adding fields to a screen, and users will fill them from top to bottom. However, there will be cases where your screen becomes over complicated and cluttered due to the sheer number of fields you need or you simply want to have a way to logically group several fields together and separate them from the rest. This is where tabs come in.

If you think of screens as the entire form a user must fill in, then tabs will be individual pages or sections that make up the whole document. Tabs go from left to right, so it is a good practice to design your tabs to flow logically from left to right. For example, the first tab can gather general information, such as summary and description. Subsequent tabs will gather more domain-specific information.

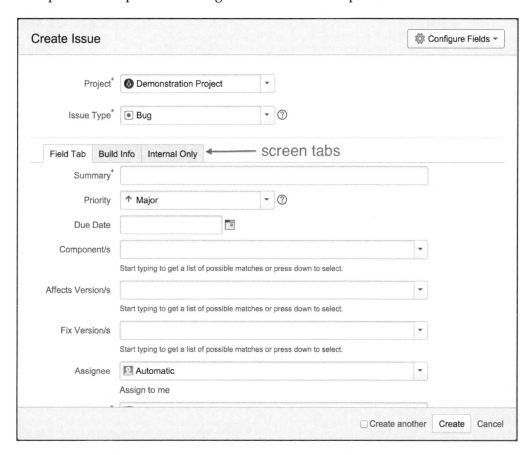

Adding a tab to a screen

You can add tabs to any screen in JIRA. In fact, by default, all screens have a default tab called **Field Tab** that is used to host all the fields. You can add new tabs to a screen to break down and better manage your screen presentation:

1. Browse to the **View Screens** page.
2. Click on the **Configure** link for the screen you wish to add a new tab for.
3. Click on the **Add Tab** link and enter a name for the tab.
4. Click on the **Add** button to create the tab.

Tabs are organized horizontally from left to right. When you add a new tab to the screen, they are appended to the end of the list. You can change the order of tabs by dragging them left and right in the list, as shown in the following screenshot:

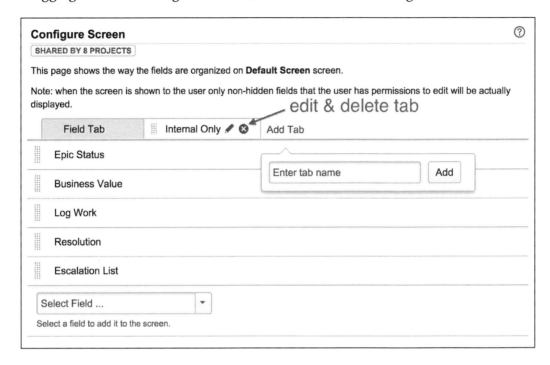

You can also move fields from one tab to another by dragging the field and hovering it over to the target tab. This will save you some time from having to manually remove a field from a tab and then add it to the new tab.

Editing/deleting a tab

Just like screens, you can maintain existing tabs by editing their names and/or removing them from the screen. Perform the following steps to edit a tab's name:

1. Browse to the **View Screens** page.
2. Click on the **Configure** link for the screen that has the tab you wish to edit.
3. Select the tab by clicking on it.
4. Click on the **Edit** icon and enter a new name for the tab.
5. Click on the **OK** button to apply the change.

When you delete a tab, the fields that are on the tab will be taken off the screen. You will need to re-add or move them to a different tab if you still want those fields to appear on the screen. You cannot delete the last tab on the screen. To delete a tab perform the following steps:

1. Browse to the **View Screens** page.
2. Click on the **Configure** link for the screen that has the tab you wish to edit.
3. Select the tab by clicking on it.
4. Click on the **Delete** icon. JIRA will ask you to confirm whether you want to delete the tab and list all the fields present.
5. Click on the **Delete** button to remove the tab from the screen.

Working with screen schemes

You have seen how we can create and manage screens and how to configure what fields to add to the screens. The next piece of the puzzle is letting JIRA know how to choose the screen that has to be displayed for each issue operation.

Screens are displayed during issue operations, and a screen scheme defines the mapping between screens and the operations. With a screen scheme, you can control the screen for displaying each of the issue operations, as follows:

*   **Create Issue**: This screen is shown when you create a new issue
*   **Edit Issue**: This screen is shown when you edit an existing issue
*   **View Issue**: This screen is shown when you view an issue

By default, all the three operations use the same screen, **Default Screen**. This is a sensible default as it displays the information to users consistently across all the three operations. However, there will be times when you would wish that certain fields should not be available for editing once the issue is created, such as **Issue Type**. You may want to have finer control over the type of issues raised for reporting and statistical measurement reasons, so it is not a good idea to let users freely change the issue type. Another example would be that certain fields are not required during the creation time, because the required information may not be available at the time. Therefore, instead of confusing and/or overwhelming your users, leave those fields out during issue creation and only ask for them to be filled in at a later time when the information becomes available.

As you can see, by dividing the screen into multiple issue operations rather than having the one-screen-fits-all approach, JIRA provides you with a new level of flexibility to control and design your screens. As always, if there are no significant differences between the screens, for example create and edit, it is recommended that you create a base screen and use the **Copy Screen** feature to reduce your workload.

Just like screens, you need to be a JIRA administrator to manage screen schemes. Perform the following steps to manage screen schemes:

1. Browse to the JIRA administration console.

2. Select the **Issues** tab and then the **Screen Schemes** option to bring up the **View Screen Schemes** page.

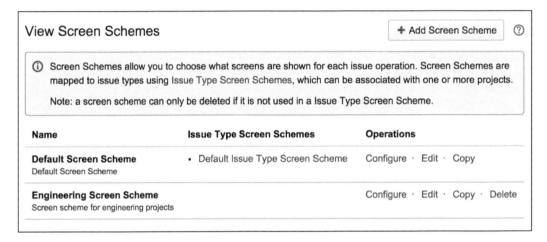

From the **View Screen Schemes** page, you will be able to see a list of all the existing screen schemes, create and manage their configurations, and view their associations with issue type screen schemes (explained in the later section).

Adding a screen scheme

JIRA ships with **Default Screen Scheme**, which uses **Default Screen** for viewing, creating, and editing issues. When you create a new project, by default, this is the screen scheme that will be used.

As your JIRA grows, different projects are created. It is a good practice to create separate, specialized screen schemes to better manage screen presentations. In this way, you will have finer control over the screens used by the different issue operations and issue types. Perform the following steps to create a new screen scheme:

1. Browse to the **View Screen Schemes** page.
2. Click on the **Add Screen Scheme** button.
3. Enter a meaningful name and description for the new screen scheme.
4. Select a default screen from the list of screens. This screen will be displayed when no specific issue operation is mapped.
5. Click on the **Add** button to create the screen scheme.

At this stage, the new screen scheme is not in use. This means that it is not associated with any issue type screen schemes yet (issue type screen schemes are covered in the later sections).

After a screen scheme is created, it will apply the selected default screen to all the issue operations. We will look at how to associate screens to issue operations in later sections.

Editing/deleting a screen scheme

You can update the details of the existing screen schemes, such as its name and description. In order for you to make changes to the default screen selection, you need to configure the screen scheme, which will be covered in later sections. Perform the following steps to edit an existing screen scheme:

1. Browse to the **View Screen Schemes** page.
2. Click on the **Edit** link for the screen scheme you wish to edit. This will take you to the **Edit Screen Scheme** page.
3. Update the name and description with new values.
4. Click on the **Update** button to apply the changes.

Inactive screen schemes can also be deleted. If the screen scheme is active (that is, associated with an issue type screen scheme), then the delete option will not be present. Perform the following steps to delete a screen scheme:

1. Browse to the **View Screen Schemes** page.
2. Click on the **Delete** link for the screen scheme you wish to edit. This will take you to the **Delete Screen Scheme** page.
3. Click on the **Delete** button to confirm that you wish to delete the screen scheme.

Copying a screen scheme

While screen schemes are not as complicated as screens, there will still be times when you would like to copy an existing screen scheme rather than creating one from scratch. You might wish to copy the scheme's screens/issue operations associations, which we will cover in the following section, or make a quick backup copy before making any changes to the scheme.

Perform the following steps to copy an existing screen scheme:

1. Browse to the **View Screen Schemes** page.
2. Click on the **Copy** link for the screen scheme you wish to copy. This will take you to the **Copy Screen Scheme** page.
3. Enter a new name and description for the screen scheme.
4. Click on the **Copy** button to copy the selected screen scheme.

Just like creating a new screen scheme, copied screen schemes are inactive by default.

Configuring a screen scheme

As mentioned earlier, when you create a new screen scheme, it will use the same screen selected as your default screen for all issue operations. Now, if you want to use the same screen to create, edit, and view, then you are all set; there is no need to perform any further configuration to your screen scheme. However, if you need to have different screens displayed for different issue operations, then you will need to establish this association.

When an issue operation does not have an association with a screen, the selected default screen will be applied. If the issue operation is later given in a screen association, then the specific association will take precedence over the general fallback default screen.

The associations between screens and issue operations are managed on a per screen scheme level. Perform the following steps to configure a screen scheme:

1. Browse to the **View Screen Schemes** page.
2. Click on the **Configure** link for the screen scheme you wish to configure. This will take you to the **Configure Screen Scheme** page.

Associating screens to issue operations

Each issue operation can be associated with one or more issue operations. Perform the following steps to associate an issue operation with a screen:

1. Browse to the **Configure Screen Scheme** page for the screen scheme to be configured.
2. Click on the **Add an Issue Operation with a Screen** button.
3. Select an issue operation to be assigned to a screen.
4. Select the screen to be associated to the issue operation.
5. Click on the **Add** button to create the association.

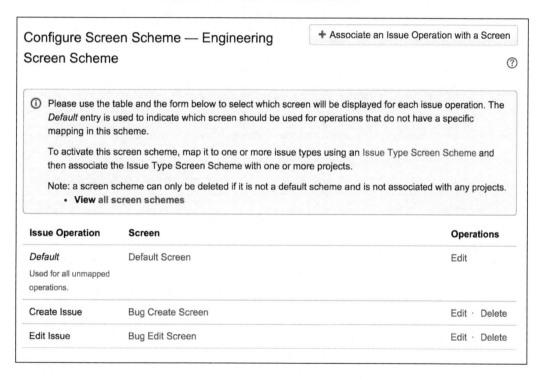

As shown in the preceding screenshot, the **Create Issue** and **Edit Issue** operations are associated with **Bug Create Screen** and **Bug Edit Screen**, respectively. Since we do not have a screen associated with the **View Issue** operation, the default association of **Default Screen** will be used.

Editing/deleting an association

After you create an association for an issue operation, JIRA prevents you from creating another association for the same issue operation by removing it from the list of available options. In order to change the association to a different screen, you need to edit the existing association, as follows:

1. Browse to the **Configure Screen Scheme** page for the screen scheme to be configured.
2. Click on the **Edit** link for the association you wish to edit. This will take you to the **Edit Screen Scheme Item** page.
3. Select a new screen to associate with the issue operation.
4. Click on the **Update** button to apply the change.

If you decide that one or more existing associations are no longer needed, then you can delete them from the screen scheme by performing the following steps:

1. Browse to the **Configure Screen Scheme** page for the screen scheme to be configured.
2. Click on the **Delete** link for the association you wish to delete.

Please note that unlike other similar operations, deleting an issue operation association does not prompt you with a confirmation page. As soon as you click on the **Delete** link, your association will be deleted immediately.

Issue type screen scheme

Screen schemes group screens together and create associations with issue operations. The next piece of the puzzle is to tell JIRA to use our screen schemes when creating, viewing, and editing specific types of issues.

We do not directly associate screen schemes to JIRA. The reason for this is that JIRA has the flexibility to allow you to define this on a per issue type level. What this means is, instead of forcing all the issue types in a given project to use the same screen scheme, you can actually use different screen schemes for different issue types. This extremely flexible and powerful feature is provided through the issue type screen scheme.

Just like screens and screen schemes, you need to be a JIRA administrator to create and manage issue type screen schemes. Perform the following steps to manage issue type screen schemes:

1. Browse to the JIRA administration console.

2. Select the **Issues** tab and then the **Issue Type Screen Schemes** option to bring up the **Issue Type Screen Schemes** page.

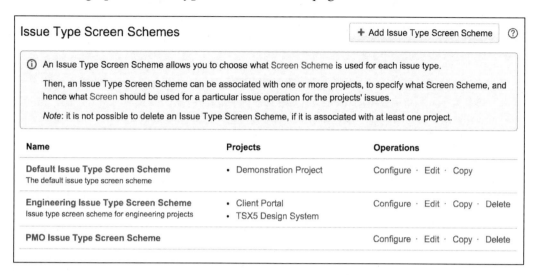

Adding an issue type screen scheme

You may have noticed by now that for any project, all of our issue types have the same screen layout. All projects, by default, use the default issue type screen scheme. Alternatively, just like anything else in JIRA, you can create your own schemes and apply them to your projects.

Perform the following steps to create a new issue type screen scheme:

1. Browse to the **Issue Type Screen Schemes** page.
2. Click on the **Add Issue Type Screen Scheme** button.
3. Enter a meaningful name for the new issue type screen scheme.
4. Enter an optional short description for the issue type screen scheme.
5. Select a default screen scheme from the list of screen schemes.
6. Click on the **Add** button to create the issue type screen scheme.

That's right, you guessed it! The new issue type screen scheme is *inactive* at this stage. It will only become active once it is applied to one or more projects, which we will look at shortly.

Editing/deleting an issue type screen scheme

You can make updates to an existing issue type screen scheme's name and descriptions. To change its screen scheme/issue type association details, you need to configure the issue type screen scheme, which will be covered in later sections. Perform the following steps to update an issue type screen scheme:

1. Browse to the **Issue Type Screen Schemes** page.
2. Click on the **Edit** link for the issue type screen scheme you wish to edit. This will take you to the **Edit Issue Type Screen Scheme** page.
3. Update the name and description with new values.
4. Click on the **Update** button to apply the changes.

Just like all other schemes in JIRA, you cannot delete issue type screen schemes that are in use. You will have to make sure that no project uses it before JIRA allows you to delete the scheme. To delete issue type screen schemes perform the following steps:

1. Browse to the **Issue Type Screen Schemes** page.
2. Click on the **Delete** link for the issue type screen scheme you wish to delete. This will take you to the **Delete Issue Type Screen Scheme** page.
3. Click on the **Delete** button to remove the issue type screen scheme.

Copying an issue type screen scheme

Issue type screen scheme cloning is also available in JIRA. You can easily make copies of the existing issue type screen schemes. One very useful application of this feature enables to you make backup copies before experimenting with new configurations. Note that copying the issue type screen scheme does not back up the screen schemes and screens that it contains.

Perform the following steps to copy an existing issue type screen scheme:

1. Browse to the **Issue Type Screen Schemes** page.
2. Click on the **Copy** link for the issue type screen scheme you wish to copy. This will take you to the **Copy Issue Type Screen Scheme** page.
3. Enter a new name and description for the issue type screen scheme.
4. Click on the **Copy** button to copy the selected scheme.

The newly created issue type screen schemes are inactive by default, while cloned schemes are not used by any projects.

Configuring an issue type screen scheme

By creating new issue type screen schemes, you can establish new associations between screen schemes and issue types. These associations are what tie the projects and issue types to the individual screens.

Each issue type screen scheme needs to be configured separately, and the associations created are specific to the configured scheme:

1. Browse to the **Issue Type Screen Schemes** page.
2. Click on the **Configure** link for the issue type screen scheme you wish to configure. This will take you to the **Configure Issue Type Screen Scheme** page.

Associating issue types to screen schemes

JIRA determines which screen scheme to use for an issue type by establishing an association between screen schemes and issue types. Each issue type can have only one screen scheme associated with it. However, each screen scheme can be associated with more than one issue types.

Perform the following steps to add a new association:

1. Browse to the **Configure Issue Type Screen Scheme** page for the issue type screen scheme you wish to configure.
2. Click on the **Associate an Issue Type with a Screen Scheme** button.
3. Select the issue type to add an association for.
4. Select the screen scheme to be associated with the issue type.
5. Click on the **Add** button to create the association.

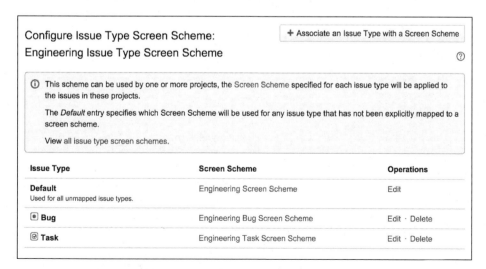

As shown in the preceding screenshot, the **Bug** and **Task** issue types are explicitly associated with **Engineering Bug Screen Scheme** and **Engineering Task Screen Scheme**, respectively. All other issues types, such as **Improvement**, will be associated with the default **Engineering Screen Scheme**.

Editing/deleting an association

You can update the existing associations such as the **Default** association, which is created automatically when you create a new issue type screen scheme:

1. Browse to the **Configure Issue Type Screen Scheme** page for the issue type screen scheme to be configured.

2. Click on the **Edit** link for the association you wish to edit. This will take you to the **Edit Issue Type Screen Scheme** page.

3. Select a new screen scheme to associate with the issue type.

4. Click on the **Update** button to apply the change.

You can also delete the existing associations for issue types if you no longer need them to be explicitly set. However, you cannot delete the **Default** association, since it is used as a catch for all the issue types that do not have an association defined. This is important because while you may have created associations for all the issue types right now, you might add new issue types down the track and forget to create associations for them. To delete an association:

1. Browse to the **Configure Issue Type Screen Scheme** page for the issue type screen scheme to be configured.

2. Click on the **Delete** link for the association you wish to delete.

Just like associations in screen schemes, you will not be taken to a confirmation dialog, and the association will be deleted immediately.

Associating an issue type screen scheme with a project

Perform the following steps in order to activate your new issue type screen scheme, which will display your new screens for the different issue operations:

1. Browse to the project you wish to associate the field configuration scheme to.

2. Click on the **Administration** tab to go to the project's administration page.

3. Click on the **Screens** option from the left panel.

4. Select **Use a different scheme** option from the **Actions** menu.

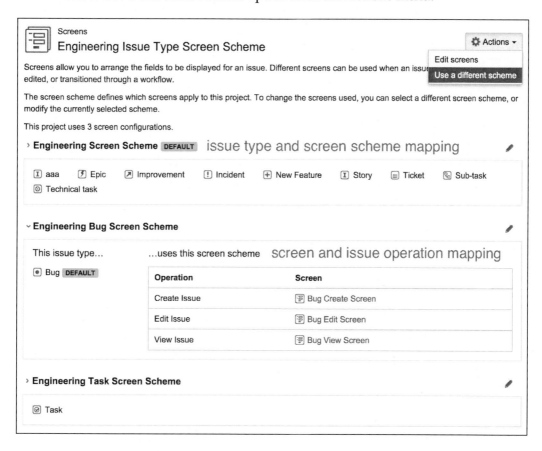

5. Select the issue type screen scheme from the **Scheme** select list.

6. Click on the **Associate** button.

Once you associate the issue type screen scheme with the project, JIRA will show you the details of the mapping, as shown in the preceding screenshot.

The Help Desk project

Armed with the new knowledge that you gathered in this chapter, together with fields from the previous chapter, it is time for you to further customize your JIRA to provide a better user experience through presentation.

What we will do this time is create new screens and apply them to our Help Desk project. We want to separate the generic fields from our specialized custom fields designed for escalation. We also want to, at this time, apply the changes to the issues of the **Incident** type only and not affect the other issue types. As with any changes to be done on a production system, it is critical that you have a backup of your current data before applying changes.

Setting up screens

In *Chapter 4, Field Management,* you created a few custom fields specifically designed for our support teams. As you learned, those fields are added to the default screen. The first thing you need to do is to create a couple of screens for your Help Desk project only, to avoid affecting any other screens used by other projects and teams.

We will be creating three screens—one for creating and viewing issues, one for updating issues, and one to transition issues through the workflow. Since workflow is covered in the next chapter, we will just create the screen and come back to it when we discuss workflows. To create a screen perform the following steps:

1. Browse to the **View Screens page** and click on **Add Screen**.
2. Name the new screen such as `Help Desk Create/View Screen`.
3. Provide a helpful description such as `Screen for create/view help desk issues`.
4. Click on the **Add** button to create the screen.

The next step is to set up the tabs for our new screen. We would like to have the default fields on the first screen to capture generic issue data, and then we will place the new custom fields that were created in *Chapter 4, Field Management,* onto a new tab called **Escalation**, as follows:

1. Rename the default tab (named **Field Tab**) to `General`.
2. Create a new tab called `Escalation`.

Now that you have your screen and tabs, it is time to place your fields onto them using the following steps:

1. Move back to the **General** tab.
2. Add the fields from the **Default** screen onto the tab (see the following table for the complete list of fields to add).
3. Move to the **Escalation** tab.

4. Add the new escalation custom fields onto the tab.

Field	Tab
Summary	General
Issue Type	General
Security Level	General
Priority	General
Due Date	General
Component/s	General
Affects Version/s	General
Fix Version/s	General
Assignee	General
Reporter	General
Environment	General
Description	General
Time Tracking	General
Attachment	General
Escalation List	Escalation
Escalation Level	Escalation
Is Escalation Required	Escalation

Of course, you might be thinking that this can be done much faster if we just clone the default screen and move the escalation fields to the new tab, and you are absolutely correct. However, we are just doing it manually this time to learn the process.

We created and configured our first create/view screen. Our new edit screen is going to look very similar to this with just a few modifications. We want to take the **Issue Type** field off since we do not want users to change the issue type all the time, and we are going to take the **Escalation Level** field off as it makes little sense to have a noneditable field on the edit screen. Since we are only taking off some fields from an existing screen, instead of going through the entire create and configure process, let's spare ourselves the tedious clicking, and copy the screen we just created, since we have already done it once:

1. Browse to the **View Screens** page.
2. Click on the **Copy** link for **Help Desk Create/View Screen**.
3. Name the new screen Help Desk Edit Screen.
4. Provide a helpful description such as Screen for edit help desk issues.
5. Click on the **Copy** button to create the new screen.

Since we copied the screen, we inherit all of the fields and tabs so there is no need to reconfigure them. All we need to do is to remove the fields we do not need:

1. Click on the **Configure** link for **Help Desk Edit Screen**.
2. Delete the **Issue Type** field in the **General** tab.
3. Delete the **Escalation Level** field in the **Escalation** tab.

The last step is to create your third screen, which we will use in the next chapter. This screen will be used during workflow transitions, and we would like to allow users to reassign the issue and also update the **Escalation List** field. Since this is going to be a fairly simple screen, we will create it from scratch:

1. Browse to the **View Screens** page and click on **Add Screen**.
2. Name the new screen as Help Desk Workflow Screen.
3. Provide a helpful description such as Screen for transition help desk issues.
4. Click on the **Add** button to create the screen.
5. Click on the **Configure** link for **Help Desk Workflow Screen**.
6. Add the **Assignee** and **Escalation List** fields to the screen.

You now have your fully configured screens set up, but they are not in use right now. The next step is to establish the associations with their respective issue operations.

Setting up screen schemes

With the screens created and configured, we now need to link them up with issue operations so that JIRA will know on which action the new screens will be displayed using the following steps:

1. Browse to the **View Screen Schemes** page and click on **Add Screen Scheme**.
2. Name the new screen scheme as Help Desk Incident Screen Scheme.
3. Provide a helpful description such as Screen scheme for Help Desk incidents.
4. Select **Help Desk Create/View Screen** as the default screen.
5. Click on the **Add** button to create the screen scheme.

With our screen scheme in place, it is time to link up our screens with their respective issue operations:

1. Click on the **Associate an Issue Operation with a Screen** button.
2. Select **Help Desk Edit Screen** for the **Edit Issue** operation.

Since we assigned **Help Desk Create/View Screen** to **Default**, this screen will be applied to the unmapped operations, **Create Issue** and **View Issue**. There are no differences if you choose to explicitly set the mappings for the preceding two operations.

Setting up issue type screen schemes

Now, you need to tell JIRA which issue type to apply the screen scheme to that you just created. We will be applying our new screens to issues of type **Incident** initially, since these are usually the type of issues that require immediate attention and appropriate escalation. For future enhancements, you can further customize your design so that each issue type will have its own screen design.

The first step is to create a new issue type screen scheme to be used specifically for our project:

1. Browse to the **Issue Type Screen Schemes** page and click on the **Add Issue Type Screen Scheme** button.

2. Name the new screen scheme `Help Desk Issue Type Screen Scheme`.

3. Provide a helpful description such as `Issue type screen scheme for Help Desk team`.

4. Select **Default Screen Scheme** as the default screen scheme.

5. Click on the **Add** button to create the issue type screen scheme.

With the scheme created, you can establish the associations between issue types and screen schemes:

1. Click on the **Associate an Issue Type with a Screen Scheme** button.

2. Select **Incident** for **Issue Type**.

3. Select **Help Desk Incident Screen Scheme** for the screen scheme to be associated.

4. Click on the **Add** button to create the association.

This will ensure that issues of type **Incident** will have your new screens applied while issues of other types will not be affected.

Putting it together

The last step is to activate all the screens and schemes you created so far in this chapter and see them in action. Remember that there is only one thing you need to do—choose your project and configure it to use your issue type screen scheme:

1. Browse to the **Project Administration** page for your Help Desk project.
2. Select the **Screens** tab on the left-hand side.
3. Click on the **Actions** drop-down menu and select **Use a different scheme**.
4. Select **Help Desk Issue Type Screen Scheme** and click on the **Associate** button.

If you are performing this on a live production system, it is recommended that you alert the users of the change and perform this when there are not many users on the system.

This is it. All done! Our final screen mapping will look something like the following screenshot:

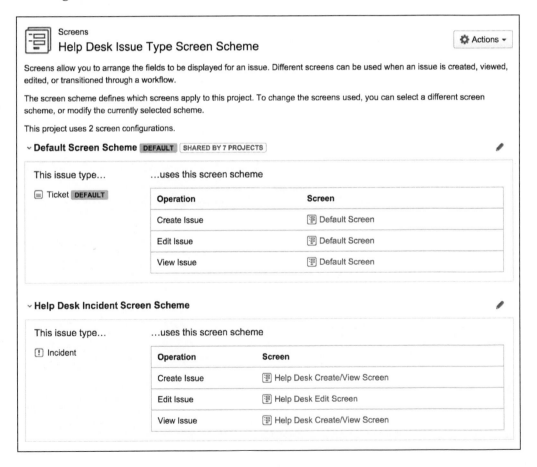

You can now take a look at your hard work and see your custom screens, fields, and tabs, all working nicely together to present you with a custom form for collecting user data. Let's go ahead and create a new incident and see what your newly customized **Create Issue** screen will look like, as shown in the following screenshot:

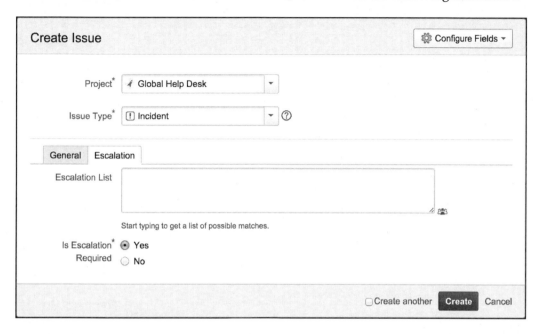

As you can see, your new screen is nicely divided into two tabs with your new custom fields on the **Escalation** tab. If you create an issue of type **Ticket**, you will see that it will not have the tabbed screen design.

Summary

In this chapter, we looked at how JIRA structures its presentation with screens. We looked at how screens are used in JIRA via screen schemes, which map screens to issue operations. We also looked at how issue type screen schemes are then used to map screen schemes to issue types. Therefore, for any given project, each issue type can have its own set of screens for create, edit, and view. We also discussed how screens can be broken down into tabs to provide a more logical grouping of fields, especially when your screen starts to have a lot of fields on it.

Together with custom fields that we saw in the previous chapter, we can now create effective screen designs to streamline our data collection. In the next chapter, we will delve into one of the most powerful features in JIRA, **workflows**.

6
Workflows and Business Processes

In the previous chapters, we learned some of the basics of JIRA and how to customize its data capture and presentation with custom fields and screens. In this chapter, we will dive in and take a look at workflows, one of the core and most powerful features in JIRA.

A workflow controls how issues in JIRA move from one status to another, as they are being worked on, often passing from one assignee to another. Unlike many other systems, JIRA allows you to create your own workflows to resemble your processes.

By the end of this chapter, you will have learned:

- What a workflow is and what it consists of
- About the relationship between workflows and screens
- What are statuses, transitions, conditions, validators, and post functions
- How to create your own workflow with the workflow designer
- How to associate a workflow with projects

Mapping business processes

It is often said that a good software system is one that adapts to your business and not one that requires your business to adapt to the software. JIRA is an excellent example of the former. The power of JIRA is that you can easily configure it to model your existing business processes through the use of workflows.

A business process flow can often be represented as a flow chart. For example, a typical document approval flow may include tasks such as document preparation, document review, and document submission, where the user needs to follow these tasks in a sequential order. You can easily implement this as a JIRA workflow. Each task will be represented as a workflow status with transitions guiding you on how you can move from one status to the next. In fact, when working with workflows, it is often a good approach to first draft out the logical flow of the process as a flow chart, and then implement this as a workflow. As we will see, JIRA provides many tools to help you visualize your workflows.

Now that we have briefly seen how you can map a normal business process to a JIRA workflow, it is time to take a closer look at the components of a workflow and how you can create your own workflows.

Understanding workflows

A workflow is what JIRA uses to model business processes. It is a flow of statuses (steps) that issues go through one by one with paths between them (transitions). All issues in JIRA have a workflow applied based on their issue type and project. Issues move through workflows from one status (for example, **OPEN**) to another (for example, **CLOSED**). JIRA lets you visualize and design workflows as a diagram, as shown in the following diagram:

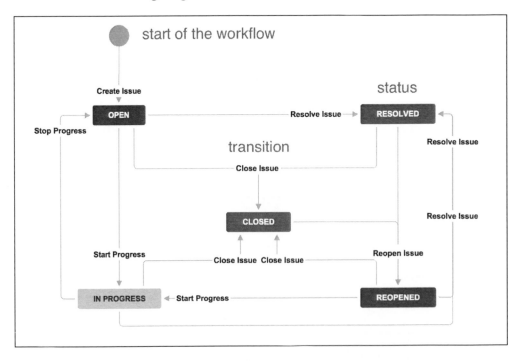

The preceding diagram shows a simple workflow in JIRA. The rectangles represent the statuses, and the arrow lines represent transitions that link statuses together. As you can see, this looks a lot like a normal flow chart depicting the flow of a process.

Issues in JIRA, starting from when they are created, go through a series of steps identified as **issue statuses**, such as **In Progress** and **Closed**. These movements are often triggered by user interactions. For example, when a user clicks on the **Start Progress** link, the issue is transitioned to the **In Progress** status, as shown in the following screenshot:

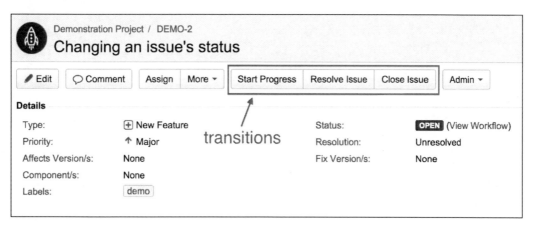

There is a definitive start of a workflow, which is when the issue is first created, but the end of a workflow can sometimes be ambiguous. For example, in the default workflow, issues can go from **Open** to **Closed** and from **Reopened** back to **Closed** again. By convention, when people talk about the end of a workflow, they are usually referring to a status named **Closed** or the status where issues are given a **resolution**. Once a resolution is given, the issue comes to a logical end. Several JIRA's built-in features follow this convention, for example, issues with resolutions set will not be displayed on the **Assigned to Me** list on the home page.

 When work for an issue is completed, it will be given a resolution.

Managing workflows

Workflows are controlled and managed centrally from the JIRA administration console, so you need to be an administrator to create and configure workflows. To manage workflows, perform the following steps:

1. Log in to JIRA as a JIRA administrator.
2. Browse to the JIRA administration console.
3. Select the **Issues** tab and then the **Workflows** option. This will bring up the **View Workflows** page.

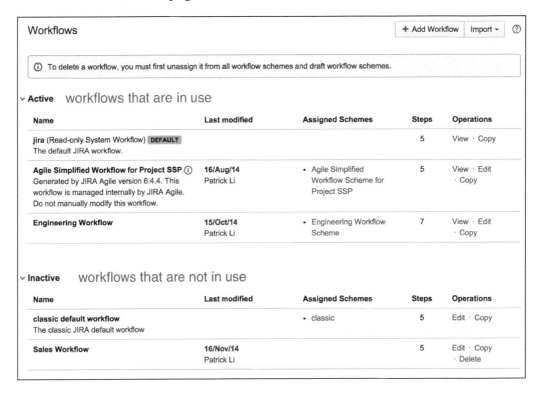

From the **View Workflows** page, you will be able to see a list of all the available workflows. You can also create new workflows and manage existing ones. The page is divided into two sections, **Active** and **Inactive**. Active workflows are being used by projects, and inactive ones are not. By default, the **Inactive** section is collapsed to display only the active workflows. This may not seem like an important change at first, but when you have many workflows, this can save you a lot of time.

JIRA comes with a default read-only workflow called **jira**. This workflow is applied to projects that do not have any specific workflow applied. For this reason, you cannot edit or delete this workflow.

Issue statuses

In a JIRA workflow, an **issue status** represents a state in the workflow for an issue. It describes the current status of the issue. If we look at a flow chart, the statuses will be the rectangles and in the diagram, they indicate the current status of the issue along the process. Just as a task can only be in one stage of a business process, an issue can be in only one status at any given time, for example, an issue cannot be both open and closed at the same time.

There is also a term called **step**, which is the workflow terminology for statuses. Since JIRA has simplified its workflow administration, step and status can be used interchangeably. For consistency, we will be using the term status in this book, unless a separation needs to be made in special cases.

Transitions

Statuses represent stages in a workflow; the path that takes an issue from one status to the next is known as a **transition**. A transition links two statuses together. A transition cannot exist on its own, meaning it must have a start and finish status, and can only have one of each. This means that a transition cannot conditionally split off to different destination statuses. Transitions are also one way only. This means that if a transition takes an issue from status A to status B, you must create a new transition if you want to go back from status B to status A.

Transitions have several components. They are as follows:

- **Conditions**: This criteria must be met before the transition is available (visible) for users to execute. It is usually used to control permissions around how users can execute the transition.

- **Validators**: These are the verifications that must pass before the transition can be executed. They are usually used together with **Transition Screens**.

- **Post Functions**: These are additional functions to be performed as part of the transition process.

- **Transition Screen**: This is an optional screen to be displayed when a user is executing the transition. It is usually used to capture additional information as a part of the transition.

- **Triggers**: JIRA 6.3 added this new feature. If you have integrated JIRA with other development tools such as Stash or GitHub, triggers can automatically execute the transition when an event happens, such as the creation of a new branch or when someone makes a code commit.

Each of the first three components defines the behavior of the transitions, allowing you to perform pre and post validations, as well as post execution processing, on the transition execution. We will discuss these components in depth in the next sections.

Triggers

As described earlier, JIRA needs to be integrated with one of the following systems before you can start using triggers:

- Atlassian Stash
- Atlassin FishEye/Crucible
- Atlassian Bitbucket
- GitHub

Triggers will listen for changes from the integrated development tools, such as code commits, and when these happen, the trigger will automatically execute the workflow transition. Note that all permissions are ignored when this happens.

Conditions

Sometimes, you might want to have control over who can execute a transition or when a transition can be executed. For example, an authorization transition can only be executed by users in the managers group, so normal employees will not be able to authorize their own requests. This is where conditions come in.

Conditions are criteria that must be fulfilled before the user is allowed to execute the transition. If the conditions on transitions are not met, the transition will not be available to the user when viewing the issue. The following table shows a list of conditions that are shipped with JIRA:

Condition	Description
Code Committed Condition	Allows the transition to execute only if code has/has not (depending on configuration) been committed against this issue.
Hide transition from user	This will hide the transition from all users, and can only be triggered from post functions. This is useful in situations where the transition will be triggered as part of an automated process, rather than manually by a user.
No Open Reviews Condition	Allows transition to execute only if there are no related open crucible reviews.
Only Assignee Condition	Only allows the issue's current assignee to execute the transition.

Condition	Description
Only Reporter Condition	Only allows the issue's reporter to execute the transition.
Permission Condition	Only allows users with the given permission to execute the transition.
Sub-Task Blocking Condition	Blocks the parent issue transition depending on all its sub-tasks' statuses.
Unreviewed Code Condition	Allows transition to execute only if there are no unreviewed change sets related to this issue.
User Is In Group	Only allows users in a given group to execute the transition.
User Is In Group Custom Field	Only allows users in a given group custom field to execute a transition.
User Is In Project Role	Only allows users in a given project role to execute a transition.

Validators

Validators are similar to conditions as they validate certain criteria before allowing the transition to complete. The most common use case for validators is to validate the user input during transition. For example, you can validate if the user has entered data for all fields presented on the workflow screen. The following table shows a list of validators that come shipped with JIRA:

Validator	Description
Permission Validator	Validates that the user has the selected permission. This is useful when checking whether the person who has executed the transition has the required permissions.
User Permission Validator	Validates that the user has the selected permission, where the OSWorkflow variable holding the username is configurable. This is obsolete.

Post functions

As the name suggests, post functions are functions that occur after (post) a transition has been executed. This allows you to perform additional processes once you have executed a transition. JIRA heavily uses post functions internally to perform a lot of its functions. For example, when you transition an issue, JIRA uses post functions to update its search indexes so your search results will reflect the change in issue status.

If a transition has failed to execute (for example, failing validation from validators), post functions attached to the transition will not be triggered. The following table shows a list of post functions that come shipped with JIRA:

Post function	Description
Assign to Current User	Assigns the issue to the current user if the current user has the assignable user permission.
Assign to Lead Developer	Assigns the issue to the project/component lead developer.
Assign to Reporter	Assigns the issue to the reporter.
Create Perforce Job Function	Creates a perforce job (if required) after completing the workflow transition.
Notify HipChat	Sends a notification to one or more HipChat rooms.
Trigger a Webhook	If this post function is executed, JIRA will post the issue content in JSON format to the URL specified.
Update Issue Field	Updates a simple issue field to a given value.

Using the workflow designer

JIRA comes with a simple to use, drag-and-drop tool called the **workflow designer**. This helps you create and configure workflows. If you are familiar with diagramming tools such as Microsoft Visio, you will feel right at home. There is also another older option, called the Text mode, available. However, since the designer is easier and has more features, we will focus on using the designer in this book.

 As your workflow becomes more complicated, the **Text** mode can be a better option to manage statuses and transitions in the workflow.

The workflow designer is shown in the following screenshot. You have the workflow layout in the main panel and a few controls on top, namely the **Add status** and **Add transition** buttons. Note that the **Diagram** option is selected; if you click on the **Text** option, JIRA will change to the old authoring tool:

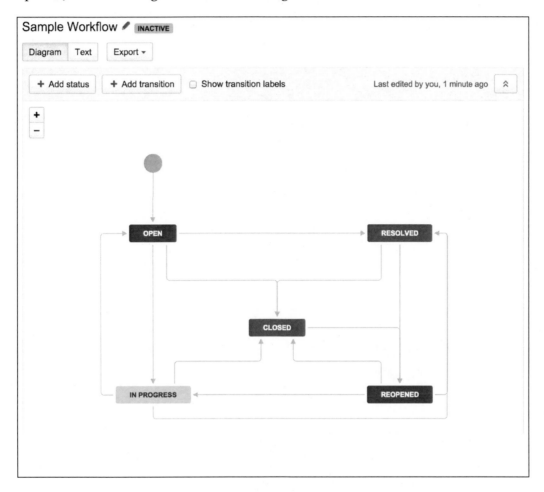

From the workflow designer, you can drag and rearrange the statuses and transitions. Clicking on each will open up its property window, as shown in the following screenshot, where the **Resolve Issue** transition is selected. From here, we can view and update its properties, such as conditions and validators:

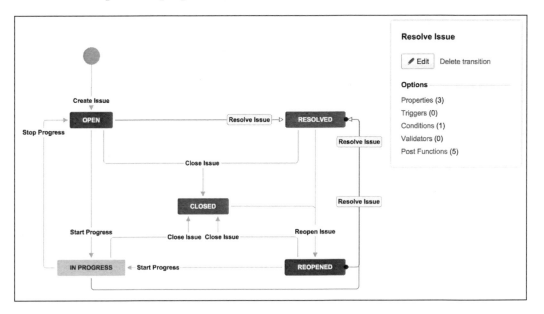

Authoring a workflow

So, let's take a look at how to create and set up a new workflow in JIRA. To create a new workflow, all you need is a name and description:

1. Browse to the **View Workflows** page.
2. Click on the **Add Workflow** button.
3. Enter a meaningful name for the new workflow in the **Add Workflow** dialog.
4. Click on the **Add** button to create the workflow.

The newly created workflow will only contain the default create and open status, so you will need to configure it by adding new statuses and transitions to make it useful. Let's start with adding new statuses to the workflow using the following steps:

1. Click on the **Add status** button.

2. Select an existing status from the drop-down list. If the status you need does not exist, you can create a new status by entering its name and pressing the *Enter* key on your keyboard.

3. Check the **Allow all statuses to transition to this one** option, if you want users to be able to move the issue into this status regardless of its current status. This is a convenient option so you do not have to manually create multiple transitions for the status, by creating a **Global Transition**.

4. Click on the **Add** button to add the status to your workflow. You can repeat these steps to add as many statuses as you want to your workflow.

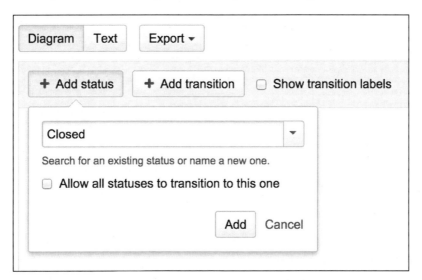

Now that the statuses are added to the workflow, they need to be linked with transitions, so issues can move from one status to the next. There are two ways to create a transition:

- Click on the **Add transition** button
- Select the originating status, then click and drag the arrow to the destination status

Both options will bring up the **Add Transition** dialog, as shown in the following screenshot:

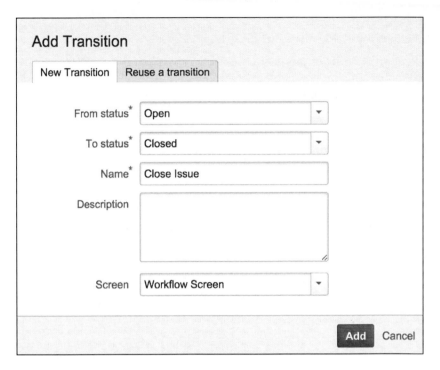

From the preceding screenshot, you can choose to either create a new transition with the **New Transition** tab or use an existing transition with the **Reuse a transition** tab.

When creating a new transition, you will need to configure the following:

- **From status**: The originating status. The transition will be available when the issue is in the selected status.

- **To status**: The destination status. Once the transition is executed, the issue will be put into the selected status.

- **Name**: Name of the transition. This is the text that will be displayed to users. It is usually a good idea to name your transitions starting with a verb, such as Close Issue.

- **Description**: An optional text description is the purpose of this transition. This will not be displayed to users.

- **Screen**: An optional intermediate screen to be displayed when users execute the transition. For example, you display a screen to capture additional data as part of the transition. If you do not select a screen, the transition will be executed immediately. The following screenshot shows a workflow screen:

If you want to reuse an existing transition, simply select the **Reuse a transition** tab, the **From** and **To** statuses, and the transition to reuse, as shown in the following screenshot:

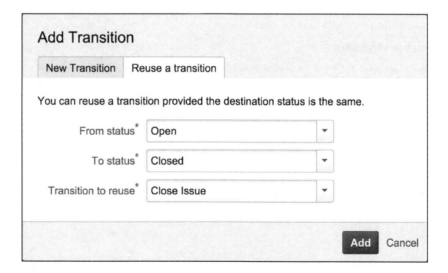

 Note that JIRA will only list valid transitions based on the **To status** selection.

You might be wondering when you should create a new transition and when you should reuse an existing transition. The big difference between the two is that when you reuse a transition, all instances of the reused transition, also known as **common transition**, will share the same set of configurations, such as conditions and validators. Also, any changes made to the transition will be applied to all instances. A good use case for this is when you need to have multiple transitions with the same name and setup, such as **Close Issue**; instead of creating separate transitions each time, you can create one transition and reuse it whenever you need a transition to close an issue. Later on, if you need to add a new validator to the transition to validate additional user input, you will only need to make the change once, rather than multiple times for each **Close Issue** transition.

Another good practice to keep in mind is to not have a *dead end* state in your workflow, for example, allowing closed issues to be reopened. This will prevent users from accidentally closing an issue and not being able to correct the mistake.

Now that we have seen how to add new statuses and transitions to a workflow, let's look at adding conditions, validators, and post functions to a transition.

Adding a trigger to a transition

You can only add triggers to transitions if JIRA is integrated with at least one of the supported development tools. To add triggers, perform the following steps:

1. Select the transition you want to add conditions to.
2. Click on the **Triggers** link.
3. Click on the **Add trigger** button. If you do not have any integrated development tools, this button will be disabled.

4. Select the trigger you want to add, as shown in the following screenshot, and click on the **Next** button:

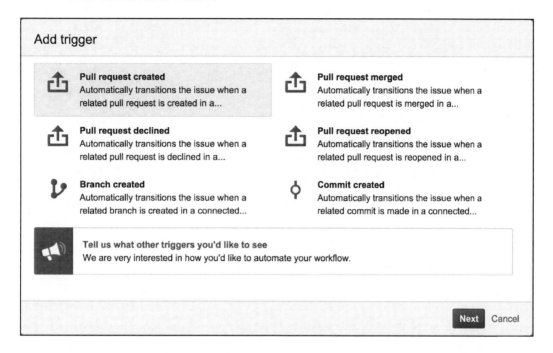

5. Confirm the trigger source detected and click on the **Add trigger** button.

Adding a condition to a transition

New transitions do not have any conditions by default. This means that anyone who has access to the issue will be able to execute the transition. JIRA allows you to add any number of conditions to the transition:

1. Select the transition you want to add conditions to.
2. Click on the **Conditions** link.
3. Click on the **Add condition** link. This will bring you to the **Add Condition To Transition** page, which lists all the available conditions you can add.
4. Select the condition you want to add.
5. Click on the **Add** button to add the condition.
6. Depending on the condition, you may be presented with the **Add Parameters To Condition** page where you can specify the configuration options for the condition. For example, the **User Is In Group** condition will ask you to select the group to check against.

Newly added conditions are appended to the end of the existing list of conditions, creating a **condition group**. By default, when there is more than one condition, logical AND is used to group the conditions. This means that all conditions must pass for the entire condition group to pass. If one condition fails, the entire group fails, and the user will not be able to execute the transition. You can switch to use logical OR, which means only one of the conditions in the group needs to pass for the entire group to pass. This is a very useful feature as it allows you to combine multiple conditions to form a more complex logical unit.

For example, the **User Is In Group** condition lets you specify a single group, but with the AND operator, you can add multiple **User Is In Group** conditions to ensure the user must exist in all the specific groups to be able to execute the transition. If you use the OR operator, then the user will only need to belong to one of the listed groups. The only restriction to this is that you cannot use both operators for the same condition group.

 One transition can only have one condition group, and each conditional group can only have one logical operator.

Adding a validator to a transition

Like conditions, transitions, by default, do not have any validators associated. This means transitions are completed as soon as they are executed. You can add validators to transitions to make sure that executions are only allowed to be complete when certain criteria are met. Use the following steps to add a validator to a transition:

1. Select the transition you want to add conditions to.
2. Click on the **Validators** link.
3. Click on the **Add validator** link. This will bring you to the **Add Validator To Transition** page, which lists all the available validators you can add.
4. Select the validator you want to add.
5. Click on the **Add** button to add the validator.
6. Depending on the validator, you may be presented with the **Add Parameters To Validator** page where you can specify configuration options for the validator. For example, the **Permissions** validator will ask you to select the permission to validate against.

Similar to conditions, when there are multiple validators added to a transition, they form a **validator group**. Unlike conditions, you can only use logical AND for the group. This means that in order to complete a transition, every validator added to the transition must pass its validation criteria. Transitions cannot selectively pass validations using logical OR. The following screenshot shows a validator (**Field Required** validator from JIRA Suite Utilities, see the *Extending workflow with workflow add-ons* section) being placed on the transition, validating if the user has entered a value for the **Resolution Details** field:

Adding a post function to a transition

Transitions, by default, are created with several post functions. These post functions provide key services to JIRA's internal operations, so they cannot be deleted from the transition. These post functions perform the following:

- Set the issue status to the linked status of the destination workflow step
- Add a comment to an issue if one is entered during a transition
- Update the change history for an issue and store the issue in the database
- Re-index an issue to keep indexes in sync with the database
- Fire an event that can be processed by the listeners

As you can see, these post functions provide some of the basic functions such as updating a search index and setting an issue's status after transition execution, which are essential in JIRA. Therefore, instead of letting users having to manually add them in and risk the possibility of leaving one or more out, JIRA adds them for you automatically when you create a new transition:

1. Select the transition you want to add post functions to.
2. Click on the **Post Functions** link.
3. Click on the **Add post function** link and select the post function you want to add.
4. Click on the **Add** button to add the post function.
5. Depending on the post function, you may be presented with the **Add Parameters To Function** page where you can specify configuration options for the post function. The following screenshot shows an example from the **Update Issue Field** post function.

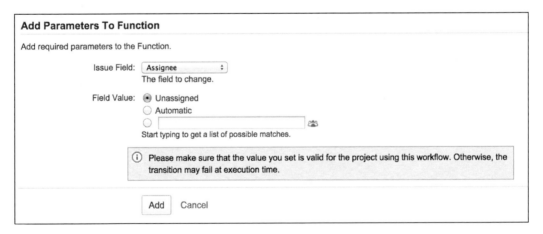

Just like conditions and validators, multiple post functions form a post function group in a transition. After a transition is executed, each post function in the group is executed sequentially as it appears in the list, from top to bottom. If any post function in the group encounters an error during processing, you will receive an error, and the remaining post functions will not be executed.

Since post functions are executed sequentially and some of them possess the abilities to modify values and perform other tasks, often, their sequence of execution becomes very important. For example, if you have a post function that changes the issue's assignee to the current user and another post function that updates an issue field's value with the issue's assignee, obviously the update assignee post function needs to occur first, so you need to make sure it is above the other post function.

You can move the positions of post functions up and down along the list by clicking on the **Move Up** and **Move Down** links. Note that not all post functions can be repositioned.

Updating an existing workflow

JIRA lets you make changes to both active and inactive workflows. However, with active workflows, there are several restrictions:

- Existing workflow steps cannot be deleted
- The associated status for an existing step cannot be edited
- If an existing step has no outgoing transitions, it cannot have any new outgoing transitions added

If you need to make these changes, you will have to either deactivate the workflow by removing the associations of the workflow with all projects or create a copy of the workflow.

 You can always make a copy of the active workflow, make your changes, and then swap the original with the copied workflow in your workflow scheme.

When editing an active workflow, you are actually making changes to a draft copy of the workflow created by JIRA. All the changes you make will not be applied until you publish your draft.

 Do not forget to publish your draft after you have made your changes.

Publishing a draft is a very simple process. All you have to do is the following:

1. Click on the **Publish Draft** button. You will be prompted if you would like to first create a backup of the original workflow. It is recommended that you create a backup in case you need to undo your changes.

2. Select either **Yes** or **No** to create a backup of the current workflow before applying the changes. This is a handy way to quickly create a backup if you have not made a copy already. If you do choose to create a backup, it is a good idea to name your workflow with a consistent convention (for example, based on a version such as Sales Workflow 1.0) to keep track.

3. Click on the **Publish** button to publish the draft workflow and apply changes, as shown in the following screenshot:

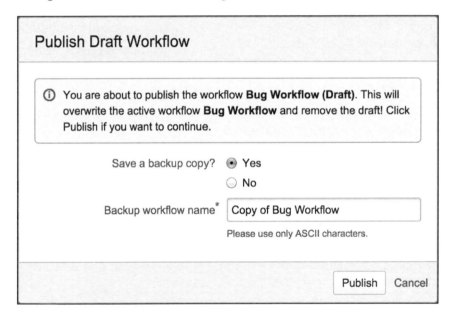

Workflow schemes

While workflows define and model business processes, there still needs to be a way to tell JIRA the situations in which to apply the workflows. As with other configurations in JIRA, this is achieved through the use of schemes. As we have seen in the previous chapters, schemes act as self-contained, reusable configuration units that associate specific configuration options with projects and optionally, issue types.

A workflow scheme establishes the association between workflows and issue types. The scheme can then be applied to multiple projects. Once applied, the workflows within the scheme become active.

To view and manage workflow schemes, perform the following steps:

1. Log in as a JIRA administrator user.
2. Browse to the JIRA administration console.
3. Select the **Issues** tab and then the **Workflow Schemes** option. This will bring up the **Workflow Schemes** page, as shown in the following screenshot:

The **Workflow Schemes** page shows each scheme's workflow association. For example, in the preceding screenshot, we can see that for **Development Workflow Scheme**, the issue type **Bug** is assigned with **Bug Workflow**, while the issue type **New Feature** is assigned to **New Feature Workflow**. It also shows what projects are using the workflow schemes.

Creating a workflow scheme

JIRA allows you to create new workflow schemes to associate workflows to issue types. This allows you to group all your associations into a single reusable unit (scheme) that can be applied to multiple projects:

1. Browse to the **Workflow Schemes** page.
2. Click on the **Add workflow scheme** button. This will take you to the **Add Workflow Scheme** dialog.
3. Enter a meaningful name for the new workflow scheme and optionally, a description. For example, you can choose to name your workflow after the project/issue type it will be applied to.
4. Click on the **Add** button to create the workflow scheme.

You will be taken back to the **Workflow Schemes** page once the new scheme has been created, and it will be listed in the table of available workflow schemes.

When you first create a new workflow scheme, the scheme is empty. This means it contains no associations of workflows and issue types, except the default association called JIRA Workflow (jira). What you need to do next is configure the associations by assigning workflows to issue types.

 You can delete the default JIRA Workflow (jira) association after you have added an association yourself.

Configuring a workflow scheme

Workflow schemes contain associations between issue types and workflows. After you have created a workflow scheme, you need to configure and maintain the associations as your requirements change. For example, when a new issue type is added to the projects using the workflow scheme, you may need to add an explicit association for the new issue type.

To configure a workflow scheme, perform the following steps:

1. Browse to the **Workflow Schemes** page.

2. Click on the **Edit** link for the workflow scheme you want to configure. This will take you to the workflow's details page, as shown in the following screenshot:

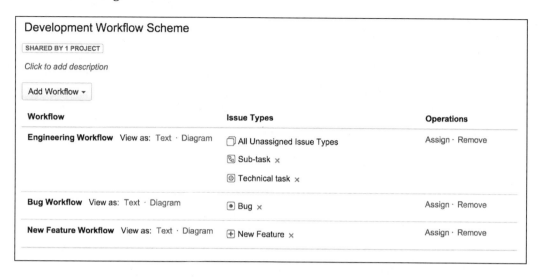

From this page, you will be able to see a list of existing associations, create new associations for issue types, and delete associations that are no longer relevant.

Assigning an issue type to a workflow

Issue type and workflow have a many-to-one relationship. This means each issue type can be associated with one and only one workflow. One workflow can be associated with multiple issue types. This rule is applied on a per workflow scheme basis, so you can have a different association of the same issue type in a different workflow scheme.

When you add a new association, JIRA will list all the issue types and all available workflows. Once you have assigned a workflow to the issue type, it will not appear in the list again until you remove the original association.

Among the list of issue types, there is an option called **All Unassigned Issue Types**. This option acts as a catch-all option for issue types that do not have an explicit association. This is a very handy feature if all issue types in your project are to have the same workflow; instead of mapping them out manually one by one, you can simply assign the workflow to all with this option. This option is also important as new issue types are added and assigned to a project; they will automatically be assigned to the catch-all workflow. If you do not have an **All Unassigned Issue Types** association, new or unassigned issue types will be assigned to use the default basic **jira** workflow. As with normal issue types, you can have only one catch-all association.

[If all issues types will be using the same workflow, use the
All Unassigned Issue Types option.]

There are two ways to assign a workflow to an issue type. If you want to assign an issue type to one of the existing associations:

1. Browse to the workflow scheme's details page for the workflow scheme you want to configure by clicking on its **Edit** link.

2. Click on the **Assign** link for the association to add an issue type to.

3. Select the issue types to add from the **Assign Issue Type to Workflow** dialog.

4. Click on the **Finish** button.

If you want to create a new association from scratch:

1. Browse to the workflow scheme's details page for the workflow scheme you want to configure.

2. Select the **Add Existing** option from the **Add Workflow** menu. This will bring up the **Add Existing Workflow** dialog.

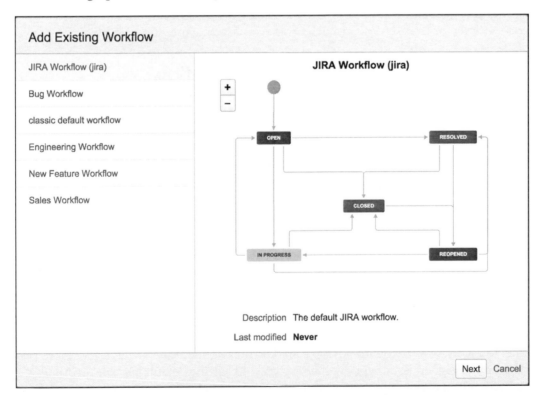

3. Select the workflow to use and click on the **Next** button.

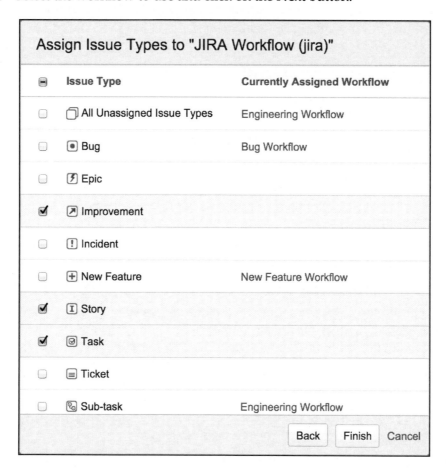

4. Select the issue types to associate with the workflow and click on the **Finish** button. If you select an issue type that is already assigned, it will be removed from the old assignment and added to the currently selected workflow.

Editing/deleting an association

Once you have associated an issue type to a workflow in a scheme, you cannot add a new association for the same issue type. There is also a no edit option to change the association. What you need to do is to delete the existing association and create a new one using the following steps:

1. Browse to the workflow scheme's details page for the workflow scheme you want to configure.
2. Click on the **Remove** link for the association you want to remove.

Once an association is deleted, you will be able to create a new one for the issue type. If you do not assign a new workflow to the issue type, the workflow with **All Unassigned Issue Types** option will be applied.

Activating a workflow scheme

Workflow schemes are inactive by default after they are created. This means there are no projects in JIRA using the workflow scheme. To activate a workflow scheme, you need to select the scheme and apply it to the project.

When assigning a workflow scheme to a project, you need to follow the three basic steps:

1. Select the project you want to apply the workflow scheme to.
2. Click on the **Administration** tab of the project and select **Workflows** from the left panel.
3. Click on the **Switch Scheme** button.
4. Select the new workflow scheme to use and click on the **Associate** button.

On the confirmation page, depending on the differences between the current and new workflow, you will be prompted to make migration decisions for existing issues. For example, if the current workflow has a status called **Reopened** and the new workflow does not (or it has something equivalent but with a different ID), you need to specify the new status to place the issues that are currently in the **Reopened** status. Once mapped, JIRA will start migrating existing issues to the new status:

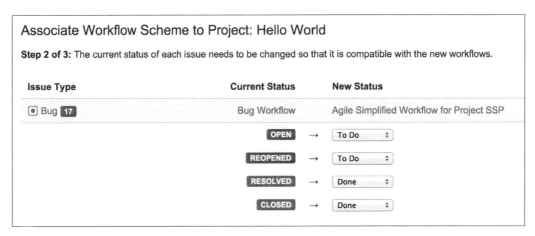

5. Select new workflow statuses for the existing issues that are in statuses that do not exist in the new workflow.
6. Click on the **Associate** button to start the migration.

Once the migration starts, JIRA will display a progress bar showing you the progress. Depending on the number of issues that need to be migrated, this process may take some time. It is recommended to allocate a time frame to perform this task as it can be quite resource-intensive for large instances.

Extending workflow with workflow add-ons

There are a number of very useful add-ons that will provide additional components such as conditions, validators, and post functions. The following list presents some of the most popular workflow-related plugins. In *Chapter 10, JIRA Service Desk*, we will talk about plugins in more detail and also how you can look for plugins yourself.

JIRA Suite Utilities

You can find a number of very useful conditions, validators, and post functions at `https://marketplace.atlassian.com/plugins/com.googlecode.jira-suite-utilities`. For example, the **Update Issue Field** post function that ships with JIRA allows you to update any issue fields such as priority and assignee when a workflow transition completes. The JIRA Suite Utilities plugin complements this by providing a very similar **Update Issue Custom Field** post function, which handles custom fields. There are many other useful components such as the **Copy Value From Other Field** post function, which will allow you to implement some amazing logics with your workflow. A must-have add-on for any JIRA.

JIRA Workflow Toolbox

As the name suggests, a workflow toolbox with a rich set of workflow conditions, validators, and post functions intends to fill many gaps when developing complex workflows. For example, it provides a condition and validator that allows you to specify the checking rules with regular expressions. You can find out more at `https://marketplace.atlassian.com/plugins/com.fca.jira.plugins.workflowToolbox.workflow-toolbox`.

JIRA Misc Workflow Extensions

This is another plugin with an assortment of conditions, validators, and post functions. Normal post functions let you alter the current issue's field values. This plugin provides post functions that will allow you to set a parent issue's field values from subtasks, along with many other features. You can find out more at `https://marketplace.atlassian.com/plugins/com.innovalog.jmwe.jira-misc-workflow-extensions`.

Workflow Enhancer for JIRA

This contains a variety of validators and conditions around comparisons of the value of a field with another field, and lets you set up validation logic to compare dates, numeric, and Boolean value. You can find out more at `https://marketplace. atlassian.com/plugins/com.tng.jira.plugins.workflowenhancer`.

Script Runner

This is a very useful and powerful add-on that allows you to create your own custom conditions, validators, and post functions by writing scripts. This does require you to have some programming knowledge and a good understanding of JIRA's API. You can find out more at `https://marketplace.atlassian.com/plugins/com. onresolve.jira.groovy.groovyrunner`.

The Help Desk project

We have seen the power of workflows and how we can enhance the usefulness of JIRA by adapting to everyday business processes. With our Help Desk project, as with most support-oriented systems, it is often the case that our Help Desk staff will require more information from the business user who has submitted the support ticket to help further diagnose and solve the problem. Our requirements for the business process would then include the following:

- Ability for support staff to request more information from the business user
- Allowing business users to reassign the ticket back after the requested information is supplied

Furthermore, as a bonus, it is ideal to automate certain aspects of this process. For example, whenever our Help Desk staff requests information, he/she will not need to decide who to assign the ticket to, but rather, let the system work it out. The same can be applied to the business user when he/she resubmits the ticket; it will be reassigned accordingly. As we will see in the next chapter, this level of automation not only enhances the user experience, but it is also very useful when facilitating communication between parties involved.

Setting up workflows

Now, it is time to create our new workflow. Since our requirements state that we need to have an extra status that will allow our Help Desk team to reassign the issue back to the business user (reporter), instead of creating a workflow from scratch, we will make a copy of the existing workflow as a template and modify its configurations. This is usually the preferred approach as it saves you time to set up some of the common transitions.

The first step is to create a workflow for the Help Desk team by performing the following steps:

1. Browse to the JIRA administration console.
2. Select **Workflows** under the **Workflows** section.
3. Click on the **Copy** link for the **jira** workflow.
4. Name the new workflow as Help Desk Workflow.
5. Enter a helpful description such as Workflow for the help desk team.
6. Click on the **Copy** button to create our workflow.

The next step is to add in the extra status we need. Make sure you are in the workflow designer by selecting the **Diagram** option:

1. Click on the **Add status** button.
2. Enter the name for our new status as, Waiting for Info, and click on **Add**. You will need to either hit the *Enter* key on your keyboard, or select the Waiting for Info (new status) option before you can click on **Add**.
3. Select a category from the **Create New Status** dialog.
4. Click on the **Create** button to create the workflow status.

Now that we have our status added to our workflow, we need a way for our Help Desk team to get there, and the answer is to add a new transition. What we need is to be able to go after the users for more information. Once our team has started working on the issue, and once the business users provide the information, the issue can then be handed back to the Help Desk team. Therefore, what we need to do is to add a new transition to the **In Progress** status that will link to the new **Waiting for Info** status:

1. Click on the **Add transition** button.
2. Select **In Progress** as the **From status**.
3. Select **Waiting for Info** as the **To status**.

4. Name the new transition as `Request for Info`.

5. Enter a helpful description such as `Request the business user for additional information`.

6. Select **Workflow Screen** for **Screen**.

7. Click on the **Add** button to create the transition.

We will also need to add another transition that will bring the issue back to **In Progress** when the business users have provided the requested information:

1. Click on the **Add transition** button again.

2. Select **Waiting for Info** as the **From status**.

3. Select **In Progress** as the **To** status.

4. Name the new transition as `Re-submit`.

5. Enter a helpful description such as `Resubmitting the ticket back to support`.

6. Select **None** for **Screen**.

7. Click on the **Add** button to create the transition.

Your workflow will look something like the one shown in the following screenshot. You can rearrange the elements in the workflow to make the diagram flow more naturally:

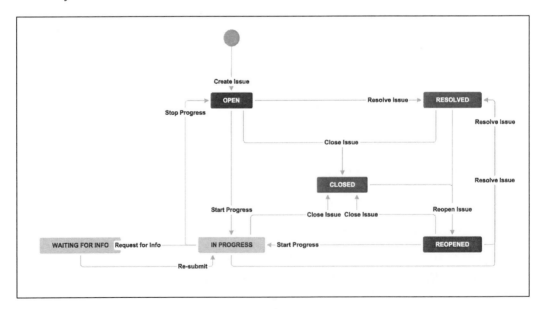

With this setup, our team can continue requesting information if required. Now, we want to make sure that only the currently assigned Help Desk team member can ask business users for more information. This will be done to automatically reassign the issue back to the business user (reporter) so that he/she will be notified. This means we need to add a condition and a post function to our transition:

1. Click on the **Request for Info** transition and click on **Conditions** from the transition property section.
2. Click on the **Add Condition** button to bring up the **Add Condition To Transition** page.
3. Select **Only Assignee Condition**.
4. Click on the **Add** button to add the condition.
5. Repeat this for all other transitions, including **Start Progress**, **Stop Progress**, **Resolve Issue**, **Close Issue**, and **Re-submit**.
6. Click on the **Post Functions** tab.
7. Click on the **Add post function** link.
8. Select **Assign to Reporter**.
9. Click on **Add** to add the post function to the transition.

Now, only the team member who is currently assigned the ticket will be able to request the business users for information, and when he/she does, the ticket will be automatically reassigned back to the business user. We will also need to do the same for the resubmit transition, so when the business user provides the requested information, the issue will be reassigned back to the Help Desk team:

1. Click on the **Re-submit** transition and click on **Conditions** from the transition property section.
2. Click on the **Add post function** link to bring up the **Add Post Function To Transition** page.
3. Select **Assign to Lead Developer**.
4. Click on **Add** to add the post function to the transition.

Setting up workflow schemes

With our workflow in place and set up, we need to let JIRA know the issue types that will be using our new workflow, so we need to create a new workflow scheme:

1. Browse to the **Workflow Schemes** page.
2. Click on the **Add Workflow Scheme** button.

3. Name the new workflow scheme as `Help Desk Workflow Scheme`.

4. Provide a helpful description such as `Workflow Scheme for the help desk team`.

5. Click on the **Add** button to create the workflow scheme.

We now need to associate our new support workflow with the appropriate issue types:

1. Click on the **Add Workflow** menu and select the **Add Existing** option.

2. Select our new **Help Desk Workflow** and click on the **Next** button.

3. Select both the **Incident** and **Ticket** issue types.

4. Click on **Finish** to create the association.

This associates our new workflow with the issue types specifically created for our Help Desk team project and uses the default workflow for the others.

Putting it together

We created a status, workflow, and workflow scheme; all we have to do now is tell our project to use them all, and this is the easiest part:

1. Browse to the **Project Administration** page for our **Global Help Desk** project.

2. Select the **Workflows** option.

3. Click on the **Switch Scheme** button.

4. Select **Help Desk Workflow Scheme** and click on the **Associate** button.

5. Click on the **Associate** button again in the next screen for JIRA to migrate all existing issues to use the new workflow.

Wait for JIRA to finish migrating the existing issue and that's it; all done! We can now create a new ticket and start testing our implementation. Since we need to simulate a scenario where a business user submits a ticket to the Help Desk team, we need to create a new business user and add him/her to the **jira-developers** group. We will look at user management and security in *Chapter 8, Securing JIRA*. For now, we will simply add a new user to our system:

1. Browse to the JIRA administration console.

2. Select the **Users Management** tab and click on the **Users** link.

3. Click on the **Create User** button to bring up the **Create New User** dialog.

4. Name the new user as `john.doe` (John Doe).

5. Set the password and e-mail address for this new user.

6. Un-check the **Send Notification Email** option.

7. Click on the **Create** button to create the user.

8. Click on the **Actions** menu and select the **Edit Groups** option.

9. Select **jira-developers** from the **Available Groups** list.

10. Click on the **Join selected groups** button.

Now, log in to JIRA as a new business user **john.doe** and create a new incident. After you create the incident issue, you will notice that you cannot execute any transitions. This is because the issue is not currently assigned to you. You need to be the assignee of the issue (member of the Help Desk team) to start working on the issue. Therefore, log out and log back in as a member of the team (**admin**).

Once logged in, you will see familiar transitions such as **Start Progress** and **Resolve Issue** are once again available. If you click on the **Workflow** drop-down box, you will also see that our new **Request for Info** transition is listed, as shown in the following screenshot:

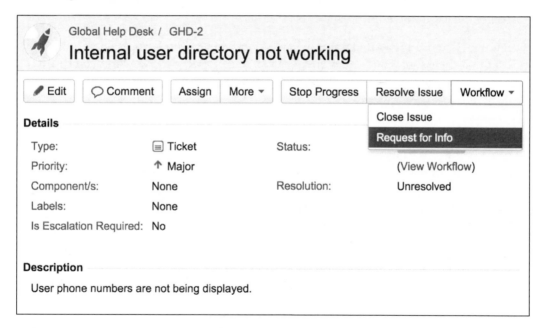

Executing that transition will place the issue in the **Waiting for Info** status, and the **Assignee** field is automatically changed to **John Doe**, the reporter of the issue, as shown in the following screenshot:

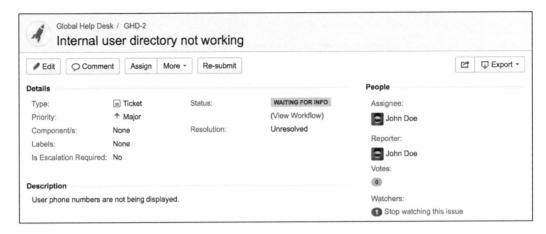

Try resubmitting the issue as the business user, and you will see that the issue will be reassigned back to the admin user.

You will notice right now that, even as a member of the Help Desk team, you are able to resubmit the issue, which is not ideal. As an additional exercise, you need to add a validation rule so that only the business user will be able to resubmit the issue back.

Summary

In this chapter, we looked at how JIRA can be customized to adapt to your organization. At the heart of this powerful feature is a robust workflow system that allows you to model JIRA workflows based on existing business processes. We also looked at the various components within a workflow, how to perform validations, and how post processing provides a level of process automation.

In the next chapter, we will look at how we can combine the power of workflow and its event-driven system to facilitate communication through JIRA notifications and the e-mail system.

7
E-mails and Notifications

So far, we have learned how to use and interact with JIRA directly from its web interface through a browser. However, you are not restricted only to a web browser; you can also communicate with JIRA through e-mails.

One powerful feature of JIRA is its ability to update users on their issue's progress through e-mails, and also create and comment on issues based on e-mails sent from users. This provides you with a whole new option of how you and your users can interact with JIRA. By the end of this chapter, you will have learned the following:

- How to set up a mail server in JIRA
- Events and how they are related to notifications
- How to configure JIRA to send out notifications based on events
- How to create custom mail templates
- What a mail handler is
- How to create issues and comments by sending e-mails to JIRA

JIRA and e-mail

E-mails have become one of the most important communication tools in today's world. Businesses and individuals rely on e-mails to send and receive information around the world almost instantly. Therefore, it comes as no surprise that JIRA is fully equipped and integrated with e-mail support.

JIRA's e-mail support comes in several flavors. Firstly, JIRA e-mails users about changes made to their issues, so people working on the same issue can be kept on the same page. Secondly, JIRA can also poll mailboxes for e-mails and create issues and comments based on their content. The last feature is the ability for users to create and subscribe to filters to set up feeds in JIRA (we will discuss filters in *Chapter 9, Searching, Reporting, and Analysis*). These features open up a whole new dimension with how users can interact with JIRA.

In the following sections, we will look at what you need to do to enable JIRA's powerful e-mail support and also explore the tools and options at your disposal to configure JIRA to e-mail it your way. The following figure shows how JIRA interacts with various mail servers:

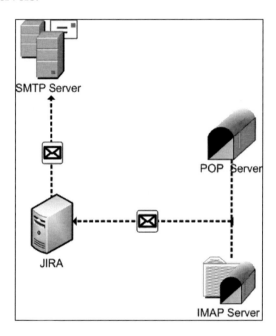

Mail servers

In order for JIRA to communicate with e-mails, you need to configure or register your mail servers in JIRA. There are two types of mail servers you need to configure:

- **Outgoing**: This mail server is used to send e-mails with an SMTP server
- **Incoming**: This mail server is used by JIRA to retrieve e-mails from a POP or an IMAP server

Working with outgoing mails

Like many settings in JIRA, you need to be a JIRA system administrator (the user created during the initial setup is a system administrator) to configure mail server details. Perform the following steps to manage the outgoing mail server:

1. Log in to JIRA as a JIRA administrator.

2. Browse to the JIRA administration console.

3. Select the **System** tab and then the **Outgoing Mail** option. This will bring up the **Outgoing Mail** page:

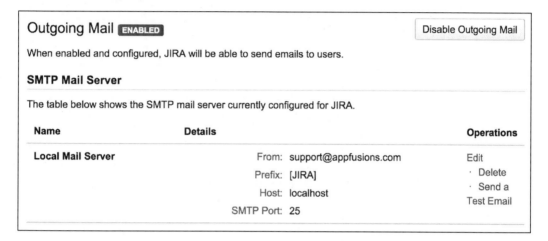

 You can have only one outgoing mail server in JIRA.

Adding an outgoing mail server

There are two ways of adding an outgoing mail server in JIRA; both options have some common configuration parameters that you will need to fill in. The following table shows those parameters:

Field	Description
Name	This specifies a name for the mail server.
Description	This specifies a brief description for the mail server.
From address	This specifies an e-mail address that outgoing e-mails will appear to have come from.

Field	Description
Email prefix	This specifies a prefix that will appear with all the e-mails sent from JIRA. This allows your users to set up filter rules in their mail clients. The prefix will be added to the beginning of the e-mail subject.
Service Provider	Select from one of the three predefined mail providers such as Google, Yahoo, or the custom SMTP server.
Host Name	This specifies the host name of your mail server (for example, `smtp.example.com`).
SMTP Port	This specifies the port number your mail server will be running on. This is optional; if left blank, the default port number `25` will be used.
Username	This is used to authenticate against the mail server if required. Note that mail servers may require authentication to relay e-mails to nonlocal users.
Password	This is used to authenticate the user against the mail server, if required.
JNDI Location	This is the JNDI lookup name if you already have a mail server configured for your application server. Please refer to the following section for details.

For the rest of the parameters, depending on which option you select to set up your mail server, you only need to fill in the ones that are appropriate.

The first option is to select from one of the built-in service providers and specify the mail server's details. For example, if you have an SMTP mail server running, you can select the **Custom** option from the **Service Provider** field and specify the host and port number. This is the approach most people will use, as it is simple and straightforward. With this approach, the administrator fills in the mail server's host information, such as the host name and port number:

1. Browse to the **Outgoing Mail** page.
2. Click on the **Configure new SMTP mail server** button. This will bring you to the **Add SMTP Mail Server** page.
3. Enter the general details of your mail server, including the name, description, from address, and e-mail prefix.
4. Select the type of mail server from the **Service Provider** field.
5. Enter the mail server's connection details.
6. Click on the **Test Connection** button to verify configuration.

7. Click on the **Add** button to register to the mail server:

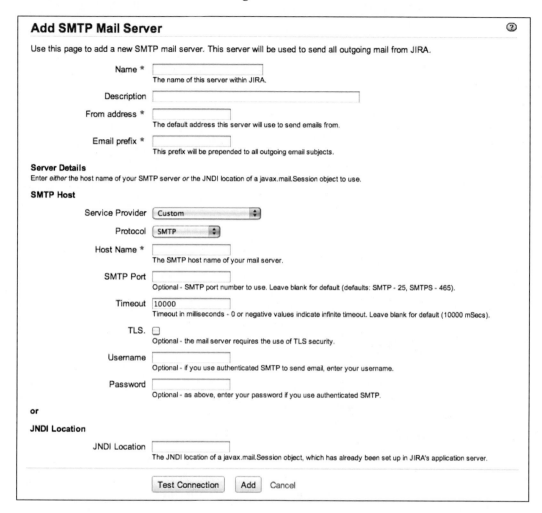

JIRA comes with support for Google and Yahoo! mail services. You can select these options in the **Service Provider** field if you are using these services.

The second option is to use JNDI. This approach is slightly more complicated as it requires configuration on the application server itself (which is different per application server), and sometimes requires a restart of the application server.

If you are using the standalone distribution, which uses Apache Tomcat, the JNDI location will be `java:comp/env/mail/JiraMailServer`. You will also need to specify the mail server details as a JNDI resource in the `server.xml` file in the `JIRA_INSTALL/conf` directory.

A sample declaration for Apache Tomcat is shown in the following code snippet. You will need to substitute in the real values for some of the parameters in the code of your mail server's details:

```
<Resource name="mail/JiraMailServer"
  auth="Container"
  type="javax.mail.Session"
  mail.smtp.host="mail.server.host"
  mail.smtp.port="25"
  mail.transport.protocol="smtp"
  mail.smtp.auth="true"
  mail.smtp.user="username"
  password="password"
/>
```

You will need to restart JIRA after saving your changes to the `server.xml` file.

Disabling outgoing mail

If you are running a test or evaluation JIRA instance or testing changes to notification rules, you might not want to flood your users with test e-mails. The easiest way for you to disable all outgoing e-mails is by just clicking on the **Disable Outgoing Mail** button in the **Outgoing Mail** page. Once you are ready to send e-mails again, you can click on the **Enable Outgoing Mail** button.

 Disabling outgoing mail will only prevent JIRA from sending out notification e-mails based on notification schemes.

Enabling SMTP over SSL

To increase security, you can encrypt the communication between JIRA and your mail server if your mail server supports SSL. There are two steps involved in enabling SSL over SMTP in JIRA.

The first step is to import your mail server's SSL certificate into Java's trust store. You can do this with Java's `keytool` utility. On a Windows machine, run the following command in a Command Prompt:

```
Keytool -import -alias mail.yourcompany.com -keystore
   $JAVA_HOME/jre/lib/security/cacerts -file yourcertificate
```

The second step is to configure your application server to use SSL for mail communication. The following declaration is for Apache Tomcat that is used by JIRA Standalone. We use the same configuration file and only need to add two additional parameters:

```
<Resource name="mail/JiraMailServer"
  auth="Container"
  type="javax.mail.Session"
  mail.smtp.host="mail.server.host"
  mail.smtp.port="25"
  mail.transport.protocol="smtp"
  mail.smtp.auth="true"
  mail.smtp.user="username"
  password="password"
  mail.smtp.atarttls.enabled="true"
  mail.smtp.socketFactory.class="javax.net.ssl.SSLSocketFactory"
/>
```

Once you import your certificate and configure your mail server, you will have to restart JIRA.

Sending a test e-mail

It is always a good idea to send a test e-mail after you configure your SMTP mail server, to make sure the server is running and you have set it correctly in JIRA:

1. Browse to the **Outgoing Mail** page.

2. Click on the **Send a Test Email** link for your SMTP mail server. This will take you to the **Send Mail** page.

3. Click on the **Send** button to send the e-mail. JIRA will autofill the **To** address based on your user profile.

If everything is correct, you will see a confirmation message in the **Mail log** section and receive the e-mail in your inbox. If there are errors, such as mail server connection, then the **Mail log** section will display the problems. This is very useful when troubleshooting any problems with JIRA's connectivity with the SMTP server:

Send Email

You can send a test email here.

To	patrick@appfusions.com
Subject	Test Message From JIRA
Message Type	Text ⬍
Body	This is a test message from JIRA. Server: Localhost SMTP Port: 25 Description: From: patrick@appfusions.com Host User Name: null
SMTP logging	☐ Log SMTP-level details

[Send] Cancel

Mail log

Log
```
An error has occurred with sending the test email:
com.atlassian.mail.MailException: javax.mail.MessagingException: Could not connect to SMTP host: localhost,
port: 25;
  nested exception is:
    java.net.ConnectException: Connection refused
    at com.atlassian.mail.server.impl.SMTPMailServerImpl.sendWithMessageId(SMTPMailServerImpl.java:201)
    at com.atlassian.mail.server.impl.SMTPMailServerImpl.send(SMTPMailServerImpl.java:149)
    at com.atlassian.jira.plugins.mail.webwork.SendTestMail.doExecute(SendTestMail.java:107)
    at webwork.action.ActionSupport.execute(ActionSupport.java:165)
    at com.atlassian.jira.action.JiraActionSupport.execute(JiraActionSupport.java:87)
    at webwork.interceptor.DefaultInterceptorChain.proceed(DefaultInterceptorChain.java:39)
    at webwork.interceptor.NestedInterceptorChain.proceed(NestedInterceptorChain.java:31)
    at webwork.interceptor.ChainedInterceptor.intercept(ChainedInterceptor.java:16)
    at webwork.interceptor.DefaultInterceptorChain.proceed(DefaultInterceptorChain.java:35)
    at webwork.dispatcher.GenericDispatcher.executeAction(GenericDispatcher.java:225)
```
Log of the events for sending mail.

In the preceding screenshot, you can see the test e-mail delivery has failed, and the error is because JIRA was unable to connect to the configured SMTP server.

Mail queues

E-mails in JIRA are not sent immediately when an operation is performed. Instead, they are placed in a mail queue, which JIRA empties periodically (every minute). This is very similar to the real-life scenario, where e-mails are placed in mailboxes and picked up everyday.

Viewing the mail queue

Normally, you do not need to manage the mail queue. JIRA automatically places e-mails into the queue and flushes them periodically. However, as an administrator, there may be times when you wish to inspect the mail queue, especially to troubleshoot JIRA notification e-mail-related problems. Sometimes, e-mails can get stuck for a number of reasons, and inspecting the mail queue will help you identify the problems and fix them.

Perform the following steps to view the content of the mail queue:

1. Browse to the JIRA administration console.

2. Select the **System** tab and then the **Mail Queue** option. This will bring up the **Mail Queue** page:

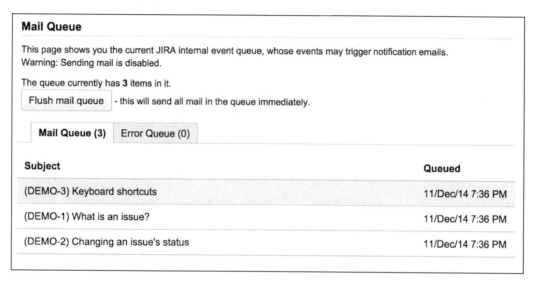

This page provides you with a one-page view of the current e-mails in the queue waiting to be delivered. There are two queues: the main mail queue and the error queue.

The **mail queue** contains all the e-mails that are pending to be delivered. If JIRA is able to successfully deliver these e-mails, they will be removed from the queue. Items listed in red indicate that JIRA has unsuccessfully attempted to send those e-mails. JIRA will retry 10 times, and if still unsuccessful, these items will be moved to the error queue.

The **error queue** contains e-mails that cannot be delivered by JIRA. You can choose to resend all the failed items in the error queue or delete them.

Flushing the mail queue

While JIRA automatically flushes the mail queue, you can also manually flush the queue if it gets stuck or to send out e-mails immediately. When you manually flush the queue, JIRA will try to send all the e-mails that are currently in the queue.

Perform the following steps to manually flush the mail queue:

1. Browse to the **Mail Queue** page.
2. Click on the **Flush mail queue** button.

If JIRA is successful in sending e-mails, you will see the queue shrink and the items disappear. If some e-mails fail to be delivered, those items will be highlighted in red.

Manually sending e-mails

Sometimes, you, as the administrator, may need to send out e-mails containing important messages to a wide audience. For example, if you are planning some maintenance work that will take JIRA offline for an extended period of time, you may want to send out an e-mail to all JIRA users to let them know of the outage.

JIRA has a built-in facility, where you can manually send out e-mails to specific groups of users. There are two options when manually sending e-mails — you can either send it based on groups or by projects.

When sending by groups, all you have to do is select one or more groups in JIRA, and all users that belong to the selected groups will receive the e-mail. Users belonging to more than one group will not get duplicated e-mails.

When sending e-mails by projects, you have to first select one or more projects and then the project roles. We will discuss project roles in more detail in the next chapter; for now, you can think of them as groups of users within projects. For example, you can send e-mails to all users that are a part of the demonstration project rather than all users in JIRA.

To send e-mails to users inside JIRA:

1. Browse to the JIRA administration console.
2. Select the **System** tab and then the **Send E-mail** option.
3. Choose if you want to send to users by **Project Roles** or **Groups**.
4. Enter the e-mail's subject and body content.
5. Click on the **Send** button to send the e-mail to all users in the selected project roles/groups.

The following screenshot shows an example of sending maintenance outage notification e-mails to everyone by selecting the **jira-users** group, which every JIRA user is a member of by default:

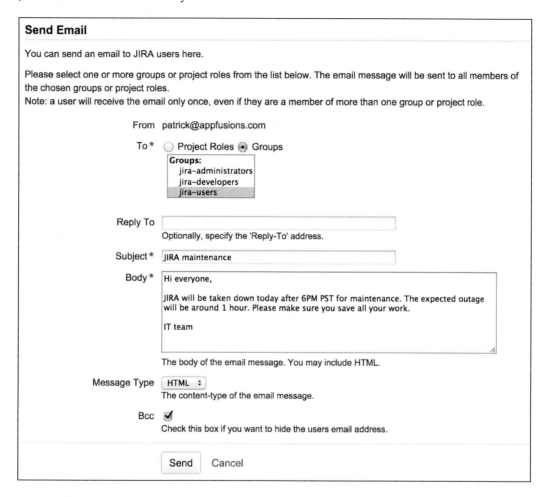

> Since JIRA does not provide a **What You See Is What You Get (WYSIWYG)** editor for composing e-mails, you may want to draft an e-mail and send it to yourself before sending it out to everyone.

Events

JIRA is an event-driven system. This means that usually when an action occurs (for example, when an issue is created), JIRA fires off a corresponding event. This event is then picked up by components that are designed to listen to the event. Not surprisingly, they are called **listeners**. When a listener picks up an event, it will perform its duty such as keeping issues up-to-date with changes or sending an e-mail to users watching the issue.

This mechanism allows JIRA to process operations asynchronously. The advantage of this model is operations, such as sending e-mails, and it's separated from JIRA's core functions like issue creation. If there is a problem with the mail server, for example, you will not want this problem to prevent your users from creating issues.

There are two types of events in JIRA:

- **System events**: These are internal events used by JIRA, and they usually represent the main functionalities in JIRA. They cannot be added, edited, or deleted.
- **Custom events**: These are events created by users. They can be added and deleted, and are fired through workflow post functions.

The following table lists all the system events in JIRA and what they are used for:

Event	Description
Issue Created	An issue has been created in JIRA.
Issue Updated	An issue has been updated (for example, changes to its fields).
Issue Assigned	An issue has been assigned to a user.
Issue Resolved	An issue has been resolved (usually applied to the resolve workflow transition).
Issue Closed	An issue has been closed (usually applied to the closed workflow transition).
Issue Commented	A comment has been added to an issue.
Issue Comment Edited	A comment has been updated.
Issue Reopened	An issue has been reopened (usually applied to the reopen workflow transition).
Issue Deleted	An issue has been deleted from JIRA.
Issue Moved	An issue has been moved (to a different or the same project).
Work Logged On Issue	Time has been logged on this issue (if time tracking has been enabled).

Event	Description
Work Started On Issue	The assignee has started working on this issue (usually applied to the start progress workflow transition).
Work Stopped On Issue	The assignee has stopped working on this issue (usually applied to the stop progress workflow transition).
Issue Worklog Updated	Worklog has been updated (if time tracking has been enabled).
Issue Worklog Deleted	Worklog has been deleted (if time tracking has been enabled).
Generic Event	A generic event that can be used by any workflow post function.
Custom Event	Events created by the user to represent arbitrary events generated by business processes.

As an administrator, you will be able to get a one-page view of all the events in JIRA. You just need to do the following:

1. Browse to the JIRA administration console.
2. Select the **System** tab and then the **Events** option. This will bring up the **View Events** page.

Like most other entities in JIRA, such as screens, events can be either active or inactive. New events are inactive by default, and they need to be associated with a notification scheme or workflow post function to become active. While you cannot edit or delete system events, you can deactivate them by removing their association with notification schemes and workflow post functions.

Each event is associated with a template, often referred to as a mail template. These templates contain the base e-mail contents when notifications are sent. For system events, you cannot change their templates (you can change the template files, however). For custom events, you can choose to use one of the existing templates or create your own mail template.

Adding a mail template

Mail templates are physical files that you create and edit directly via a text editor; you can not edit mail templates in the browser. Each mail template is made up of three files:

- **Subject template**: This file contains the template used to generate the e-mail's subject.

- **Text template**: This file contains the template used by JIRA when the e-mail is sent as plain text.

- **HTML template**: This file contains the template used by JIRA when the e-mail is sent as HTML.

Mail templates are stored in the `<JIRA_INSTALL>/atlassian-jira/WEB-INF/classes/templates/email` directory. Each of the three files listed are placed in their respective directories called `subject`, `text`, and `html`.

While creating new mail templates, it is a good practice to name your template files after the issue event. This will help future users understand the purpose of the templates.

Mail templates use Apache's Velocity template language (`http://velocity.apache.org`). For this reason, creating new mail templates will require some understanding of HTML and template programming.

If your templates only contain static text, you can simply use standard HTML tags for your template. However, if you need to have dynamic data rendered as part of your templates, such as the issue key or summary, you will need to use the **Velocity syntax**. A full explanation of Velocity is beyond the scope of this book. The following section provides a quick introduction to creating simple mail templates for JIRA. You can find more information on Velocity and its usage in JIRA mail templates at `https://confluence.atlassian.com/x/dQISCw`.

In a Velocity template, all the text will be treated as normal. Anything that starts with a dollar sign (\$), such as `$issue`, is a Velocity statement. The \$ sign tells Velocity to reference the item after the sign, and when combined with the period (`.`), you are able to retrieve the value specified. For example, the following command will get the issue key and summary from the current issue, separated by a "-" character:

```
$issue.key - $issue.summary
```

JIRA provides a range of Velocity references that you can use for creating mail templates. You can find a comprehensive list at `https://developer.atlassian.com/display/JIRADEV/Velocity+Context+for+Email+Templates`.

Now that you have a brief understanding of how Velocity works, you first need to create a template for the mail subject. The following command shows a typical subject template:

```
$eventTypeName: ($issue.key) $issue.summary
```

When the template is processed, JIRA will substitute in the actual values for the event type (for example, Issue Created), issue key, and issue summary (for example, Issue Escalated: HD-11–Database server is running very slow).

You then need to create a template for the actual e-mail content. You need to create a text and HTML version. The following code shows a simple example of a text-based template, which displays the key for the escalated issue:

```
Hello,

The ticket $issue.key has been escalated and is currently being worked
on.  We will contact you if we require more information.

Regards
Support team.
```

Before JIRA sends out the e-mail, the preceding text will be processed, where all Velocity references, such as `$issue.key`, will be converted into proper values, for example, DEMO-1.

After creating your mail templates, register them with JIRA. To register your new templates, locate and open the `email-templates-id-mappings.xml` file in the `<JIRA_INSTALL>/atlassian-jira/WEB-INF/classes` directory in a text editor. Add a new entry to the end of the file before closing the `</templatemappings>` tag, as follows:

```
<templatemapping id="10001">
  <name>Example Custom Event</name>
  <template>examplecustomevent.vm</template>
  <templatetype>issueevent</templatetype>
</templatemapping>
```

Here, we register a new custom mail template entry and the details are given in the following table:

Parameter	Description
id	The unique ID for the template.
name	A human-readable name for JIRA to display.
template	The mail template file names for `subject`, `text`, and `html`. All three template files must be named as specified here.
type	Template type. For events generated from an issue, the value will be `issueevent`.

After creating your templates and registering them in the mapping file, you will have to restart JIRA for the changes to be picked up. The new templates will be available when we create new events, as covered in the following section.

Adding a custom event

JIRA comes with a comprehensive list of system events focused around issue-related operations. However, there will be times when you will need to create custom-designed events representing specialized business operations, or when you simply need to use a custom e-mail template.

Perform the following steps to add a new custom event:

1. Browse to the **View Events** page.
2. Enter a meaningful name and description for the new event in the **Add New Event** section.
3. Select the mail template for the new event.
4. Click on the **Add** button to create a new event:

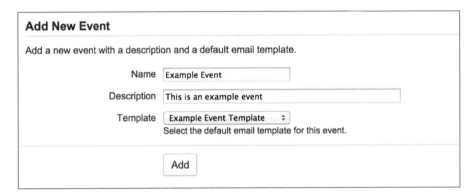

New events are inactive by default. Associating them with a notification scheme or workflow post function will activate them.

Firing a custom event

Unlike system events, with custom events, you need to tell JIRA when it can fire a custom event.

Custom events are mostly fired by workflow transitions. If you recall from *Chapter 6, Workflows and Business Processes*, you can add post functions to workflow transitions. Almost all JIRA's transitions will have a post function that fires an appropriate event. It is important to understand that just because an event is fired does not mean that there needs to be something to listen to it.

If you skipped *Chapter 6, Workflows and Business Processes*, or still do not have a good understanding on workflows, now would be a good time to go back and revisit the chapter.

Perform the following steps to fire a custom event from a workflow post function:

1. Browse to the **View Workflows** page.
2. Click on the **Edit** link for the workflow that will be used to fire the event.
3. Click on the transition that will fire the event when executed.
4. Click on the **Post Functions** tab.
5. Click on the **Edit** link for the post function that reads **Fire a <event name> event that can be processed by the listeners**:

6. Select the custom event from the drop-down list.
7. Click on the **Update** button to apply the changes to the post function.
8. Publish the workflow.

Now, whenever the workflow transition is executed, the `post` function will run and fire the selected event. Each transition can fire only one event, so you cannot have **both Issue Created** and **Issue Updated** events being fired from the same transition.

Notifications

Notifications associate events (both system and custom) to e-mail recipients. When an event is fired and picked up, e-mails will be sent out. Notification recipients are defined by notification types. For example, you can set it to only send e-mails to a specific user or all members from a given user group. You can add multiple notifications to a given event.

JIRA ships with a comprehensive list of notification types (that is, the recipients) that will cover many of your needs. The following table lists all the notification types available and how they work:

Notification type	Description
Current Assignee	The current assignee of the issue.
Reporter	The reporter of the issue (usually the person who originally created the issue).
Current User	The user who fired the event.
Project Lead	Lead of the project the issue belongs to.
Component Lead	Lead of the component the issue belongs to.
Single User	Any user that exists in JIRA.
Group	All users that belong to the specified group.
Project Role	All users that belong to the specified project role.
Single Email Address	Any e-mail address.
All Watchers	All users that are watching this issue.
User Custom Field Value	The users specified in the user-type custom field. For example, if you have a **User Picker** custom field called **Recipient**, the user selected in the custom field will receive notifications if he/she has access to the issue.
Group Custom Field Value	All users that belong to the group in the group-type custom field. For example, if you have a **Group Picker** custom field called **Approvers**, all users from the group (with access to the issue) selected in the custom field will receive notifications.

As you can see, the list includes a wide range of options from issue reporters to values contained in custom fields. Basically, anything that can be represented as a user in JIRA can have notifications set up.

If a user belongs to more than one notification for a single event, JIRA will make sure that only one e-mail will be sent so the user does not receive duplicates. In order for a user to receive notifications, the user must have permission to view the issue. The only exception to this is when using the **Single Email Address** option (we will discuss security in *Chapter 8, Securing JIRA*). If the user does not have permission to view the issue, JIRA will not send a notification e-mail.

We will look at how you can add notifications to events so that users can start receiving e-mails; however, before that, you need to first take a look at the notification scheme.

The notification scheme

The notification scheme is a reusable entity that links events with notifications. In other words, it contains the associations between events and their respective e-mail recipients:

1. Browse to the JIRA administration console.

2. Select the **Issues** tab and then the **Notification Schemes** option. This will bring up the **Notification Schemes** page:

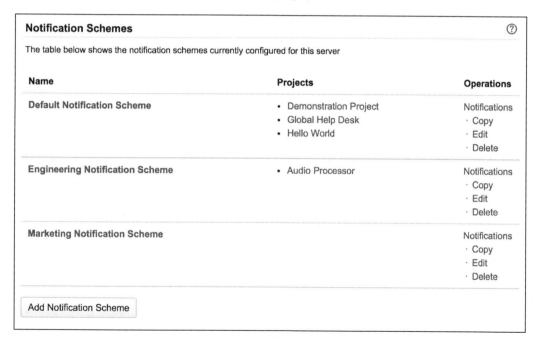

From this screen, you can see a list of all the notification schemes and what projects are currently using them.

JIRA comes with a generic default notification scheme. The default scheme is set up with notifications set for all the system events. This allows you to quickly enable notifications in JIRA. The default setup has the following notifications:

- **Current Assignee**
- **Reporter**
- **All Watchers**

You can modify the default notification scheme to add your own notification rules, but as you grow your JIRA adoption, it is a better idea to create a new scheme from scratch or copy the default scheme and make your modifications.

Adding a notification scheme

As with all other aspects in JIRA, you are not forced to use the default configurations provided. JIRA allows you to create your own custom notification schemes to set up customized notification rules that can be applied to your projects. Perform the following steps to create a new notification scheme:

1. Browse to the **Notification Schemes** page.
2. Click on the **Add Notification Scheme** button at the bottom. This will bring you to the **Add Notification Scheme** page.
3. Enter a meaningful name and description for the new notification scheme.
4. Click on the **Add** button to create the notification scheme.

When you create a new notification scheme, you create a blank scheme that can be configured later to add your own notification rules in. It is important that after you create a new notification scheme, you configure its notification rules before applying the scheme to projects; otherwise, no notifications will be sent out. We will look at how to configure notification rules later in this chapter.

Editing a notification scheme

You can keep your notification scheme's name and description up-to-date by editing it. Do not confuse this with updating the scheme's configuration. Just like other schemes, a notification scheme's name and description details are kept and managed separately from its configuration contents.

Perform the following steps to edit a notification scheme:

1. Browse to the **Notification Schemes** page.
2. Click on the **Edit** link for the notification scheme you wish to update. This will bring up the **Edit Notification Scheme** page.
3. Enter a new name and description.
4. Click on the **Update** button to apply the changes.

You can make updates to the notification scheme at any time, regardless of whether it is being used by projects.

Deleting a notification scheme

Unlike most other schemes, such as workflow, JIRA allows you to delete notification schemes even when they are being used by projects. However, JIRA does prompt you with a warning when you attempt to delete a notification scheme that is in use.

Perform the following steps to delete a notification scheme:

1. Browse to the **Notification Schemes** page.
2. Click on the **Delete** link for the notification scheme you wish to remove. This will bring up the **Delete Notification Scheme** page.
3. Click on the **Delete** button to remove the notification scheme.

Once you delete a notification scheme, the projects that were previously using the scheme will have no notification schemes, so you will have to reapply schemes individually. When you delete a notification scheme, you remove all the notifications you set up in the scheme.

Copying a notification scheme

It is always a good idea to make a backup copy of your notification schemes before making changes or deleting them. This allows you to quickly roll back your changes if problems are detected. Another benefit of copying an existing notification scheme is the amount of time it can save. As you have seen, when you create a new notification scheme from scratch, it will contain no notifications. Most of the time, it will be more efficient to use the default notification scheme provided by JIRA as a base and modify the notification rules accordingly.

Whatever the reason may be, you will find the ability to make copies of existing notification schemes to be handy from time to time. Perform the following steps to copy a notification scheme:

1. Browse to the **Notification Schemes** page.

2. Click on the **Copy** link for the notification scheme you wish to copy. A copy of the notification scheme will be made immediately with the name **Copy of** appended to the original notification scheme.

Once you copy a notification scheme, you can edit its name and description to better describe its purpose and configure its notifications as explained in the next sections.

Managing a notification scheme

Notification schemes contain notifications that are set on events in JIRA. Perform the following steps to configure a notification scheme:

1. Browse to the **Notification Schemes** page.

2. Click on the **Notifications** link for the notification scheme you wish to configure. This will bring you to the **Edit Notifications** page.

This page lists all the existing events in JIRA and their corresponding notification recipients. If you configure a new notification scheme, there will be no notifications set for the events.

Adding a notification

There are two ways you can add a new notification. You can add a notification for a specific event or you can add a notification for multiple events. Perform the following steps to add a new notification:

1. Browse to the **Edit Notifications** page for the notification scheme you wish to configure.

2. Click on the **Add notification** link or the **Add** link for the event you wish to add a notification for. This will bring you to the **Add Notification** page. If you click on the **Add** link, the **Events selection** list will preselect the event for you.

3. Select the events you want to add the notification type to.

4. Select the notification type from the available options.

5. Click on the **Add** button. For example, the following screenshot shows setting up notification for JIRA to send out e-mails to the project lead, when issues are created and edited in the project:

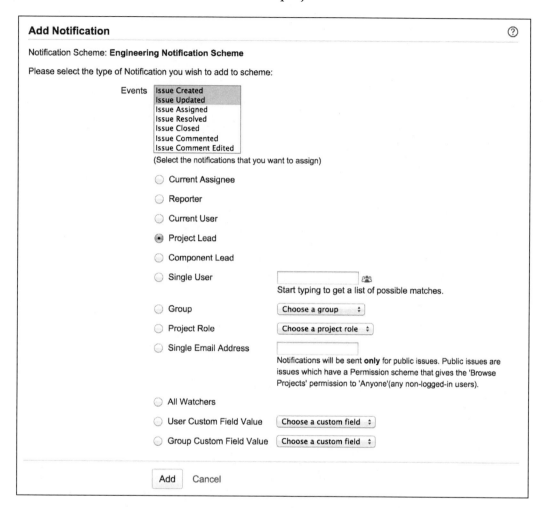

Once added, the notification will be listed against the events selected. You can continue adding notifications for the events by repeating the same steps.

> You can select multiple events to add a notification type to.

Deleting a notification

When notifications are no longer required for certain events, you can also have them removed. To remove notifications, you will need to do it one by one, per event:

1. Browse to the **Edit Notifications** page for the notification scheme you wish to configure.
2. Click on the **Delete** link for the notification you wish to remove. This will bring you to the **Delete Notification** page.
3. Click on the **Delete** button to remove the notification for the event.

After you remove a notification, users affected by that notification will stop receiving e-mails from JIRA. However, you need to pay attention to your configurations, as there may be other notifications for the same event that will continue to send e-mails to the same user. For example, if you created two notifications for the **Issue Created** event—one set to a **Single User** John (who belongs to the jira-administrator group) and another set to **Group** (jira-administrator). If your goal is to prevent e-mails being sent to the user John, you will need to remove both notifications from the event instead of simply the **Single User** option.

Assigning a notification scheme

When new projects are created, they are automatically assigned to use the default notification scheme. If you want your project to use a different scheme, you will need to go to the **Notifications** section of your project's administration console:

1. Select the project you want to apply the workflow scheme to.

2. Click on the **Administration** tab of the project and select **Notifications** from the left panel:

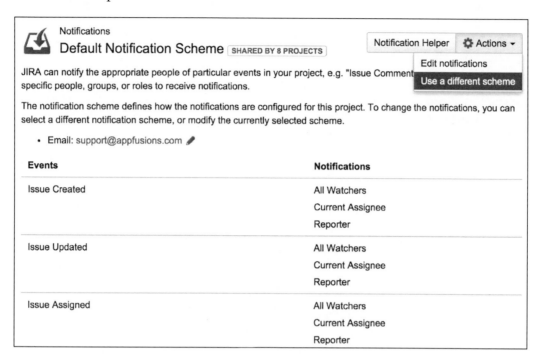

3. Select **Use a different scheme** in the **Actions** menu. This will bring up the **Associate Notification Scheme to Project** page.

4. Select the notification scheme to use.

5. Click on the **Associate** button.

As soon as a notification scheme is applied to the project, it will take effect immediately, and you will see e-mails being sent out for the events that have been configured in the scheme. Like any other schemes in JIRA, notification schemes can be assigned to multiple projects to share the same notification behavior.

Troubleshooting notifications

Often, when people do not receive notifications from JIRA, it can be difficult and frustrating to find the cause. The two most common causes for notification-related problems are either outgoing mail server connectivity, or misconfiguration of the notification scheme.

Troubleshooting outgoing mail server problems is quite simple. All you have to do is try to send out a test e-mail as described in the *Sending a test mail* section. If you receive your test e-mail, then there will be no problems with your outgoing mail server configuration, and you can focus on your notification configurations.

Troubleshooting notifications are not as straightforward, since there are a number of things that you will need to consider. To help with this challenge, JIRA 5 has introduced a new feature called **Notification Helper**. The notification helper can save the JIRA administrators time by helping them to pinpoint why a given user does or does not receive notifications. All the administrator has to do is tell the helper who the user is, which issue (or an example issue from a project) the user will or will not be receiving notifications for, and the event that is triggering the notification:

1. Browse to the JIRA administration console.
2. Select the **Add-ons** tab and then the **Notification Helper** option at the bottom.
3. Specify the user that will or will not receive notifications in the **User** field.
4. Specify the issue to test with.
5. Select the type of notification event.
6. Click on **Submit**.

Notification Helper will then process the input and report back if the user will be receiving notifications and why, based on notification scheme settings:

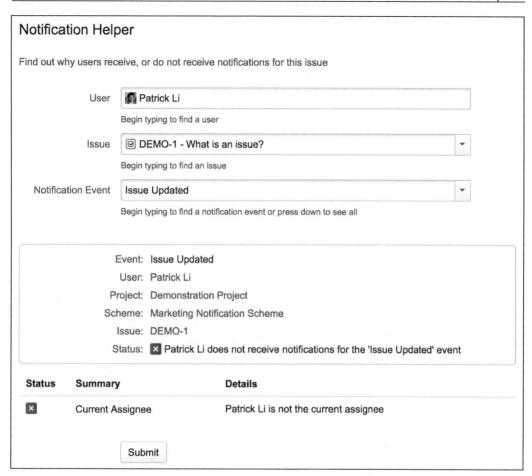

As you can see from the preceding screenshot, the user **Patrick Li** is currently not receiving notifications for **DEMO-1** issue because the notification is set up to have only the **Current Assignee** receive e-mails, and **Patrick Li** is not the assignee.

Incoming e-mails

We have seen how you can configure JIRA to send e-mails to notify users about updates on their issues. Although, this is only half of the story when it comes to JIRA's e-mail support.

You can also set up JIRA for it to periodically poll mailboxes for e-mails and create issues based on the e-mails' subject and content. This is a very powerful feature with the following benefits:

- Hides the complexity of JIRA from business users so they can log issues more efficiently and leave the complexity to your IT team

- Allows users to create issues even if JIRA can only be accessed within the internal network. Users can send e-mails to a dedicated mailbox for JIRA to poll

Adding an incoming mail server

For JIRA to retrieve e-mails and create issues from them, you need to add the POP/IMAP mail server configurations to JIRA. POP and IMAP are mail protocols used to retrieve e-mails from the server. E-mail clients, such as Microsoft Outlook and Mozilla Thunderbird, can use one of these protocols to retrieve your e-mails.

Unlike outgoing mail servers, JIRA allows you to add multiple incoming mail servers. This is because while you only need one mail server to send e-mails, you may have multiple mail servers or multiple mail accounts (on the same server) that people will use to send e-mails to. For example, you might have one dedicated to support and another one for sales. It is usually a good idea to create separate mail accounts to make it easier when trying to work out which e-mail can go into which project. For this reason, adding POP/IMAP mail servers can be thought of as adding multiple mail accounts in JIRA:

Perform the following steps to add an incoming mail server:

1. Browse to the JIRA administration console.
2. Select the **System** tab and then the **Incoming Mail** option; this will display the **Incoming Mail** page.
3. Click on the **Configure POP/IMAP mail server** button. This will bring you to the **Add POP/IMAP Mail Server** page.
4. Enter a meaningful name and description for the mail server.
5. Select the type of mail service provider. For example, if you are using your own hosted mail service or one of the recognized cloud provider such as Google.
6. Specify the host name of the POP/IMAP server if you are using your own (custom provider).
7. Enter the username/password credentials for the mail account.

8. Click on the **Add** button to create the POP/IMAP mail server:

Add POP / IMAP Mail Server

Use this page to add a new POP / IMAP server for JIRA to retrieve mail from.

Name *	
	The name of this server within JIRA.
Description	
Service Provider	Custom
Protocol	POP
Host Name *	
	The host name of your POP / IMAP server.
POP / IMAP Port	
	Optional - The port to use to retrieve mail from your POP / IMAP account. Leave blank for default. (defaults: POP - 110, SECURE_POP - 995, IMAP - 143, SECURE_IMAP - 993)
Timeout	10000
	Timeout in milliseconds - 0 or negative values indicate infinite timeout. Leave blank for default (10000 ms).
Username *	
	The username used to authenticate your POP / IMAP account.
Password *	
	The password for your POP / IMAP account.

Test Connection   Add   Cancel

 You can have multiple incoming servers.

Mail handlers

Mail handlers are what JIRA uses to process retrieved e-mails. Each mail handler is able to process e-mails from one incoming mail server and periodically scan for new e-mails.

JIRA ships with a number of mail handlers, each with their own features. In the following sections, we will discuss each of the handlers in detail.

Creating a new issue or adding a comment to an existing issue

Creating a new issue or adding a comment to an existing issue mail handler (also known as the **Create or Comment Handler** in previous versions of JIRA) is the most used mail handler. It will create new issues from the received e-mails and also add comments to existing issues if the incoming e-mail's subject contains a matching issue key. If the subject does not contain a matching issue key, a new issue is created. The following table lists the parameters required when creating the mail handler:

Parameter	Description
Project	The project in which issues will be created. This is not used for commenting where the e-mail subject will contain the issue key.
Issue Type	The issue type for newly created issues.
Strip Quotes	If present in the parameters, quoted text from the e-mail will not be added as a part of the comment.
Catch Email Address	Specifies if JIRA is to only handle e-mails that are sent to the specified address.
Bulk	This specifies how to handle autogenerated e-mails such as those generated by JIRA. It is possible to create a loop, if JIRA sends e-mails to the same mailbox where it also picks up e-mails. In order to prevent this, you can specify either of the following: • `ignore`: Ignore these e-mails • `forward`: Forward these e-mails to another address • `delete`: Delete these e-mails altogether Generally, you can set it to `forward`.
Forward Email	If specified, then the mail handler is unable to process an e-mail message it receives. An e-mail message indicating this problem will be forwarded to the e-mail address specified in this field.
Create Users	If the e-mail is sent from an unknown address, JIRA will create a new user based on the e-mail "from" address and randomly generate a password. An e-mail will be sent to the "from" address informing the new JIRA account user.
Default Reporter	Specifies the username of a default reporter, which will be used if the e-mail address in the **From** field of any of the received messages does not match the address associated with that of an existing JIRA user.

Parameter	Description
Notify Users	Uncheck this option if you do not want JIRA to notify new users created as per the **Create Users** parameter.
CC Assignee	JIRA will assign the issue to the user specified in the **To** field first. If no user can be matched from the **To** field, JIRA will then try the users in the **CC** and then **BCC** list.
CC Watchers	JIRA will add users in the **CC** list (if they exist) as watchers of the issue.

Adding a comment with the entire e-mail body

This mail handler extracts text from an e-mail's content and adds it to the issue with a matching issue key in the subject. The author of the comment is taken from the **From** field.

It has a similar set of parameters to **Create and Comment handler**.

Adding a comment from the non-quoted e-mail body

Adding a comment from the non-quoted e-mail body is very similar to the Full Comment handler, but only extracts non-quoted texts and adds them as comments. Texts that start with ">" or "|" are considered to be quoted.

It has a similar set of parameters to **Create and Comment handler**.

Creating a new issue from each e-mail message

Creating a new issue from each e-mail message is very similar to **Create and Comment handler**, except this will always create a new issue for every received e-mail.

It has a similar set of parameters to **Create and Comment handler**.

Adding a comment before a specified marker or separator in the e-mail body

Adding a comment before a specified marker or separator in the e-mail body is a more powerful version of the comment handlers. It uses regular expressions to extract texts from e-mail contents and add them to the issue:

Parameter	Description
Split Regex	The regex expression is used to extract contents. There are two rules for the regex expression: • It must start and end with a delimiter character, usually with "/" • It cannot contain commas, for example, `/-{}{}{}{}{}\s*Original Message\s*{}-/` or `/_____*/`

Adding a mail handler

You can set up as many mail handlers as you want. It is recommended that you create dedicated mailboxes for each project you wish to allow JIRA to create issues from e-mails. For each account, you will then need to create a mail handler. The mailbox you set up needs to be accessible through POP or IMAP.

Perform the following steps to add a mail handler:

1. Browse to the **Incoming Mail** page.
2. Click on the **Add incoming mail handler** button. This will bring up the **Mail Handler** dialog box.
3. Provide a meaningful name to the new mail handler.
4. Select an incoming mail server or **Local Files**.
5. Specify how long JIRA can wait to poll the mailbox for new e-mails (in minutes). You will want to keep this long enough to allow enough time for JIRA to process all the e-mails, but not too long as you may end up having to wait for a long time to see your e-mails converted into issues in JIRA.
6. Select the type of handler you want to add.

7. Click on the **Next** button:

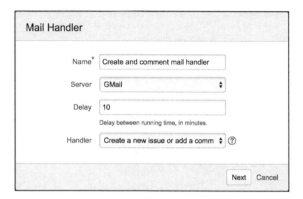

Depending on the handler type you select, the next screen will vary. On the next screen, you will need to provide the required parameters for the mail handler, as described in the preceding section. The following screenshot shows an example configuration dialog box, where new issues will be created in the **Demonstration** project as **Bugs**:

You can always use the **Test** button to test out your configuration. JIRA provides you with helpful hints if there are problems.

Editing and deleting a mail handler

You can update the details of your mail handlers at any time. You will often need to tune your handler parameters a few times until you get your desired results. Perform the following steps to update a mail handler:

1. Browse to the **Incoming Mail** page.
2. Click on the **Edit** link for the mail handler you wish to update.
3. Update the configure options.

Once updated, the changes will be applied immediately and JIRA will use the new handler parameters for the next polling run.

You can also delete mail handlers that are no longer required at any time. Perform the following steps to delete a mail handler:

1. Browse to the **Incoming Mail** page.
2. Click on the **Delete** link for the mail handler you wish to remove.

 You will not be prompted with a confirmation page. The mail handler will be removed immediately, so think carefully before you delete it.

The Help Desk project

Users will often want to get progress updates on their issues after they have logged them. So, instead of business users having to ask for updates, we will proactively update them through our newly acquired knowledge, that is, JIRA notifications.

In *Chapter 4, Field Management*, we added a custom field called **Escalation List**, which allows users to add who else will receive notifications along with the issue's reporter and assignee.

The other customization we have made in *Chapter 6, Workflows and Business Processes*, is the addition of new transitions in the workflow. We need to make sure those transitions fire appropriate events and also send out notifications. In summary, we need to do the following:

- Send out notifications for the new custom events fired by our custom workflow transitions
- Send out notifications to users specified in our **Escalation List** custom field

While you can achieve both using other JIRA features, such as adding users as watchers to the issue and reusing existing JIRA system events, this exercise will explore the options available to you. In later chapters, you will see there are other criteria to consider while deciding on the best approach.

Setting up mail servers

The first step to enable e-mail communication, as you will have guessed, is to register mail servers in JIRA. If you are using the standalone distribution of JIRA, it is recommended that you add your mail server by entering the host information:

1. Log in to JIRA as a JIRA administrator.
2. Browse to the JIRA administration console.
3. Select the **System** tab and then the **Outgoing Mail** option.
4. Click on the **Configure new SMTP mail server** button.
5. Enter in your mail server information.

After adding your mail server, you can try sending yourself a quick test e-mail to see if JIRA is able to access your server successfully.

Setting up custom events

In *Chapter 6, Workflows and Business Processes*, we created two new workflow transitions. One is for the Help Desk staff to request additional information from the business user and another for the business user to supply the requested information. What you need to do now is create custom events for the transitions when they are executed:

1. Browse to the **View Events** page.
2. Go to the **Add New Event** section at the end of the page.
3. Name the new event **Info Requested**.
4. Provide a description for the event—This is the request information event.

5. Select the **Issue Updated** template.

6. Click on the **Add** button to create the new event.

With your event created, you now need to update your workflow so that your transitions can fire the correct event:

1. Browse to the **View Workflows** page.

2. Click on the **Edit** link for **Help Desk Workflow**.

3. Click on the **Request for Info** transition.

4. Update the post function to fire our **Info Requested** event rather then the **Generic Event**.

5. Publish the draft workflow. You can save a backup copy in case you want to revert back.

In this case, you can reuse the **Issue Updated** event and it will work just as fine. However, there are advantages to having your own custom events as it helps to distinguish exactly what the nature of the update is. When you have the listeners' components in JIRA, having specialized events helps to distinguish the origin and act accordingly.

Setting up a notification scheme

Now, you need to have your own notification scheme, so you can start adding notifications to your events. We will base our notification scheme on the default scheme to help us get things set up quickly:

1. Select the **Issues** tab and then the **Notification Schemes** option.

2. Click on the **Copy** link for **Default Notification Scheme**. A new notification scheme named **Copy of Default Notification Scheme** will be created.

3. Click on the **Edit** link of **Copy of Default Notification Scheme**.

4. Rename it to `Help Desk Notification Scheme` and click on **Update**.

This will create a new notification scheme with the basic notifications prepopulated. All you need to do now is modify the events and add your own notification needs.

Setting up notifications

There are two rules you need to follow to add notifications. First, you need to add notifications for your custom events so that e-mails will be sent out when they are fired. Second, you will want users specified in the **CC** list custom field to also receive e-mails along with the assignee and reporter of the issue:

1. Click on the **Notifications** link for **Help Desk Notification Scheme**.
2. Click on the **Add notification** link.
3. Select all the event types.
4. Select **User Custom Field Value** for the notification type and select **Escalation List** from the drop-down list.
5. Click on the **Add** button.

Nice and easy. With just a few clicks, JIRA has allowed you to add a new notification to not only all the system events, but also our new custom events.

Putting it together

The last step, as always, is to associate your scheme with projects for activation:

1. Browse to the **Global Help Desk** project.
2. Click on the **Administration** tab and select **Notifications** from the left panel.
3. Select **Use a different scheme** in the **Actions** menu.
4. Select **Help Desk Notification Scheme**.
5. Click on the **Associate** button.

With just a few clicks, you enable JIRA to automatically send out e-mails to update users with their issue's progress. Not only this, but you have tied in the custom fields you created from earlier chapters to manage who, along with the issue assignee and reporter, will also get these notifications. So let's put this to the test!

1. Create a new issue in the Global Help Desk project.
2. Select one or more users for the **Escalation List** custom field. It is a good idea not to select yourself since the reporter will get notifications by default. Also make sure that the user selected has a valid e-mail address.
3. Transition the issue to **In Progress** status and execute the **Request for Info** transition on the new issue.
4. You will receive e-mails from JIRA within minutes.

If you do not receive e-mails from JIRA, check your mail queue and see if the mail is being generated, and follow the steps from the *Troubleshooting notifications* section in this chapter.

Summary

In this chapter, we looked at how JIRA can stay in touch with its users through e-mails. Indeed, with today's new gadgets, such as smartphones and tablets, being able to keep users updated with e-mails is a powerful feature, and JIRA has a very flexible structure in place to define the rules on who will receive notifications.

We also very briefly mentioned some of the security rules about who can receive notifications. JIRA performs security checks prior to sending out notifications for two very good reasons—one, there is no point sending out an e-mail to a user who cannot view the issue; two, you will not want unauthorized users to view the issue and receive updates that they will not know about.

In the next chapter, we will look into the security aspects of JIRA and how you can secure your data to prevent unauthorized access.

8
Securing JIRA

In the previous chapters, you learned how to store data in JIRA by creating issues. As you can see, as an information system, JIRA, is all about data. It should come as no surprise to you that security plays a big role in JIRA not only to ensure the right people will get access to our data, but also to maintain data integrity by preventing accidental changes.

By the end of the chapter, you will have learned the following:

- User directories and how to connect JIRA to LDAP
- General access control in JIRA
- Managing fine-grained permission settings
- How to troubleshoot permission problems

Before we delve into the deep end of how JIRA handles security, let's first take a look at how JIRA maintains user and group memberships.

User directories

User directories are what JIRA uses to store information about users and groups. A user directory is backed by a user repository system, such as LDAP, a database, or a remote user management system, such as Atlassian Crowd.

You can have multiple user directories in JIRA. This allows you to connect your JIRA instance to multiple user repositories. For example, you can have an LDAP directory for your internal users and a database directory (a JIRA internal directory) for external users. A example is given, in the following screenshot, is that, we have two user directories configured. The first user directory is the built-in JIRA **Internal** directory running on the JIRA database. The second user directory is connected to **Microsoft Active Directory** in read-only mode. The last user directory is connected to **Crowd**, a user identity management software from Atlassian:

User Directories ⓘ

The table below shows the user directories currently configured for JIRA.

The order of the directories is the order in which they will be searched for users and groups. Changes to users and groups will be made in the first directory where JIRA has permission to make changes. It is recommended that each user exist only in a single directory.

Directory Name	Type	Order	Operations
JIRA Internal Directory	Internal	⬆ ⬇	Disable | Edit
Active Directory Server	Microsoft Active Directory (Read Only)	⬆ ⬇	Disable | Edit | Test | Synchronise Last synchronised at 10/1/14 2:39 PM (took 2s). Incremental synchronisation completed successfully.
Crowd Server You cannot edit this directory because you are logged in through it, please log in as a locally authenticating user to edit it.	Atlassian Crowd	⬆ ⬇	Test | Synchronise Last synchronised at 10/1/14 3:39 PM (took 10s). Incremental synchronisation completed successfully.

Add Directory

Additional Configuration & Troubleshooting

• Directory Configuration Summary

Perform the following steps to access the user directories' interface:

1. Browse to the JIRA administration console.
2. Select the **User management** tab and then the **User Directories** option. This will bring up the **User Directories** page.

While adding a new user directory, you need to first decide on the directory type. There are several different user directory types within JIRA:

• **JIRA internal directory**: This is the built-in default user directory when you first install JIRA. With this directory, all the user and group information is stored in the JIRA database.

- **Active directory (AD)/LDAP**: This is used when you want to connect JIRA to an LDAP server. With this directory, JIRA will use the backend LDAP to query user information and group membership. This is also known as **LDAP Connector**, and should not be confused with Internal and LDAP Authentication directories.

JIRA supports a wide range of LDAP servers including Microsoft Active Directory, OpenLDAP, and Novell eDirectory server. If a particular LDAP is not listed as one of the options, then there is also a **Generic Directory Server** option.

When using the AD/LDAP connector directory type, you can choose to connect with one of the permission options:

- **Read only**: JIRA cannot make any modifications to the LDAP server.
- **Read only, with local groups**: Information retrieved from LDAP will be read-only, but you can also add users to groups created within JIRA. These changes will not be reflected in LDAP.
- **Read/Write**: JIRA will be able to retrieve and make changes to the LDAP server.
- **Internal with LDAP authentication**: This is also known as **Delegated LDAP**. With this directory type, JIRA will only use LDAP for authentication and will keep all user information internally in the database (retrieved from LDAP when the user successfully authenticates for the first time). This approach can give a better performance. Since LDAP is only used for authentication, this avoids the need to download larger numbers of groups from LDAP.
- **Atlassian Crowd**: If you are also using Atlassian Crowd, a user management and **Single Sign-On (SSO)** solution, you can use this directory type to connect to your crowd instance. With this option, you can also configure your JIRA instance to participate in the SSO session.
- **Atlassian JIRA**: JIRA is capable of acting as a user repository for other compatible applications. If you have another JIRA instance running, you can use this directory type to connect to the other JIRA instance and for user information.

Managing user directories

When you have multiple user directories configured for JIRA, there are a few important points to keep in mind.

The order of the user directories is important, as it will directly affect the order JIRA will use to search users and apply changes made to users and groups. For example, if you have two user directories and both have a user called **admin** with different passwords, this will have the following effects:

- When you log in to JIRA with the user admin, you will be logged in as the admin user from the first user directory that is able to validate the password, in the order of listed directories.

- After logging in, you will be granted with group membership from the directory that has validated your password. Any other directories will be skipped.

- If you make a change to the admin user, such as changing the full name, then the changes will only be applied to the first directory JIRA has write access to.

Another important point to remember when working with user directories is that you cannot make changes to the user directory when you are logged in with a user account that belongs to the said directory. For example, if you are logged in with an LDAP account, then you will not be able to make changes to JIRA's LDAP settings, since there is a potential for the new change to actually lock you out of JIRA.

> Always have an active administrator user account ready in the default JIRA internal directory, for example, the account created during the initial setup. This will provide you with an administrator account that can help you fix user directory problems such as the preceding scenario. If you have a user account with the same name in the other user directory, then the internal directory should also be the first one in the list.

Connecting to LDAP

In the days prior to user directories, connecting to LDAP was a tedious process of manually editing configuration files and restarting the system. With user directories, it is much easier to connect JIRA to an LDAP server for user management.

To connect your JIRA to LDAP, all you have to do is add a new user directory:

1. Browse to the **User Directories** page.
2. Click on the **Add Directory** button and select **either Microsoft Active Directory** or **LDAP** from the **Directory Type** select list.
3. Provide your LDAP server information.

Since every LDAP is different, the exact parameters that are required will vary. At a minimum, you need to provide the following information:

Parameter	Description
Name	This is the name of the user directory.
Directory Type	Select the flavor of your LDAP. This will help JIRA to prefill some of the parameters for you.
Hostname	This is the hostname of your LDAP server.
Port	This is the port number of your LDAP server. JIRA will prefill this based on your directory type selection.
Base DN	This is the root node for JIRA to search for users and groups.
LDAP Permissions	This helps choose whether JIRA should be able to make changes to LDAP.
Username	This is the username JIRA will use to connect to LDAP for user and group information.
Password	This is the password JIRA will use to connect to LDAP.

You can see these sections filled in the following screenshot:

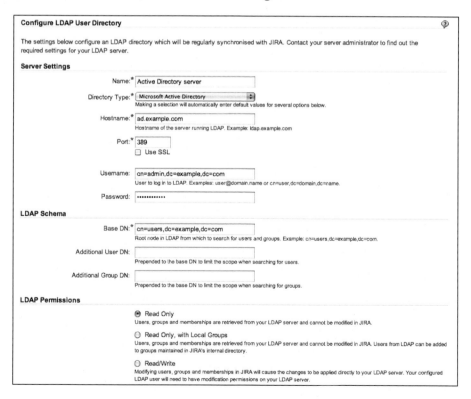

Apart from the preceding parameters are additional advanced settings such as **User Schema Settings** and **Group Schema Settings**. After filling in the form, you can click on the **Quick Test** button to verify that JIRA is able to connect to your LDAP server and authenticate with the username and password provided. Note that this does not test for things such as the user lookup. If the initial quick test is successful, then you can go ahead and click on the **Save and Test** button. This will add the user directory and take you to the test page where you can test the settings with a proper user credential (this will be different than the one used by JIRA to connect to LDAP):

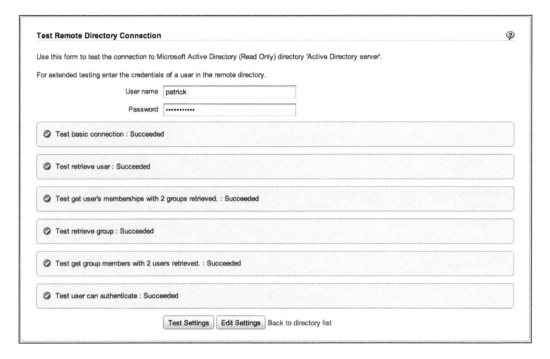

After the new user directory is added, JIRA will automatically synchronize with the LDAP server and pull in users and groups. Depending on the size of your LDAP server, this may take some time to complete. After the initial synchronization, JIRA will periodically synchronize with LDAP for any changes.

Users

In JIRA, each user needs to have an account for him/her to access JIRA, unless JIRA is configured to allow anonymous access (by selecting the **Anyone** group in the **Browse Project** permission scheme; please refer to the *Permission Schemes* section in this chapter for details). Each user is identified by his/her username, starting with JIRA 6, which can be changed after the account is created.

User Browser

User Browser is where you will be able to see a list of all the users in JIRA, including their usernames, e-mail addresses, last login attempt, and which user directory they belong to. **User Browser** also provides you with search capabilities. You will be able to search for users that fit in the criteria such as username, full name, e-mail address, and group association. Perform the following steps to access the user browser:

1. Browse to the JIRA administration console.
2. Select the **User management** tab and then the **Users** option. This will bring up the **User Browser** page.

By default, the results will be paginated to show 20 users per page, but you can change this setting to show up to 100 users per page. When dealing with large deployments having hundreds of users, these options will become very useful to quickly find the users you need to manage.

Other than providing the ability for you to effectively search for users, **User Browser** also serves as the portal for you to add new users to JIRA and manage a user's group/role associations:

Adding a user

New users can be added to JIRA in a number of ways:

- Direct creation by the JIRA administrator
- Invitation by the JIRA administrator to create an account
- By signing up for an account if the public signup option is enabled
- Synchronization of user accounts from an external user repository such as LDAP

The first and second options have centralized management, where only the JIRA administrators can create and maintain user accounts. This option is applicable to the most private JIRA instances designed to be used by an organization's internal users.

The third option allows users to sign up for accounts by themselves. This is most useful when you run a public JIRA instance, where manually creating user accounts is not scalable enough to handle the volume. We will be looking at how to enable public signup options in later sections in this chapter. For now, we will examine how administrators can create user accounts manually:

1. Browse to the **User Browser** page.
2. Click on the **Create User** button. This will bring you to the **Create New User** dialog box.
3. Enter a unique username for the new user.
4. Enter the password, full name, and e-mail address for the user. If you do not enter a password, a random password will be generated. You should select the **Send Notification Email** option in the following step for the new user to reset his/her password.
5. Optionally, select the **Send Notification Email** option if you have an outgoing mail server configured for JIRA (see *Chapter 7, E-mails and Notifications*). If checked, JIRA will send an e-mail to the user with a link for them to set his/her password.

6. Click on the **Create** button to create the new user.

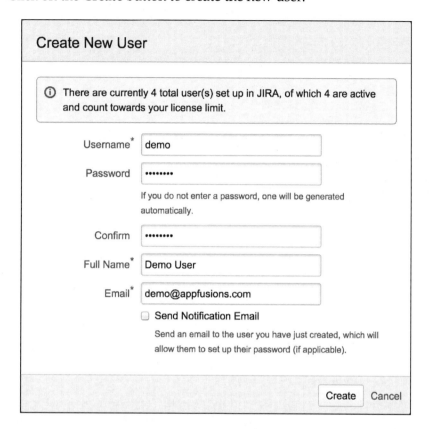

Alternatively, the administrator can also choose to invite users so that they can create their accounts themselves. This is different than the public signup option, since only recipients of the invitations will be able to create accounts. For this feature to work, you will need to have an outgoing mail server configured as the invitations will be sent as e-mails. Perform the following steps to invite users to sign up:

1. Browse to the **User Browser** page.

2. Click on the **Invite Users** button. This will bring you to the **Invite Users** dialog box.

3. Specify the e-mail addresses for the people you wish to invite. You can invite multiple people at once.

4. Click on the **Send** button to send out the invitations.

Enabling public signup

If your JIRA is public (for example, a public support system), then creating user accounts individually as explained earlier will become a very demanding job for your administrator. For this type of JIRA setup, you can enable public signup to allow users to create accounts by themselves. Perform the following steps to enable public signup in JIRA:

1. Browse to the JIRA administration console.
2. Select the **Systems** tab and then the **General Configuration** option.
3. Click on the **Edit Settings** button.
4. Select **Public** for the **Mode** field.
5. Click on the **Update** button to apply the setting.

Once you have set JIRA to run in the **Public** mode, users will be able to sign up and create their own accounts from the login page:

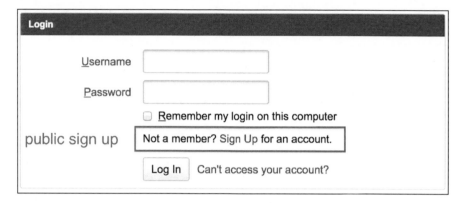

As you will see in the later section *Global permissions* in this chapter, once a user signs up for a new account, he/she will automatically join groups with JIRA users' global permission. If you have set JIRA to run in the **Private** mode, then only the administrator will be able to create new accounts.

Enabling CAPTCHA

If your running JIRA in the **Public** mode, you run the risk of having automated spam bots creating user accounts on your system. To counter this, JIRA provides the CAPTCHA service, where potential users will be required to type a word represented in an image into a text field. Perform the following steps to enable the CAPTCHA service:

1. Browse to the JIRA administration console.
2. Select **Systems** tab and then the **General Configuration** option.
3. Click on the **Edit Settings** button.
4. Select **On** for the **CAPTCHA on sign up** field.
5. Click on the **Update** button to apply the setting.

Now, when someone tries to sign up for an account, JIRA will present him/her with a CAPTCHA challenge that must be verified before the account is created:

Sign up

Full Name*	
Email*	
Username*	
Password*	
Confirm Password*	

Please enter the word as shown below

ꙅ

seculed

Sign up   Cancel

Groups

Groups are a common way of managing users in any information system. A group represents a collection of users, usually based on their positions and responsibilities within the organization. In JIRA, groups provide an effective way to apply configuration settings to users, such as permissions and notifications.

Groups are global in JIRA, which is something that should not be confused with project roles (discussed later). This means if you belong to the `jira-administrators` group, then you will always be in that group regardless of which project you are accessing. You will see in later sections how this is different from project roles and their significance.

Group Browser

Similar to User Browser, **Group Browser** allows you to search, add, and configure groups within JIRA:

1. Browse to the JIRA administration console.

2. Select the **User management** tab and then the **Groups** option. This will bring up the **Group Browser** page.

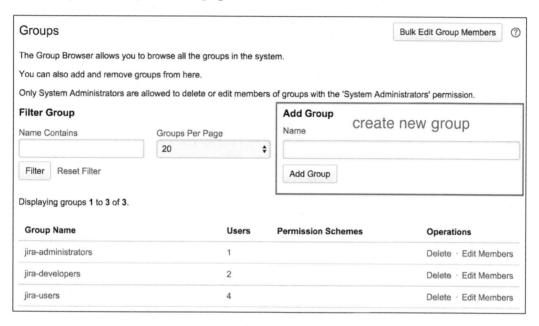

JIRA comes with three default groups. These groups are created automatically when you install JIRA:

Group	Description
jira-administrators	Administrators of JIRA. By default, this group lets you access the administration console.
jira-developers	Usually developers or people that work on issues. By default, this group lets you edit and work on issues.
jira-users	Normal users in JIRA. By default, this group lets you log into JIRA.

You can, as we will learn, change this default behavior to have your custom groups have the same permissions.

Adding a group

Other than the three groups that come by default with JIRA, you can create your own groups. It is important to note that once you create a group, you cannot change its name. Therefore, make sure you think about the name of the group carefully before you create it:

1. Browse to the **Group Browser** page.
2. Enter a unique name of the new group in the **Add Group** section.
3. Click on the **Add Group** button to create the new group.

After a group is created, it will be empty and have no members; you will need to manually add users to the group.

Editing group memberships

Often, people move around within an organization, and your JIRA needs to be kept up to date with the movement. In **Group Browser**, there are two ways to manage group memberships. The first option is to manage the membership is on a per group level, and the second option is to manage several groups at the same time. Both these options are actually similar, so we will be covering both at the same time.

Perform the following steps to manage individual groups:

1. Browse to the **Group Browser** page.
2. Click on the **Edit Members** link for the group you wish to manage members on. This will bring you to the **Bulk Edit Group Members** page.

Perform the following steps to manage multiple groups:

1. Browse to the **Group Browser** page.
2. Click on the **Bulk Edit Group Members** button at the top. This will bring you to the **Bulk Edit Group Members** page.

You will notice that both options will take you to the same page. The difference is if you have chosen the individual group option, JIRA will auto-select the group to update, and if you have chosen the bulk edit option, then no groups will be selected. However, regardless of which option you choose, you can still select one or all the groups to apply your changes to:

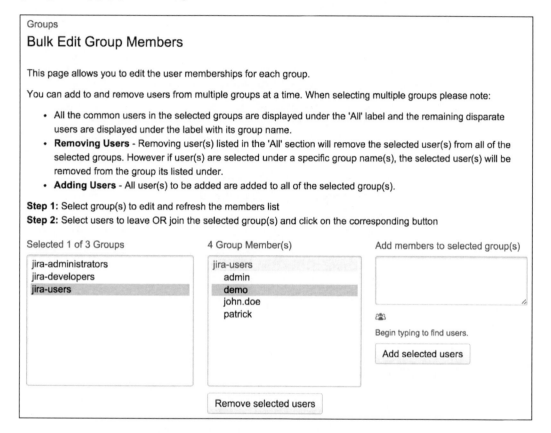

Perform the following steps to update the membership in one or more groups:

1. Browse to the **Bulk Edit Group Members** page.

2. Select one or more groups to update.

3. Select users from the middle box and click on the **Remove selected users** button to take users out of the groups.

4. Specify users (by typing usernames) in the right-hand box and click on the **Add selected users** button to add users to the groups.

Deleting a group

If a group has become redundant, you can remove it from JIRA:

1. Browse to the **Group Browser** page.

2. Click on the **Delete** link for the group you wish to remove. This will take you to the **Delete Group** page.

3. Click on the **Delete** button to permanently remove the group.

Once you remove the group, all the users who previously belonged to it will have their group associations updated to reflect the change.

Project roles

As you have seen, groups are collections of users and are applied globally. JIRA also offers another way of grouping users, which is applied on the project level only. JIRA comes with three default project roles out of the box:

Project role	Description
Administrators	This project role represents the administrator of the project (for example, the project manager).
Developers	This project role represents the developer of the project.
Users	This project role represents the user of the project (for example, the tester).

Project Role Browser

Similar to users and groups, project roles are maintained by the JIRA administrator through the **Project Role Browser** page. There is a slight difference, however, because since project roles are specific to projects, JIRA administrators only define what roles are available in JIRA and their default members. Each project's administrators (discussed in later sections) can further define each role's membership for their own projects, overriding the default assignment. We will first look at what JIRA administrators can control through the **Project Role Browser** page and then look at how project administrators can fine-tune the membership assignment later. Perform the following steps to access the **Project Role Browser** page:

1. Browse to the JIRA administration console.

2. Select the **System** tab and then the **Roles** option. This will bring up the **Project Role Browser** page.

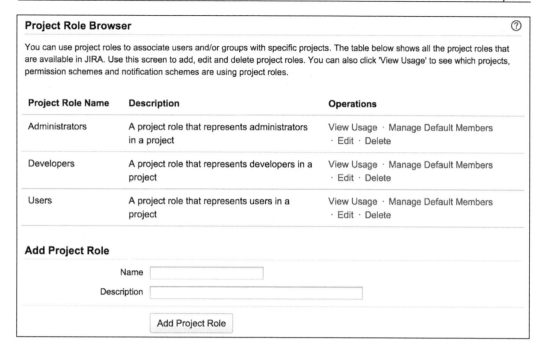

Adding a project role

To start creating your own project roles, you will first need to add the role as an administrator, and then each project administrator will be able to add users to it. Perform the following steps to create a new project role:

1. Browse to the **Project Role Browser** page.
2. Enter a unique name for the new project role in the **Add Project Role** section.
3. Click on the **Add Project Role** button to create the project role.

Once you add a new project role, it will appear for all the projects.

Editing a project role

You can update a project role's name and description as follows:

1. Browse to the **Project Role Browser** page.
2. Click on the **Edit** link for the project role you wish to update. This will take you to the **Edit Project Role** page.
3. Enter a new name and description.
4. Click on the **Update** button to apply the changes.

Deleting a project role

Existing project roles can be deleted if they are no longer used as follows:

1. Browse to the **Project Role Browser** page.
2. Click on the **Delete** link for the project role you wish to remove. This will bring up the **Delete Project Role** page.
3. Click on the **Delete** button to remove the project role.

Managing default members

You can assign default members for project roles, so newly created projects will have project roles assigned to them. Default members are an efficient way for JIRA administrators to assign project role members automatically, without having to manually manage each new project as it comes in.

For example, by default, users in the `jira-administrators` group will have the **Administrators** project role. This not only increases the efficiency of the setup by creating a baseline for new projects, but also offers the flexibility to allow modifications to the default setup to cater to unique requirements.

Perform the following steps to set default members for a project role:

1. Browse to the **Project Role Browser** page.
2. Click on the **Manage Default Members** link for the project role you wish to edit. This will take you to the **Edit Default Members for Project Role: Administrators** (name of the project role) page.

The following screenshot shows the **Administrators** project role has a default user (**Patrick Li**) and a default group (**jira-administrators**):

Edit Default Members for Project Role: Administrators   ⑦

The table below shows the default members (i.e. users, groups) for a project role.

NOTE: When a new project is created, it will be assigned these 'default members' for the 'Administrators' project role. Note that 'default members' apply only when a project is created. Changing the 'default members' for a project role will not affect role membership for existing projects.

- **Return to Project Role Browser**

Default Users	Default Groups
Patrick Li Edit	jira-administrators Edit

In this page, you will see all the default members assigned to the selected project role. You can assign default memberships based on individual users or groups.

Perform the following steps to add a default user/group for the project role:

1. Click on the **Edit** link for the default member option (either the user or group).
2. Use the User Picker/Group Picker function to select the users/groups you wish to assign to the project role.
3. Click on the **Add** button to assign the role. The following screenshot shows the **jira-administrators** group is the default group for the **Administrators** project role.

Assign Default Groups to Project Role: Administrators

You can add and remove default groups from the project role **Administrators** by using the 'Join' and 'Leave' buttons below.

- **<< Return to viewing project role Administrators**

Add group(s) to project role:

☐ **Groups in Project Role**

☐ jira-administrators

Remove

Add

Once added, any new projects created will have the specified users/groups assigned to the project role. It is important to note that after you have set default members, only new projects will have the settings applied. Existing projects will not retrospectively have the default members applied.

> The default membership changes the project roles only to affect new projects.

Assigning project role members

As you have seen, JIRA allows you to assign default members to projects when they are created. This might be sufficient for most projects when they start, but changes will often need to be made due to staff movements throughout the project life cycle. While it is possible for the JIRA administrator to continue maintaining each project's membership, it can easily become an overwhelming task, and in most cases, since project roles are specific to each project, it makes sense to delegate this responsibility to the owner of each project.

In JIRA, an owner of a project is someone with the **Administer Projects** permission. By default, members of the administrators' project role will have this permission. We will see in a later section how to manage permissions in JIRA.

As a project administrator, you will be able to assign members to various project roles for your project. You can assign roles from the project administration page, as follows:

1. Select the project whose project role memberships you want to update.
2. Click the **Administration** tab of the project, and select **Roles** from the left panel.
3. Click directly on either the **Users** or **Groups** column for the role you want to update in the assignment.
4. Start typing the user's username or the group's name; JIRA will auto-search for results as you type.
5. Click on the **Update** button once you have found the user/group you want to add.

The users and groups assigned to the project role will be for the current project only. Each project administrator can configure this for his/her own projects. In this way, you can maintain project role memberships separately for each project.

If you are a JIRA administrator, you can also manually set the user's project role membership:

1. Browse to the **User Browser** page.

2. Click the **Project Roles** link for the user to you want to set project role membership for. This also brings up the **View Project Roles for User** page.

3. Click the **Edit Project Roles** button.

4. Select the checkboxes for the project roles you want to add the user to and click on the **Save** button.

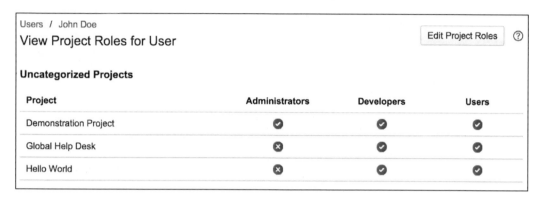

The **View Project Role for User** page is a very useful way to get a summary view of a user's project role membership.

JIRA permissions hierarchy

JIRA manages its permissions in a hierarchical manner. Each level is more fine-grained than the one above it. For a user to gain access to a resource, for example to view an issue, he/she needs to satisfy all three levels of permission (if they are all set on the issue in question):

- **JIRA global permission**: This permission controls the overall access rights to JIRA, for example, who can access JIRA

- **Project-level permission**: This permission controls the project-level permissions

- **Issue-level security**: This permission controls the view access on a per issue level

We will now look at each of the permission levels and how you can configure them to suit your requirements, starting from the most coarse-grained permission level — global permissions.

Global permissions

Global permissions, as the name suggests, is the highest permission level in JIRA. These are coarse-grained permissions applied globally across JIRA, controlling broad security levels such as the ability to access JIRA and administer configurations.

Since they are not fine-grained security, global permissions are applied to groups rather than users. The following table lists all the permissions and what they control in JIRA:

Global permission level	Description
JIRA System Administrators	Permission to perform all JIRA administration functions. This is akin to the `root` mode in other systems.
JIRA Administrators	Permission to perform most JIRA administration functions that are not related to system-wide changes. (For example, to configure the SMTP server and to export/restore JIRA data).
JIRA Users	Permission to log in to JIRA. Newly created users will automatically join the groups with this permission.
Browse Users	Permission to view the list of JIRA users and groups. This permission is required if the user needs to use the User Picker/Group Picker function.
Create Shared Object	Permission to share filters and dashboards with other users.
Manage Group Filter Subscriptions	Permission to manage group filter subscriptions. Filters will be discussed in *Chapter 9, Searching, Reporting, and Analysis*.
Bulk Change	Permission to perform bulk operations including the following: • Bulk edit • Bulk move • Bulk delete • Bulk workflow transition

JIRA system administrator versus JIRA administrator

For people who are new to JIRA, it is often confusing when it comes to distinguishing between the JIRA system administrator and the JIRA administrator. For the most part, both are identical, and they can carry out most of the administrative functions in JIRA.

The difference is JIRA administrators cannot access functions that can affect the application environment or network, while the JIRA system administrator has access to everything.

While it can be useful to separate these two, in most cases, it is not necessary. By default, the `jira-administrators` group has both the JIRA system administrators' and JIRA administrators' permission.

The following list shows examples of system operations that are only available to people with JIRA system administrators' permission:

- Configure SMTP server details
- Configure CVS source code repository
- Configure listeners
- Configure services
- Configure where JIRA stores index files
- Import data into JIRA from an XML backup
- Export data from JIRA to an XML backup
- Configure attachment settings
- Access JIRA license details
- Grant/revoke JIRA system administrators' global permission
- Delete users with JIRA system administrators' global permission

Configuring global permissions

Global permissions are configured and maintained by JIRA administrators and JIRA system administrators as follows:

1. Browse to the JIRA administration console.

2. Select the **System** tab and then the **Global Permissions** option to bring up the **Global Permissions** page.

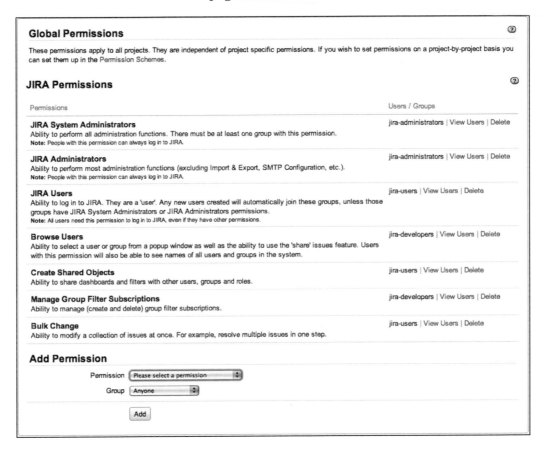

Users with JIRA Administrators' global permission cannot grant himself/herself JIRA System Administrators' global permission.

Granting global permissions

Global permissions can only be granted to groups. For this reason, you will need to organize your users into logical groups for global permissions to take effect. For example, you will want to have all your users belong to a single group, such as the `jira-users` group, so you can grant them permission to access JIRA:

1. Browse to the **Global Permissions** page.
2. Select the permission you wish to assign from the **Add Permission** section.

3. Choose the group to be given the permission.
4. Click on the **Add** button to add the assignment.

The **Group** drop-down list will list all the groups in JIRA. It will also have an extra option called **Anyone**. This option refers to all users, including those that do not need to log in to access JIRA. You cannot select this option when granting the **JIRA Users** permission as they are required to log in, and **Anyone** refers to a non-logged-in user. For a production system, it is recommended to take care when granting any global permission to **Anyone** (non-logged-in users) as this can lead to security and privacy concerns. For example, by granting **Anyone** as the global permission for **Browse Users**, anyone with access to your JIRA instance will be able to get your registered users' information.

Revoking global permissions

Global permissions can also be revoked. There are, however, a few rules and restrictions you need to be aware of:

- Both the JIRA system administrators and JIRA administrators can revoke global permissions, but JIRA administrators cannot revoke the JIRA system administrators' global permission

- If you revoke JIRA users' permission, you are effectively disallowing the affected users from accessing JIRA (they will not be able to log in to JIRA)

- You will not be able to grant additional JIRA users permission if you exceed the number of users permitted by your license

Perform the following steps to delete a global permission from a group:

1. Browse to the **Global Permissions** page.
2. Click on the **Delete** link for the group you wish to remove from the global permission. This will take you to the **Delete Global Permission** page.
3. Click on the **Delete** button to remove the global permission.

JIRA has built-in validation rules to prevent you from accidentally locking yourself out by mistakenly removing the wrong permissions. For example, JIRA will not let you delete the last group from JIRA system administrators' global permission as doing so will effectively prevent you from adding yourself back (since only JIRA system administrators can assign/revoke global permissions).

Project permissions

As you have seen, global permissions are rather coarse in what they control and are applied globally. Since they can only be applied to groups, they are rather inflexible when it comes to deciding whom to grant the permissions to.

To provide a more flexible way of managing and designing permissions, JIRA allows you to manage permissions on the project level, which allows each project to have its own distinctive permission settings. Furthermore, permissions can be assigned to one of the following:

- **Reporter**: This is the user who submitted the issue
- **Group**: These are all users that belong to the specified group
- **Single user**: This is any user in JIRA
- **Project lead**: This is the lead of the project
- **Current assignee**: This is the user currently assigned to the issue
- **User custom field value**: This user is specified in a custom field of type **User Custom Field**
- **Project role**: These are all users that belong to the specified role
- **Group custom field value**: These are users within the specified group in a **Group Custom Field**

The list of permissions is also more fine-grained and designed more around controlling permissions on a project level. The only catch to this is that the list is final, and you cannot add new permission types:

Project permissions	Description
Administer Project	Permission to administer a project. Users with this permission are referred to as project administrators. Users with this permission are able to edit the project role membership, components, versions, and general project details such as name and description.
Browse Project	Permission for users to browse and view the project and its issues. If a user does not have the browse project permission for a given project, the project will be hidden from him/her, and notifications will not be sent.
View Development Tools	Permission for users to have access to information from JIRA's development tools integration, such as code commits and build results.
View Read-Only Workflow	Permission for users to view a read-only diagram of the workflow. When the user has this permission, there will be a View Workflow link next to the issue's status.

Issue permissions	Description
Assignable User	Users that can be assigned to issues.
Assign Issues	Permission for users to assign issues to different users.
Close Issues	Permission for users to close issues.
Create Issues	Permission for users to create issues.
Delete Issues	Permission for users to delete issues.
Edit Issues	Permission for users to edit issues.
Link Issues	Permission for users to link issues together (if issue linking is enabled).
Modify Reporter	Permission for users to change the value of the **Reporter** field.
Move Issues	Permission for users to move issues.
Resolve Issues	Permission for users to resolve issues and set values for the **Fix For Version** field.
Schedule Issues	Permission for users to set and update due dates for issues.
Set Issue Security	Permission for users to set issue security levels to enable issue-level security. Please see the next sections to learn more about issue security.
Transition Issues	Permission to transition issues through the workflow.

Voters and Watchers permissions	Description
Manage Watchers	Permission to manage the watchers' list of issues (add/remove watchers).
View Voters and Watchers	Permission to view the voters and watchers' list of issues.

Comments permissions	Description
Add Comments	Permission for users to add comments to issues.
Delete All Comments	Permission to delete all comments.
Delete Own Comments	Permission to delete your own comments.
Edit All Comments	Permission for users to edit comments made by all users.
Edit Own Comments	Permission to edit your own comments.

Attachments permissions	Description
Create Attachments	Permission to add attachments to issues (if attachment is enabled).
Delete All Attachments	Permission to delete all attachments to issues.
Delete Own Attachments	Permission to delete attachments to issues added by you.

Time tracking permissions	Description
Delete Own Worklogs	Permission to delete worklogs made by you.
Delete All Worklogs	Permission to delete all worklogs.
Edit Own Worklogs	Permission to edit worklogs made by you.
Edit All Worklogs	Permission to edit all worklogs.
Work On Issues	Permission to log work done on issues (if time tracking is enabled).

As you can see, even though the list cannot be modified, JIRA provides you with a very comprehensive list of permissions that will cover almost all your permission needs.

With this many permissions, it will be highly inefficient if you have to create them individually for each project you have. With permission schemes, JIRA lets you define your permissions once and apply them to multiple projects.

Permission schemes

Permission schemes, like other schemes such as notification schemes, are collections of associations between permissions and users or a collection of users. Each permission scheme is a reusable, self-contained entity that can be applied to one or more projects.

Like most schemes, permission schemes are applied at the project level. This allows you to apply fine-grained permissions for each project. Just like project roles, JIRA administrators oversee the creation and configuration of permission schemes, and it is up to each project's administrator to choose and decide which permission scheme to use. This way, administrators are encouraged to design their permissions, that can be reused based on the common needs of an organization. With meaningful scheme names and descriptions, project administrators will be able to choose the scheme that will fit their needs the best, instead of requesting a new set of permissions to be set up for each project.

We will first look at how JIRA administrators manage and configure permission schemes and then how project administrators can apply them in their projects.

Perform the following steps to start managing permission schemes:

1. Browse to the JIRA administration console.

2. Select the **Issues** tab and then the **Permission Schemes** option to bring up the **Permission Schemes** page.

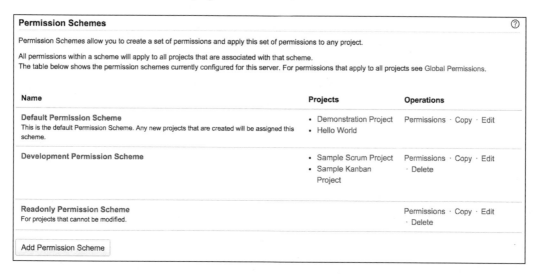

On the **Permission Schemes** page, you will see a list of all the permission schemes. From here, you will be able to create new schemes, edit and delete existing schemes, as well as configure each scheme's permission settings.

Adding a permission scheme

JIRA comes with a preconfigured permission scheme called **Default Permission Scheme**. This scheme is suitable for most simple software development projects. However, it is often not enough, and it is usually a good practice to not modify the Default Permission Scheme directly so that you can create your own permission schemes:

1. Browse to the **Permission Schemes** pages.

2. Click on the **Add Permission Scheme** button. This will take you to the **Add Permission Scheme** page.

3. Provide a meaningful name and description for the new permission scheme.

4. Click on the **Add** button to create the permission scheme.

For new permission schemes, all of the permissions will have no permission configured. This means if you start using your new scheme straightaway, you will end up with a project that nobody can access. We will look at how to configure permissions in later sections of this chapter.

Editing a permission scheme

You can keep a permission scheme's name and description up to date. You will often need to do this after making a copy of an existing permission scheme. As you will see in the following section, when you copy a permission scheme, JIRA automatically generates a name for your new scheme:

1. Browse to the **Permission Schemes** pages.
2. Click on the **Edit** link for the permission scheme you wish to update. This will take you to the **Edit Permissions Scheme** page.
3. Update the name and description with new values.
4. Click on the **Update** button to apply the changes.

Deleting a permission scheme

Unlike some other types of schemes, you can delete permission schemes even if they are being used by projects:

1. Browse to the **Permission Schemes** pages.
2. Click on the **Delete** link for the permission scheme you wish to remove. This will take you to the **Delete Permissions Scheme** page.
3. Click on the **Delete** button to remove the permission scheme.

If you are deleting a permission scheme that is being used by one or more projects, JIRA will prompt you with the list of projects that are currently using the scheme. If you delete it, all the projects will automatically be updated to use the Default Permission Scheme.

 You cannot delete the Default Permission Scheme.

Copying a permission scheme

It is not always desirable to create permission schemes from scratch, as there are around thirty permissions you will need to set for a new one. JIRA allows you to easily clone existing permission schemes with the **copy** function:

1. Browse to the **Permission Schemes** pages.

2. Click on the **Copy** link for the permission scheme you wish to clone. This will immediately create a copy of the permission scheme with the name **Copy** appended to the front of the original scheme's name.

One good use of the copy function is to create a backup of an existing permission scheme before you make changes. It is sometimes a good practice to name your permission schemes with a version number, and every time you need to make a change, create a copy and increment the version number in the name. This way, it helps you to keep track of your changes and roll them back if things do not work out as planned.

[It is often quicker to clone from an existing permission scheme than to start from scratch.]

Configuring a permission scheme

Just like most other schemes in JIRA, you need to further fine-tune your permission scheme to make it useful:

1. Browse to the **Permission Schemes** pages.

2. Click on the **Permissions** link for the permissions scheme you wish to configure. This will take you to the **Edit Permissions** page.

On this page, you will be presented with a list of project-level permissions, along with short descriptions for each, and the users, groups, and roles that are linked to each of the permissions. You will notice that for the Default Permission Scheme, most of the permission options have default users linked to them through project roles. If you are looking at a new permission scheme, there will be no users linked to any of the permissions. This is your one-page view of permission settings for projects, and you will also be able to add and delete users.

Unlike some other schemes, such as the notification schemes, which allow you to add additional options (through custom events), you cannot define new permissions for a permission scheme:

Edit Permissions — Default Permission Scheme ⑦

SHARED BY 8 PROJECTS

On this page you can edit the permissions for the "Default Permission Scheme" permission scheme.
- Grant permission
- **View all** permission schemes

Project Permissions	Users / Groups / Project Roles	Operations
Administer Projects Ability to administer a project in JIRA.	• Project Role (Administrators) (Delete)	Add
Browse Projects Ability to browse projects and the issues within them.	• Project Role (Users) (Delete)	Add
View Development Tools Allows users to view development-related information on the view issue screen, like commits, reviews and build information.	• Project Role (Developers) (Delete)	Add
View Read-Only Workflow Users with this permission may view a read-only version of a workflow.	• Project Role (Users) (Delete)	Add
Issue Permissions	**Users / Groups / Project Roles**	**Operations**
Assignable User Users with this permission may be assigned to issues.	• Project Role (Developers) (Delete)	Add

Granting a permission

Like the notification schemes, JIRA offers you a range of options to specify which users should have certain permissions. You can specify users through some of the most common options such as groups, but you also have some advanced options, such as using users specified in a custom field.

Again, you have two options to grant permissions to a user. You can add them to specific permissions or multiple permissions at once. Both options will present you with the same interface and there is no difference between the two:

1. Browse to the **Edit Permissions** page for the permission scheme you wish to configure.
2. Click on the **Grant permission** link or the **Add** link for a specific permission. This will take you to the **Add New Permission** page.
3. Select the permissions you wish to grant the user.
4. Select the user option to specify whom to grant the permission to.
5. Click on the **Add** button to grant the selected permission.

Permission options such as **User Custom Field Value** is a very flexible way to allow end users to control access. For example, you can have a custom field called **Editors**, and set up your **Edit Issues** permission to allow only users specified in the custom field to be able to edit issues.

The custom field does not have to be placed on the usual view/edit screens for the permission to be applied. For example, you can have the custom field appear on a workflow transition called **Submit to Manager**; once the user has selected the manager, only the manager will have permission to edit the issue.

Revoking a permission

You can easily revoke a permission given to a user, as follows:

1. Browse to the **Edit Permissions** page for the permission scheme you wish to configure.
2. Click on the **Delete** link for the permission you wish to revoke. This will take you to the **Delete Permission** page.
3. Click on the **Delete** button to revoke the permission.

When you are trying to revoke permissions to prevent users from gaining certain access, you need to make sure no other user options are granted the same permission that might be applied to the same user. For example, if you have both the **Single User** and **Group** options set for the **Browse Projects** permission, then you will need to make sure to revoke the **Single User** option and also make sure that the user does not belong to the **Group** option selected, so you do not have a loophole in your security settings.

Applying a permission scheme

All this time, we have been saying how permission schemes can be selected by project managers to set permissions for their projects; now we will look at how to apply the scheme to your projects. There really is nothing special, permission schemes are applied to projects in the same way as notification and workflow schemes:

1. Select the project you want to apply the workflow scheme to.
2. Click the **Administration** tab of the project and select **Permissions** from the left panel.
3. Select the **Use a different scheme** option in the **Actions** menu.
4. Select the permission scheme you want to use.
5. Click on the **Associate** button.

Permission schemes are applied immediately, and you will be able to see the permissions take effect.

Issue security

We have seen how JIRA administrators can restrict general access to JIRA with global permissions, and what project administrators can do to place fine-grained permissions on individual projects through permission schemes. JIRA allows you to take things to yet another level to allow ordinary users to set the security level on the issues they are working with, with **Issue security**.

Issue security allows users to set view permissions (not edit) on issues by selecting one of the preconfigured issue security levels. This is a very powerful feature as it allows the delegation of security control to the end users and empowers them (to a limited degree) to decide who can view their issues.

On a high level, issue security works in a similar way to permission schemes. The JIRA administrator will start by creating and configuring a set of issue security schemes with security levels set. Project administrators can then apply one of these schemes to their projects, which allow the users (with **Set Issue Security** project permission) to select the security levels within the scheme and apply them to individual issues.

Issue security scheme

As explained earlier, the starting point of using issue security is the issue security scheme. It is the responsibility of the JIRA administrator to create and design the security levels so they can be reused as much as possible:

1. Browse to the JIRA administration console.
2. Select the **Issues** tab and then the **Issue Security Schemes** option to bring up the **Issue Security Schemes** page.

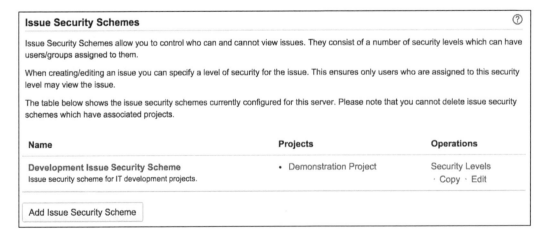

Adding an issue security scheme

JIRA does not come with any predefined issue security schemes, so you will have to create your own from scratch. Perform the following steps to create a new issue security scheme:

1. Browse to the **Issue Security Schemes** page.
2. Click on the **Add Issue Security Scheme** button. This will bring up the **Add Issue Security Scheme** page.
3. Provide a meaningful name and description for the new scheme.
4. Click on the **Add** button to create the new issue security scheme.

Since the issue security scheme does not define a set of security levels like the permission scheme, you will need to create your own set of security levels right after you create your scheme.

Configuring an issue security scheme

Unlike permission schemes that have a list of predefined permissions, with issue security schemes, you are in full control over how many options you want to add to the schemes.

The options within an issue security scheme are known as **Security levels**. These represent the levels of security that users need to meet before JIRA will allow them access to the requested issue. Please note that even though they are called security levels, it does not mean that there are any forms of hierarchy amongst the set of levels you create.

Perform the following steps to configure an issue security scheme:

1. Browse to the **Issue Security Schemes** page.

2. Click on the **Security Levels** link for the issue security scheme you wish to configure. This will bring up the **Edit Issue Security Levels** page.

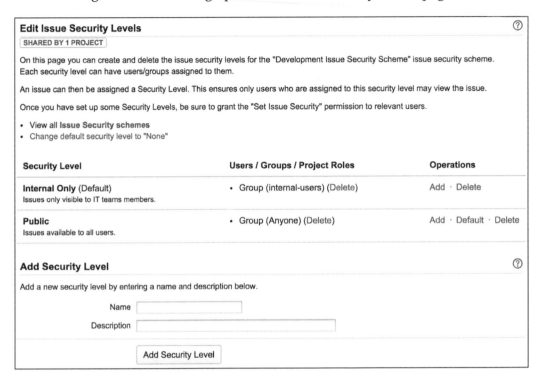

From here, you can create new security levels and assign users to existing security levels.

Adding a security level

Since issue security schemes do not define any security levels, the first step to configure your scheme would be to create a set of new security levels:

1. Browse to the **Edit Issue Security Levels** page for the issue security scheme you wish to configure.

2. Provide a meaningful name and description for the new security level in the **Add Security Level** section.

3. Click on the **Add Security Level** button.

You can add as many security levels as you like in a scheme. One good practice is to design your security levels based on your team or project roles.

Assigning users to a security level

Similar to permission schemes, once you have your security levels in place, you will need to assign users to each of the levels. Users assigned to the security level will have permissions to view issues with the specified security level:

1. Browse to the **Edit Issue Security Levels** page.
2. Click on the **Add** link for the security level you wish to assign users to. This will bring up the **Add User/Group/Project Role to Issue Security Level** page.
3. Select the option you wish to assign to the security level.
4. Click on the **Add** button to assign the users.

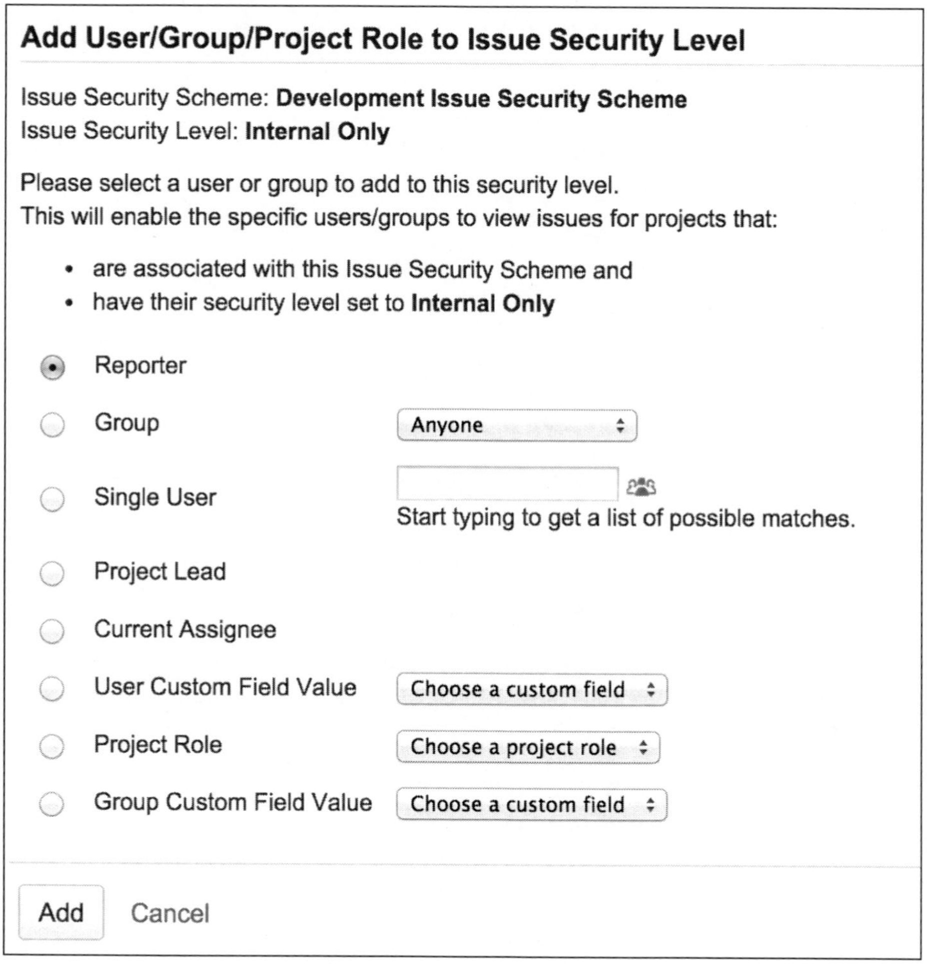

Add User/Group/Project Role to Issue Security Level

Issue Security Scheme: **Development Issue Security Scheme**
Issue Security Level: **Internal Only**

Please select a user or group to add to this security level.
This will enable the specific users/groups to view issues for projects that:

- are associated with this Issue Security Scheme and
- have their security level set to **Internal Only**

- ◉ Reporter
- ○ Group   [Anyone ⬍]
- ○ Single User   [👥]
  Start typing to get a list of possible matches.
- ○ Project Lead
- ○ Current Assignee
- ○ User Custom Field Value   [Choose a custom field ⬍]
- ○ Project Role   [Choose a project role ⬍]
- ○ Group Custom Field Value   [Choose a custom field ⬍]

[Add]   Cancel

While it may be tempting to use the **Single User** option to add individual users, it is a better practice to use other options such as **Project Role and Group** as it is more flexible by not tying the permission to individual users and allows you to control permission with options such as group association.

Setting a default security level

You can set a security level to be the default option for issues if none are selected. This can be a useful feature for projects with a high-security requirement to prevent users (with **Set Issue Security** permission) from forgetting to assign a security level for their issues:

1. Browse to the **Edit Issue Security Levels** page.
2. Click on the **Default** link for the security level you with to set as default.

Once set as default, the security level will have **Default** next to its name. Now, when the user creates an issue and does not assign a security level, the default security level will be applied.

Deleting a security level

You can revoke users assigned to security levels or remove the security level completely. When you revoke a user, he/she will no longer have access to the issue unless there is another user setting, which the user also belongs to, applied to the same security level.

Perform the following steps to revoke a user from a security level:

1. Browse to the **Edit Issue Security Levels** page.
2. Click on the **Delete** link for the users/groups/project roles you wish to remove. This will take you to the **Delete Issue Security** page.
3. Click on the **Delete** button to revoke the user.

When you delete a security level, you will be affecting all the issues that are currently set to the security level. JIRA allows you to update these issues to use a different security level (if one is available) or have no security level applied:

1. Browse to the **Edit Issue Security Levels** page.
2. Click on the **Delete** link for the security level you wish to remove. This will take you to the **Delete Issue Security Level** page. If there are issues set to the security level, JIRA will list the issues and also ask you to change their security level settings.
3. Select a new security level for the issues affected.
4. Click on the **Delete** button to remove the security level.

Applying an issue security scheme

Just like permission schemes, the project administrators apply issue security schemes to projects. Applying the issue security scheme is similar to applying the workflow scheme, where there is an intermediate migration step involved. This is to ensure that existing issues with set issue security levels can be successfully migrated over to the new security levels in the scheme:

1. Select the project you want to apply the workflow scheme to.
2. Click the **Administration** tab of the project and select **Issue Security** from the left panel.
3. Select **Use a different scheme** option in the **Actions** menu.
4. Select the permission scheme to use.
5. Click on the **Next** button to move to step 2 of the process.
6. Select the new security level to apply to the existing issue that may be affected by this change.
7. Click on the **Associate** button to apply the new issue security scheme.

Troubleshooting permissions

Just like notifications, it can be very frustrating to troubleshoot permission settings. To help with this, JIRA also provides a Permission Helper to assist administrators with pinpointing settings that prevent users from accessing certain features.

The Permission Helper works similarly to the Notification Helper:

1. Browse to the JIRA administration console.
2. Select the **Add-ons** tab and then the **Permission Helper** option at the bottom.
3. Specify the user that is having access problems in the **User** field.
4. Specify the issue to test with.
5. Select the permission the user does not have (for example, **Edit issue**).

6. Click on **Submit**.

Permission Helper

Discover why a user does or does not have certain permissions...

User	🧑 Patrick Li
	Begin typing to find a user, leave blank for Anonymous user
Issue	⊚ DEMO-1 - What is an issue? ▾
	Begin typing to find an issue
Permission	Edit Issues ▾
	Begin typing to find a permission or press down to see all

Permission name: Edit Issues

User: Patrick Li

Project: Demonstration Project

Permission scheme: Default Permission Scheme

Issue: DEMO-1

Status: ☒ Patrick Li does not have the 'Edit Issues' permission

Status	Summary	Details
☒	Project Role	Patrick Li is not a member of the Developers project role
		You can change this by going to the 'Demonstration Project' project roles and adding Patrick Li to the missing role(s)

Submit

As shown in the preceding screenshot, the user **Patrick Li** cannot edit issues for the **DEMO** project because he is not a member of the **Developer** project role, which is required as per the **Default Permission Scheme** used.

Workflow security

The security features we have looked at thus far are not applied to workflows. When securing your JIRA, you will also need to consider who will be allowed to perform certain workflow transitions. For example, only users in the managers' group will be able to execute the **Authorize** transition on issues. For you to enforce security on workflows, you will have to set it on each transition you have by adding workflow conditions. Please refer to *Chapter 6, Workflows and Business Processes*, which discusses workflows and conditions in more detail.

The Help Desk project

In the previous chapters, you configured your JIRA to capture data with customized screens and fields, and processed the captured data through workflows. What you need to do now is secure the data you have gathered to make sure that only the authorized users can access and manipulate issues.

Since your Help Desk project is used by the internal team, what you really need to do is put enough permission around your issues to ensure the data they hold do not get modified by other users, usually by mistake. This allows us to mitigate human errors by handling access accordingly.

To achieve this, you need to have the following requirements:

- Be able to tell who belongs to the Help Desk team
- Restrict issue assign operations to only the user that has submitted the ticket and members of the Help Desk team
- Do not allow tickets to be moved to other projects
- Limit the assignee of tickets to the reporter and members of the Help Desk team

Of course, there are a lot of other permissions we can apply here; the preceding four requirements will be a good starting point for us to build on further.

Setting up groups

The first thing you need to do is to set up a new group for your Help Desk team members. This will help you distinguish normal JIRA users from your Help Desk staff:

1. Browse to the **Group Browser** page.
2. Name the new group `help-desk-team` in the **Add Group** section.
3. Click on the **Add Group** button.

You can create more groups for other teams and departments for your scenario here. Since anyone can log a ticket in your project, there is no need to make that distinction.

Setting up user group association

With your group set up, you can start assigning members of your team to the new group:

1. Browse to the **Group Browser** page.
2. Click on the **Edit Members** link for the `help-desk-team` group.

3. Select users with the user picker or simply type in the usernames separated with a comma. This time, let's add our admin user to the group.

4. Click on the **Add selected users** button.

Setting up permission schemes

The next step is to set up permissions for our Help Desk project, so you need to have your own permission scheme. As always, it is more efficient to copy the Default Permission Scheme as a baseline and make your modifications on top, since we are only making a few changes here:

1. Browse to the **Permission Schemes** pages.

2. Click on the **Copy** link for **Default Permission Scheme**.

3. Click on the **Edit** link for the new copy of **Default Permission Scheme** we just created.

4. Name the new permission scheme `Help Desk Permission Scheme`.

5. Change the description to `Permission scheme designed for Help Desk team projects`.

Now that we have our base permission scheme set up, we can start on the fun part, interpreting requirements and implementing them in JIRA.

Setting up permissions

The first thing you need to do when you start setting up permissions is to try and match up with the existing JIRA permissions to your requirements. In our case, we want to restrict the following:

• Who can assign issues?

• Who can be assigned to an issue?

• Disable issues from being moved

Looking at the existing list of JIRA permissions; you can see that we can match up the requirements with the **Assign Issues**, **Assignable Users**, and **Move Issues** permissions, respectively.

Once you work out what permissions you need to modify, the next step is to work out a strategy to specify the users that should be given the permissions. Restricting the move issue options is simple. All you have to do is remove the permission for everyone, thus effectively preventing anyone from moving issues in your project.

The next two requirements are similar, as they are both granted to the reporter (the user that submitted the ticket) and our new `help-desk-team` group:

1. Browse to the **Permission Schemes** pages.
2. Click on the **Permissions** link for **Help Desk Permission Scheme**.
3. Click on the **Grant permission** link.
4. Select both **Assign Issues** and **Assignable Users** permissions.
5. Select the **Reporter** option.
6. Click on the **Add** button.
7. Repeat the steps and grant the `help-desk-team` group both permissions.

By selecting both the permissions in one go, you have quickly granted multiple permissions to users. Now, you need to remove all the users granted with the **Move Issues** permission. There should be only one granted at the moment, **Project Role (Developer)**, but if you have more than one, you will need to remove all of them:

1. Browse to the **Permission Schemes** page.
2. Click on the **Permissions** link for **Help Desk Permission Scheme**.
3. Click on the **Delete** link for all the users that have been granted **Move Issues** permission.

That's it! You've addressed all our permission requirements with just a few clicks.

Putting it together

Last but not least, you can now put on our project administrator's hat and apply your new permission scheme to your Help Desk project:

1. Browse to the **Project Administration** page for your Help Desk project.
2. Click on the **Select** link for **Permission Scheme**.
3. Select **Help Desk Permission Scheme**.
4. Click on the **Associate** button.

By associating the permission scheme with our project, you have applied all your permission changes. Now, if you create a new issue or edit an existing issue, you will notice that the list of assignees will no longer include all the users in JIRA.

Summary

In this chapter, we first looked at how we can integrate JIRA with user repositories such as LDAP through user directories. We then looked at JIRA's user management options with groups and project roles. Though both are very similar, groups are global, while project roles are specific to each project. We also learned how JIRA hierarchically manages permissions. We discussed each permission level in detail and how to manage them.

In the next chapter, we will take a different approach and start looking at another powerful use of JIRA—getting your data out through reporting.

9
Searching, Reporting, and Analysis

From *Chapter 2, Project Management*, to *Chapter 5, Screen Management*, we looked at how JIRA can be used as an information system to gather data from users. In *Chapter 6, Workflows and Business Processes*, and *Chapter 7, E-mails and Notifications*, we discussed some of the features that JIRA provides to add values to the gathered data through workflows and notifications. In this chapter, we will look at the other half of the equation, getting the data out, and presenting it as useful information to the users.

By the end of this chapter, you will have learned the following:

- Utilizing the search interface in JIRA
- Learning the different search options available in JIRA
- Getting to know about filters and how you can share search results with other users
- Generating reports in JIRA
- Sharing information with dashboards and gadgets

Search interface and options in JIRA

As an information system, JIRA comes fully loaded with features and options to search for data. JIRA comes with three search options:

- Quick/text search: This allows you to search for issues quickly through simple text-based search queries
- Basic/simple search: This lets you specify issue field criteria via intuitive UI controls

- Advanced search: This lets you construct powerful search queries with JIRA's own search language, JIRA Query Language (JQL)

However, before we start looking into the in-depth details of all the search options JIRA provides, let's first take a look at the main search interface that you will be using in JIRA while performing your searches.

Issue navigator

The **Issue Navigator** is the primary location where you will be performing all of your searches in JIRA. You can access the issue navigator by clicking on the **Issues** menu in the top menu bar and then select **Search for issues**.

The issue navigator is divided into several sections. The first section is where you will specify all of your search criteria, such as the project you want to search in and the issue type you are interested in. The second section shows the search results brought back. The third section includes the operations that you can perform on the search results, such as exporting them in a different format. The fourth and last section lists a number of useful, preconfigured, and user-created filters.

When you access the issue navigator for the first time, you will be in **basic search** (we will discuss the different search options in more detail later in this chapter). If you previously visited the issue navigator and chose to use a different search option, such as **advanced search**, then JIRA will remember this and open up advanced search instead.

The following screenshot shows the issue navigator in the basic search mode. In basic search, you specify your search criteria with menu bars and fields, selecting the values for each field.

Basic search

This is also known as **simple search**. Basic search allows you to construct your search criteria with a simple-to-use interface. The basic search interface lets you select the fields you want to search with, such as projects and issue types, and specify the values for these fields. As shown in the following screenshot, we are searching for issues of the **Bug** type in the **Demonstration Project** project, and with the status as **Open**.

With basic search, JIRA will prompt you for the possible search values for the selected field. This is very handy for fields such as status- and select list-based custom fields, so you do not have to remember all the possible options. For example, for the status field, JIRA will list all the available statuses.

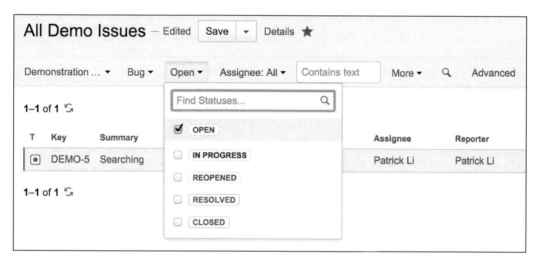

While working with the basic search interface, JIRA will have the default fields of project, issue type, status, and assignee visible. You can add additional fields to the search by clicking on the **More** button and then selecting the field you want to use in the search. Perform the following steps to construct and run a basic search:

1. Browse to **Issue Navigator**. If you do not see the basic search interface and the **Basic** link is showing, click on it to switch to basic search.

2. Select and fill in the fields in the basic search interface. You can click on **More** to add more fields to search criteria.

JIRA will automatically update the search results every time you make a change to the search criteria.

 When working with basic search, one thing to keep in mind is that the project and issue type context of the custom fields are taken into consideration (please see *Chapter 4, Field Management*, for field configuration). If a custom field is set to be applicable to only specific projects and/or issue types, then you have to select the project and issue type as part of your search for the custom field to show up.

Advanced search with JQL

Basic search is useful and will fulfill most of the users' search needs. However, there are still some limitations. One such limitation is that basic search allows you to perform searches based on inclusive logic but not exclusive logic. For example, if you need to search for issues in all but one project, with basic search, you will have to select every project except for the one to be excluded, since the basic search interface does not let you specify exclusions, and this is where advanced search comes in.

With advanced search, instead of using a field selection-based interface as in basic search, you will be using what is known as the **JIRA Query Language (JQL)**. JQL is a custom query language developed by Atlassian. If you are familiar with the **Structured Query Language (SQL)**, then you will notice that it has a similar syntax; however, JQL is not the same as SQL.

One of the most notable differences between JQL and SQL is that JQL does not start with a select statement. A JQL query consists of a field, followed by an operator, and then by a value or a function (which will return a value). You cannot specify what fields to return from a query with JQL, which is different to SQL. You can think of a JQL query as the part that comes after the `where` keyword in a normal SQL `select` statement. The following table summarizes the components in JQL:

JQL component	Description
Keyword	Keywords in JQL are special reserved words that do the following: • Join queries together, such as AND • Determine the logic of the query, such as NOT • Have special meaning, such as NULL • Provide specific functions, such as ORDER BY

JQL component	Description
Operator	Operators are symbols or words that can be used to evaluate the value of a field on the left and the values to be checked on the right. Examples include the following: • **Equals**: = • **Greater than**: > • **IN**: When checking whether the field value is in one of the many values specified in parentheses
Field	Fields are JIRA system and custom fields. When used in JQL, the value of the field for issues is used to evaluate the query.
Functions	Functions in JQL perform specific calculations or logic and return the results as values that can be used for evaluation with an operator.

Each JQL query is essentially made up of one or more components. A basic JQL query consists of the following three elements:

- **Field**: This can be an issue field (for example, status) or a custom field
- **Operator**: This defines the comparison logic (for example, = or >) that must be fulfilled for an issue to be returned in the result
- **Value**: This is what the field will be compared to, it can be a literal value expressed as text (for example, Bug) or a function that will return a value

Queries can then be linked together to form a more complex query with keywords such as logical AND or OR. For example, a basic query to get all the issues with a status of Resolved will look similar to the following:

```
status = Resolved
```

A more complex query to get all the issues with a Resolved status and Bug issue type, which is assigned to the currently logged-in user, will look similar to the following (where currentUser() is a JQL function):

```
issuetype = Bug and status = Resolved and assignee = currentUser()
```

Discussing each and every JQL function and operator is out of the scope of the book, but you can get a full reference by clicking on the **Syntax Help** link in the advanced search interface. The full JQL syntax reference can be found at https://confluence.atlassian.com/x/ghGyCg.

You can access the advanced search interface from the **Issue Navigator** page, as follows:

1. Browse to the **Issue Navigator** page.

2. Click on the **Advanced** link on the right.

3. Construct your JQL query.

4. Click on the **Search** button or press the *Enter* key on your keyboard.

As JQL has a complex structure and it takes some time to get familiar with, the advanced search interface has some very useful features to help you construct your query. The interface has an **autocomplete** feature (which can be turned off) that can help you pick out keywords, values, and operators to use. It also validates your query in real time and informs you if your query is valid, as shown in the following screenshot:

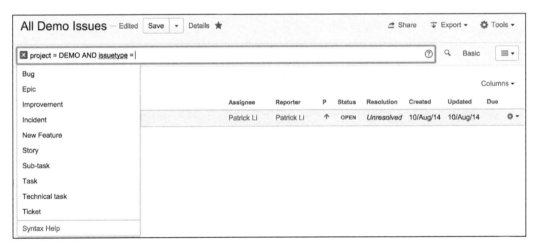

If there are no syntax errors with your JQL query, JIRA will display the results in a table below the JQL input box.

You can switch between the basic and advanced search by clicking on the **Basic/ Advanced** link while running your queries, and JIRA will automatically convert your search criteria into and from JQL. In fact, this is a rather useful feature and can help you learn the basic syntax of JQL when you are first starting up, by first constructing your search in basic and then seeing what the equivalent JQL is. You need to a take note, however, that not all JQLs can be converted into basic search since you can do a lot more with JQL than with the basic search interface.

Switching between the simple and advanced search can help you get familiar with the basics of JQL.

Quick search

JIRA provides a quick search functionality, which allows you to perform quick simple searches based on the text contained in the issue's summary, description, or comments. This allows you to perform quick text-based searches on all issues in JIRA.

The quick search function has several additional features to let you perform more specialized searches with minimal typing, through smart querying. JIRA has a list of built-in queries, which you can use as your quick search terms to pull up issues with a specific issue type and/or statuses. Some useful queries are included in the following table:

Smart query	Result
Issue key (for example, `HD-12`)	Takes you directly to the issue with the specified issue key.
Project key (for example, `HD`)	Displays all the issues in the project specified by the key in the **Issue Navigator** page.
`my` or `my open bugs`	Displays all the issues that are assigned to the currently logged-in user.
`overdue`	Displays all issues that are due before today.
Issues with a particular status (for example, `open`)	Displays all issues with the specified status.
Issues with a particular resolution (for example, `resolved`)	Displays all issues with the specified resolution.

You can combine these queries together to create quick and yet powerful searches in JIRA. For example, the following query brings back all the resolved issues in the Help Desk project:

```
HD resolved
```

Running a quick search is much simpler than either basic, or advanced searches. All you have to do is to type in either the text you want to search with, or the smart query in the **Quick Search** box in the top-right corner, and click *Enter* on your keyboard.

As you can see, the goal of quick search is to allow you to find what you are looking for in the quickest possible way. With smart query, you are able to perform more than just simple text-based searches.

It is important to note that quick search is case-sensitive. For example, searching with the term My instead of my will become a simple text search, rather than issues that are assigned to the currently logged-in user.

Working with search results

You have seen how you can execute searches in JIRA. With the exception of using the issue key smart query, which will take you directly to the target issue, all other search results will be shown in the issue navigator.

The issue navigator is capable of more than letting you run searches and presenting you with the results; it also has other features including the following:

- Display search results in different view options
- Export search results into different formats
- Select the columns you want to see for the issues in the results
- Share your search results with other people
- Create and manage filters

Switching result views

The issue navigator can display your search results in two different views. The default view is **Detail View**, where issues from results are listed on the left-hand side, and the currently selected issue's details are displayed on the right. This view allows you to view the issue's contents right on the same page as the search result.

The second view is **List View**, where issues are listed in a tabular format. Issue's field values are displayed as table columns. As we will see later, you can configure the table columns as well as how they are ordered. You can switch between the two views by selecting the options from the **Views** menu underneath the **Tools** menu from the right-hand side.

Exporting search results

From the **Issue Navigator** page, JIRA allows you to export your search results in a variety of formats, such as MS Word and Excel. JIRA is able to present your search results in different formats such as XML or print-friendly pages. When you select formats such as Word or Excel, JIRA will generate the appropriate file and let you download it directly. Perform the following steps to export your results to a different format:

1. Browse to the **Issue Navigator** page.
2. Execute a search.
3. Select the **Export** drop-down menu in the top-right corner.
4. Select the format you wish to see your search results in.

Depending on the format you select, some formats will be on screen (for example, printable), while others will prompt you with a download dialog box (for example, Excel).

Customizing the column layout

If you are using the **List View** option to display your search results, you configure the field columns to be displayed. In JIRA, you can customize your issue navigator for all your personal searches and also on a per search level with filters (see later in this chapter). If you are an administrator, you can set the column layout for other users too (which can be overwritten by each user's own column layout settings).

Perform the following steps to customize your global issue navigator's column layout:

1. Browse to the **Issue Navigator** page.
2. Change your result view to **List View**.
3. Select the **Columns** drop-down menu and a column layout option.

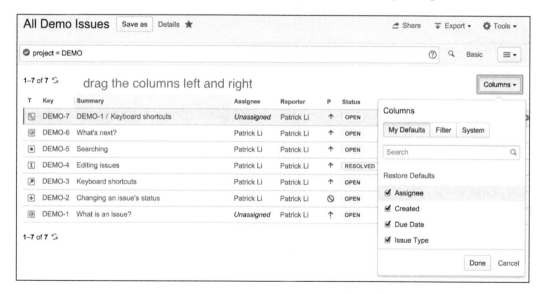

The following options can be used to layout the columns:

- **My Defaults**: This column layout will be applied to all your searches
- **Filter**: This column layout will only be applied to the current filter
- **System**: This column layout will be applied to all searches

To add or remove a field column, simply check or uncheck the field from the list. To reorder the column layout, you can drag the columns left and right to their appropriate locations.

Sharing search results

After completing a search, you may want to share the results with your colleagues. Now, you can tell your colleagues to run the same search or, as we will see later in the chapter, save your search as a filter and then share it with people. Alternatively, a more convenient way is to use the built-in **share feature**, especially if this is a one-off sharing.

To share your current search results, all you have to do is click on the **Share** button in the top-right corner and type in the user's name or an e-mail address (using an e-mail address lets you share your search results with people who are not JIRA users), and you can add multiple users or e-mail addresses, so you can share this with more than one person. You can also add a quick note, letting people know why you are sharing the search results with them, and JIRA will send out e-mails to all the selected users and e-mail addresses.

Filters

After you have run a search query, sometimes it will be useful to save the query for later use. For example, you may have created a query to list all the open bugs and new features in a project that are to be completed by a certain date in several projects, so you can keep an eye on their progress. Instead of recreating this search query every time you want to check up on the statuses, you can save the query as a filter, which can be reused at a later stage. You can think of filters as named search queries that can be reused.

Other than being able to quickly pull up a report without having to recreate the queries, saving search queries as filters provides you with other benefits, including the following:

- Share saved filters with other users
- Use the filters as a source of data to generate reports
- Display results on a dashboard as a gadget
- Subscribe to the search queries to have results e-mailed to you automatically

We will explore all of the advanced operations you can perform with filters and explain some of the new terms and concepts, such as dashboard and gadgets, in later sections. However, let's look at how we can create and manage filters first.

Creating a filter

To create a new filter, you will first have to construct and execute your search query. You can do this with any of the three available search options provided in JIRA, but please note that the search result must bring you to the **Issue Navigator** page. If you are using the quick search option and search by issue key, you will not be able to create a filter. Once you have executed your query, regardless of whether it brings back any result, you will be able to create a new filter based on the executed search:

1. Browse to **Issue Navigator**.
2. Construct and execute a search query in JIRA.
3. Click on the **Save as** button at the top.
4. Enter a meaningful name for the filter.
5. Click on the **Submit** button to create the filter.

Once you have created the filter, all your search parameters will be saved. In future, when you rerun the saved filter, JIRA will retrieve the updated results based on the same parameters.

Take note that you need to click on the **New filter** button to start a new search if you created a filter. Since issue navigator remembers your last search, if you were working with an existing filter, without starting a new search, you will in fact be modifying the current filter instead.

 Always click on the **New filter** button to start a new search session to avoid accidentally modifying an existing filter.

Managing filters

As the number of created filters grows, you will need a centralized location to manage and maintain them. There are two ways to access the **Manage Filters** page. You can access the page through the issue navigator, as follows:

1. Browse to **Issue Navigator**.
2. Click on the **Find Filters** link at the left-hand side. This will bring you to the **Manage Filters** page. You can also access the **Manage Filters** page by going through the top navigator bar.
3. Bring the drop-down menu from **Issues**.
4. Click on the **Manage Filters** option at the bottom of the list.

The **Manage Filters** page displays the filters that are visible to you in three main categories, as set out in the tabs to the left, along with the option to search for existing filters:

- **Favorite**: This option lists filters with a gray star next to their names. These filters will be listed in the **Issues** drop-down menu. You can mark a filter as a favorite by clicking on the star directly.

- **My**: This option lists the filters that are created by you.

- **Popular**: This option lists the top 20 filters that have the most people marking them as favorite.

- **Search**: This option searches for existing filters that are shared by other users.

As shown in the following screenshot, both the **All Demo Issues** and **Critical Issues** filters are marked as a favorite:

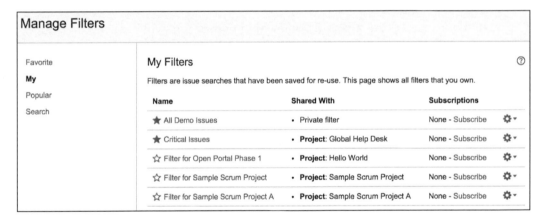

Editing and sharing a filter

After creating a filter, you can update its details such as name and description, sharing permission, and search parameters:

1. Browse to the **Manage Filters** page.
2. Click on the **Edit** link for the filter you wish to edit. This will bring up the **Edit Current Filter** dialog.
3. Update the details of the filter.
4. Select the **group/project** role to share the filter with.

5. Click on the **Save** button to apply the changes.

 Make sure you click on the **Add** link after you have chosen a group or a project to share the filter with.

For you to be able to share a filter, you will also need to have the **Create Shared Object** global permissions (please refer to *Chapter 8, Securing JIRA*, for more information on global permissions).

After you have shared your filter, other users will be able to search for it and subscribe to it. However, they will not be able to make changes to your filter. Only the owner of the filter is able to make changes to its search parameters. As we will see later, JIRA administrators can also change the ownership of filters.

Subscribing to a filter

You have seen in *Chapter 7, E-mails and Notifications,* that JIRA is able to send out e-mails when certain events occur to keep the users updated. With filters, JIRA takes this feature one step further, by allowing you to subscribe to a filter.

When you subscribe to a filter, JIRA will run a search based on the filter and send you the results in an e-mail. You can specify the schedule of when and how often JIRA should perform this. For example, you can set up a subscription to have JIRA send you the results every morning before you come to work, so when you open up your mail inbox, you will have a full list of issues that require your attention.

To subscribe to a filter, you will need to be able to see the filter (either created by you, or shared with you by other users):

1. Browse to the **Manage Filters** page.
2. Locate the filter you wish to subscribe to.
3. Click on the **Subscribe** link for the filter. This will bring up the **Filter Subscription** dialog.
4. Select the recipient of the subscription. Normally, this will be you (**Personal Subscription**). You can also create subscriptions for other people by selecting a group.
5. Select the **Email this filter even if there are no issues found** option and whether you wish to have an e-mail sent to you if there are no results returned from the filter. This can be useful to make sure that the reason you are not getting e-mails is not due to other errors.
6. Specify the frequency and time when JIRA can send you the e-mails.
7. Click on the **Subscribe** button. This will create the subscription and take you back to the **Manage Filters** page. The **Subscribe** link will now change to **1 Subscription**.
8. Click on the **1 Subscription** link to verify the subscription is created correctly.

9. Click on the **Run Now** link to test your new subscription.

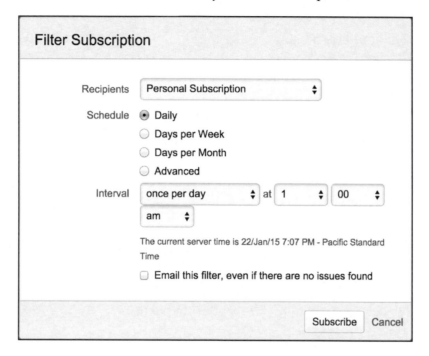

Deleting a filter

You can delete a filter when it is no longer needed. However, since you can share your filters out with other users and they can create subscriptions, you need to keep in mind that if you are deleting a shared filter, you may impact other users. Luckily, when you delete a filter, JIRA will inform you if other people are using the filter:

1. Browse to the **Manage Filters** page.

2. Click on the **Delete** link for the filter you wish to remove. This will bring up the **Delete Filter** confirmation dialog box.

3. Make sure that the removal of the filter will not impact other users.

4. Click on the **Delete** button to remove the filter.

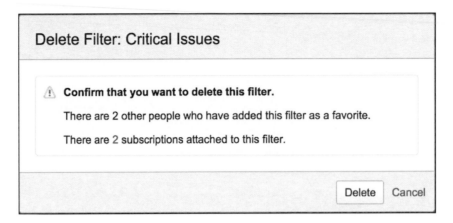

In your example, the **Critical Issues** filter is shared and there are two users subscribing to it. JIRA informs you of that and by clicking on the **2** link, you will be taken to the **View Subscription** page, where you can see a list of users that are subscribed to the filter. You can then decide either to proceed with deleting the filter and letting the other users know, or leave the filter in JIRA.

Changing the ownership of a filter

JIRA only allows the filter's owner to make changes, such as in the search criteria. This is usually not a problem in most cases, but when a filter is shared with other users, this can be problematic when the owner leaves the organization. Perform the following steps to change a filter's ownership:

1. Browse to the JIRA Administration console.
2. Select the **System** tab and then the **Shared Filters** option.
3. Search for the filter you wish to change ownership of.
4. Click on the **Actions** menu for the filter and select the **Change Owner** option.
5. Search and select the user that will be the new owner.

6. Click on the **Change Owner** button.

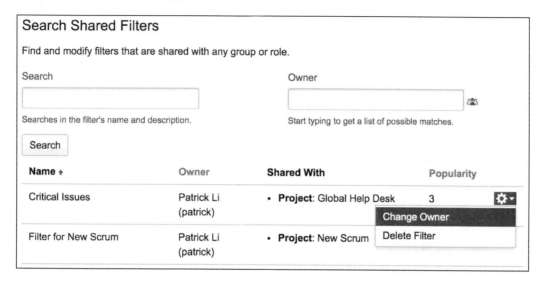

Reports

Apart from JQL and filters, JIRA also provides specialized reports to help you get a better understanding of the statistics for your projects, issues, users, and more.

Most reports in JIRA are designed to report on issues from a specific project; however, there are some reports that can be used globally across multiple projects, with filters. The following table shows all the reports that come with JIRA out of the box:

Report type	Description
User Workload Report	This shows how much work a user has been allocated and how long it is estimated to take based on values in the estimate fields.
Version Workload Report	This shows how much outstanding work there is (per user and per issue) before a given version is complete.
Single Level Group By Report	This shows the search results from an issue filter, grouped by a field of your choice.
Created versus Resolved Issues Report	This shows the number of issues created versus the number of issues resolved over a given period of time.
Resolution Time Report	This shows the average time taken to resolve issues.

Report type	Description
Pie Chart Report	This shows the search results from a specified issue filter (or project) in a pie chart based on a statistic of your choice.
Average Age Report	This shows the average age (in days) of unresolved issues.
Recently Created Issues Report	This shows the rate at which issues are being created in the current project.
Time Since Issue Report	This shows the number of issues for which your chosen date field (for example, **Created**) was set on a given date.
Time Tracking Report	This shows the time since a chosen field for each issue for a project or a saved filter is tracked.

Generating a report

All JIRA reports are accessed from the **Browse Project** page of a specific project, regardless of whether the report is project-specific or global. The difference between the two types of report is that a global report will let you choose a filter as a source of data, while a project-specific report will have its source of data predetermined based on the project you are in.

When generating a report, you will often need to supply several configuration options. For example, you may have to select a filter, which will provide the data for the report, or select a field to report on. The configuration options vary from report to report, but there will always be hints and suggestions to help you work out what each option is.

Perform the following steps to create a report; you will first need to get to a project's browse page:

1. Select the project you wish to report on or **View All Projects** if the project does not show up in the list.
2. Click on the **Reports** tab.
3. Select the report you wish to create under the **Reports** heading. This will often bring you to the **Report Configuration** page.
4. Specify the configuration options for the report.
5. Click on the **Next** button to create the report.

In the following example, we will create a pie chart report. We will first select the type of report to be generated by selecting it from a list of available report types that come with JIRA, as shown in the following screenshot:

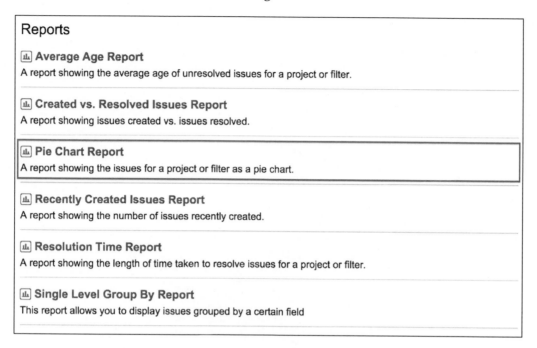

We will then configure the necessary report parameters. In this case, you need to specify whether you are generating a report based on a project or an existing filter; by default, the current project will be preselected. You also need to specify which issue field you will be reporting on.

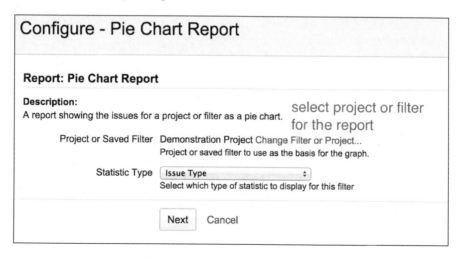

Once you have configured the report and click on the **Next** button, JIRA will generate the report and present it on the screen.

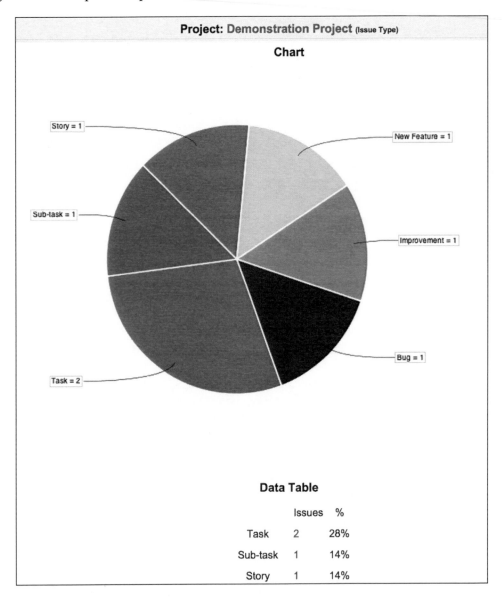

The report type determines the report's layout. Some reports have a chart associated with it (for example, **Pie Chart Report**), while other reports will have a tabular layout (for example, **Single Level Group By Report**). Some reports will even have an option for you to export its content into formats such as Microsoft Excel (for example, **Time Tracking Report**).

Dashboard

The dashboard is the first page you see when you access JIRA. Dashboards host mini-applications known as **Gadgets**, which provide various data and information from your JIRA instance. The dashboard acts as a portal, which provides users with a quick one-page view of information that is relevant or of interest to them.

Managing dashboards

When you first install JIRA, the default dashboard you see is called the **system dashboard**, and it is preconfigured to show some useful information, such as all issues that are assigned to you:

1. Since everyone shares the system dashboard, you as a user cannot make changes to it but can create your own dashboards. Each dashboard's functions are configured independently.

2. Bring down the drop-down menu from **Dashboards**.

3. Select the **Manage Dashboards** option. This will bring you to the **Manage Dashboards** page.

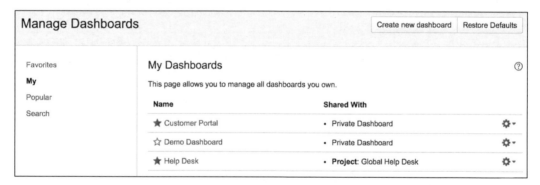

From this page, you can edit and maintain dashboards created by you, search dashboards created and shared by others, and mark them as favorite so that they will be listed as tabs for easy access.

When a dashboard is marked as favorite by clicking on the star icon in front of its name, the dashboard will be accessible when you click on the **Dashboards** link at the top menu bar. If you have more than one favorite dashboard, each will be listed in the tabs and you can select which one to display.

Creating a dashboard

The default **System Dashboard** cannot be changed by users, so if you want to have a personalized dashboard displaying information that is specific to you, you will need to create a new dashboard. Perform the following steps to create a new dashboard:

1. Go to your JIRA home page.
2. Bring up the drop-down menu from **Tools**.
3. Select the **Create Dashboard** option. This will bring you to the **Create New Dashboard** page.
4. Enter a meaningful name and description for the new dashboard.
5. Select whether you wish to copy from an existing dashboard or start with a blank one. This is similar to creating a new screen from scratch or copying an existing screen.
6. Select whether or not the new dashboard will be a favorite dashboard (for easy access) by clicking on the star icon.
7. Select whether you wish to share the dashboard with other users. If you share your dashboard with the **Everyone** option, then users that are not logged in will also be able to see your dashboard.
8. Click on the **Add** button to create the dashboard.

The following screenshot shows how you can create a new dashboard from scratch (blank dashboard) and shares it with the members of the `jira-users` group, which by default, are all logged-in users:

Once you created the new dashboard, you will be taken immediately to it. As the owner of the new dashboard, you will be able to edit its layout and add gadgets to it. We will be looking at these configuration options in the next section.

Editing and sharing a dashboard

For dashboards created by you, you can edit its name and description and choose to share it with other users so that they can access the dashboard by choosing it as a favorite:

1. Browse to the **Manage Dashboards** page.
2. Click on the **Edit** option for the dashboard you wish to edit. This will bring you to the **Edit and Share Dashboard** page.
3. Update the details of the dashboard.
4. Select the group/project role to share the dashboard with.
5. Click on the **Update** button to apply the changes.

For you to be able to share a dashboard, you will also need to have the Create Shared Object global permissions (please refer to *Chapter 8, Securing JIRA*, for more information on global permissions).

Deleting a dashboard

Dashboard creators can also delete dashboards they created. However, it is important to note that if you have shared the dashboard, by removing it from JIRA, all other users that are using it will be affected:

1. Browse to the **Manage Dashboards** page.
2. Click on the **Delete** option for the dashboard you wish to remove. This will bring up the **Delete Dashboard** confirmation dialog box.
3. Click on the **Delete** button to remove the dashboard.

The **Delete Dashboard** dialog box will alert you if there are users who have added the dashboard as favorite.

Configuring a dashboard

All custom created dashboards can be configured once they have been created. As the owner, there are two aspects of a dashboard you can configure:

- **Layout**: This describes how the dashboard page will be divided
- **Contents**: This describes the gadgets that are to be added to the dashboard

Setting a layout for the dashboard

You have to be the owner of the dashboard (created by you) to set the layout. Setting a dashboard's layout is quite simple and straightforward. If you are the owner, you will have the **Edit Layout** option at the top-right corner while you view the dashboard.

JIRA comes with five layouts that you can choose from. These layouts differ in how the dashboard page's onscreen real estate is divided. By default, new dashboards have the second layout that divides it into two columns of equal size:

1. Bring up the drop-down menu from **Dashboards**.
2. Select the dashboard you wish to edit the layout for.
3. Click on the **Edit Layout** option at the top-right corner. This will bring up the **Edit Layout** dialog.
4. Select the layout you wish to change to.

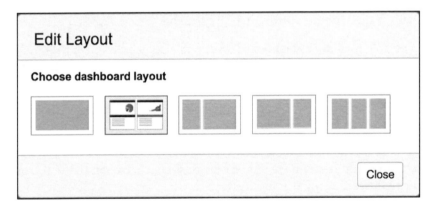

After selecting a layout from the dialog box, it will be immediately applied to the dashboard. Any existing contents will automatically have their size and positions adjusted to fit within the new layout.

After you have decided on your dashboard's layout, you can start adding contents, known as **gadgets**, onto your dashboard. Before you get to that, let's first take a brief look at what gadgets are.

Gadgets

Gadgets are like mini applications that live on a dashboard in JIRA. They are similar to widgets on most of the smart phones we have today or portlets on most portal applications. Each gadget has its own unique interface and behavior. For example, the **Pie Chart** gadget displays data in a pie chart, while the **Assigned to Me** gadget lists all the unresolved issues that are assigned to the current user in a table.

To discuss the in-depth details of gadgets and its underlying technology (OpenSocial) is beyond the scope of this book, but there is much information on this topic available on the Internet, if you are interested in creating your own gadgets to use with JIRA. A good place to start will be the Atlassian documentation at `https://developer.atlassian.com/x/IgA3`.

Placing a gadget on the dashboard

All gadgets are listed in **Gadget Directory**. JIRA comes with a number of useful gadgets, such as the **Assigned to Me** gadget that you see on the **System Dashboard**. The following screenshot shows the gadget directory, listing all the bundled gadgets in JIRA.

Perform the following steps to place a gadget onto your dashboard:

1. Bring up the drop-down menu from **Dashboards**.
2. Select the dashboard you wish to add a gadget to.
3. Click on the **Add Gadget** option at the top-right corner. This will bring up the **Gadget Directory** window.
4. Click on the **Add it Now** button for the gadget you wish to add.
5. Click on the **Close** link to return to the dashboard.

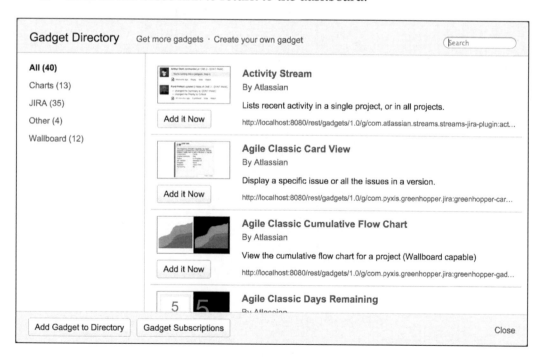

Depending on the gadget you selected, some gadgets will require additional options to be configured. For these gadgets, you will be presented with their configuration screen on the dashboard. Fill in the options and click on the **Save** button.

The following screenshot shows the configuration screen for the **Filter Results** gadget, where you can select the search filter to display and control the number of results to show and the fields to include. One common parameter is the **Refresh Interval** option, where you can decide how often the gadget can refresh its content or stay static if you choose never. Whenever you refresh the entire dashboard, all gadgets will load the latest data, but if you stay on the dashboard for an extended period of time, each gadget can automatically refresh its data, so the content will not become stale overtime.

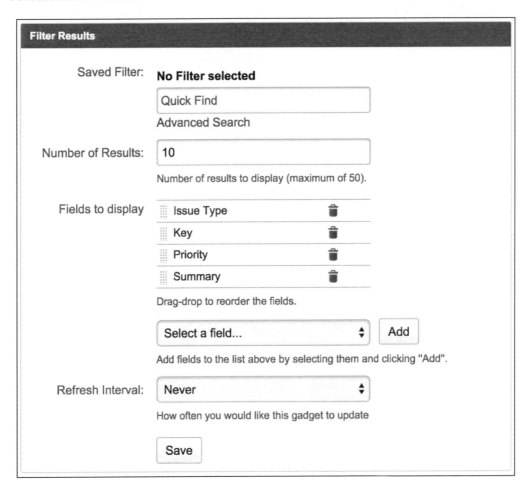

Moving a gadget

When you add a gadget, it's usually added to the first available spot on the dashboard. This sometimes might not be where you want to display the gadget on the dashboard, and in other cases, you might want to move the existing gadgets around from time to time. As the owner of the dashboard, you can easily move gadgets on a dashboard through a simple drag-and-drop interface:

1. Browse to the dashboard that has gadgets you wish to move.
2. Click on the gadget's title and drag it to the new position on the dashboard.

As soon as you drop the gadget to its new location (release your mouse button), the gadget will be moved permanently until you decide to move it again.

Editing a gadget

After configuring your gadget when you first place it on your dashboard, the gadget will remember this and use it to render its content. You can update the configuration details or even its look and feel, as follows:

1. Browse to the dashboard that has gadgets you wish to update.
2. Hover over the gadget and click on the down arrow button at the top-right corner of it. This will bring up the gadget configuration menu.
3. Click on the **Edit** option.
4. This will change the gadget into its configuration mode.
5. Update the configuration options.
6. Click on the **Save** button to apply the changes.

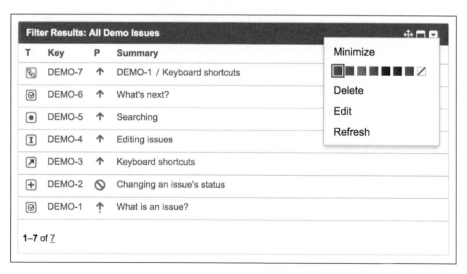

The preceding screenshot shows the edit menu for the **Assigned to Me** gadget. You can force a refresh with the **Refresh** option. Since gadgets retrieve their data asynchronously through AJAX, you can use this option to refresh the gadget itself, without refreshing the entire page. The edit, delete, and color options are only available to the owner of the dashboard.

Deleting a gadget

As the owner of the dashboard, you can remove the existing gadgets from the dashboard when they are no longer needed. When you remove a gadget from a dashboard, please note that all the other users who have access to your dashboard will no longer see it:

1. Browse to the dashboard that has gadgets you wish to delete.
2. Hover over the gadget and click on the down arrow button at the top-right-hand corner of it. This will bring up the gadget configuration menu.
3. Click on the **Delete** option.
4. Confirm the removal when prompted.

Once removed, the gadget will disappear from the dashboard. If you choose to re-add the same gadget again at a later stage, you will have to reconfigure it again.

The Help Desk project

In our previous chapters and exercises, we have built and customized a JIRA project to collect data from users. What we need to do now is to process and present this data back to the users. The goal we are trying to achieve in this exercise is to set up a portal page for our Help Desk team, which will have useful information such as statistics and issue listings that can help our team members to better organize themselves, to provide better services to other departments.

Setting up filters

The first step is to create a useful filter that can be shared with the other members of the team and also act as a source of data to feed our gadgets. We will use the advanced search to construct our search:

1. Browse to **Issue Navigator**.
2. Click on the **Switch to searching** link to bring up the JQL interface.
3. Type the following in the JQL search query:

```
project = GHD and issuetype = Incident and status != Resolved
   and status != Closed order by priority
```

4. Click on the **Search** button to execute the search.

5. Click on the **Save as** button to bring up the **Save Filter** dialog.

6. Name the filter as `Unresolved Incidents GHD` and click on the **Submit** button.

7. Share the filter with the HelpDesk-team group setup from *Chapter 8, Securing JIRA*, by clicking on the **Details** link next to the **Save as** button.

This filter searches and returns a list of unresolved issues of type **Incident** from our Help Desk project. The search results are then ordered by their priority so that the users can determine the urgency. As you will see in the later steps, this filter will be used as the source of data for your gadgets to present information on your dashboard.

Setting up dashboards

The next step is to create a new dashboard for your help desk team. What you need is a dashboard specifically for your team so that you can share information easily. For example, you can have the dashboard displayed in a large overhead projector showing all the high priority incidents that need to be addressed:

1. Browse to the **Manage Dashboards** page.

2. Click on the **Create new dashboard** button. This will bring you to the **Create New Dashboard** page.

3. Name the new dashboard as `Help Desk.`

4. Select **Blank** dashboard as your base.

5. Tick the new dashboard as favorite.

6. Share the filter with the HelpDesk team group.

7. Click on the **Add** button to create the dashboard.

In your example, we will use the default two columns layout for your new dashboard. Alternatively, you are free to experiment with other layouts and find the ones that best suit your needs.

Setting up gadgets

Now that you have set up your portal dashboard page and shared it with the other members of the team, you need to start adding some useful information to it. One example would be to have the dashboard display all the unresolved incidents that are waiting to be processed. JIRA has an **Assigned to Me** gadget, which shows all the issues that are assigned to the currently logged-in user, but what you need is a global list irrespective of the assignee of the incident.

Luckily, JIRA also has a **Filter Results** gadget, which displays search results based on a search filter. Since you have already created a filter that returns all the unresolved incidents in your Help Desk project, the combination of both will nicely solve your problem:

1. Browse to the **Help Desk** dashboard you have just created.
2. Click on the **Add Gadget** option at the top-right corner. This will bring up the **Gadget Directory** window.
3. Click on the **Add it Now** button for the **Filter Results** gadget.
4. Click on the **Close** link to close the **Gadget Directory** and return to the dashboard.
5. Select the **Unresolved Incidents** filter you created.
6. Select **Default Columns** and any additional fields you wish to add.
7. Set **Refresh Interval** to 15 minutes.
8. Click on the **Save** button.

This will add a new **Filter Results** gadget to your new dashboard, using your filter as the source of data. The gadget will auto-refresh its contents every 15 minutes, so you will not need to refresh the page all the time. You can add some other gadgets to the dashboard to make it more informative and useful. Some other useful gadgets include the **Activity Stream** and **Assigned to Me** gadgets.

Putting it together

This is pretty much all you have to do to set up and share a dashboard in JIRA. After you have added the gadget to it, you will be able to see it in action. The great thing about this is, since you have shared the dashboard with others in the team, they will be able to see the dashboard too. Members of the team will be able to search for your new dashboard or mark it as a favorite to add it to their list of dashboards.

You do have to keep in mind that, if you are using a filter as a source of data for your gadget, you have to share the filter with other users too, or they will not be able to see anything from the gadget.

Summary

We covered how users can search and report on the data they have put into JIRA, which is an essential component for any information system. JIRA provides a robust search facility by offering many different search options to users, including quick, simple, and advanced searches. You can save and name your searches by creating filters that can be rerun at later stages to save you from recreating the same search again.

JIRA also allows you to create configurable reports on projects or results brought back from search filters. Information can be shared with others through a dashboard, which acts as a portal for users to quickly get a glance of the data kept in JIRA.

In the next chapter, we will start to expand our usage of JIRA beyond the out-of-the-box features, by installing add-ons. We will start with the JIRA Service Desk add-on, which helps to change JIRA into a fully functional service desk with powerful features, such SLA management.

10
JIRA Service Desk

JIRA was originally designed and intended as a tool for developers. It was also designed to be an issue-tracking tool to capture bugs and tasks as they build a software. However, its flexibility and extensibility allowed users to use and adapt it into almost any other use cases. Recognizing this and JIRA's potential, a new product called JIRA Service Desk from Atlassian has been released, which was built on top of the JIRA platform, transforming it into a fully-fledged service desk solution.

By the end of the chapter, you will learn the following:

- Installing the JIRA Service Desk
- Creating and branding a new service desk
- Defining and setting up service-level agreement
- Creating custom queues for agents to work from
- Integrating with Confluence to set up a knowledge base

Introducing JIRA Service Desk

In each of our previous chapters, we have been building JIRA as a support system, which is a part of our end of chapter exercise. While JIRA is more than capable of handling the requirements of a service desk, there are still a number of things left to be desired.

For example, the user interface is often too complicated and confusing for business users to simply create a support ticket. Despite our best efforts, there are still way too many options on the screen, most of which are not useful in a service desk environment. Another example will be the lack of ability to set up any sort of service-level agreement to ensure a consistent quality of service.

This is where JIRA Service Desk comes in. It addresses all the shortcomings of JIRA that is out of the box by providing a clean, intuitive, and user-friendly interface for both the end customers and support team. It also provides many features that you can expect from a service desk solution. As shown in the following screenshot, JIRA Service Desk lets you serve your customers in four easy steps:

<table>
<tr><td>1</td><td>2</td><td>3</td><td>4</td></tr>
<tr><td>1 - Customer needs assistance and submits a request to JIRA Service Desk.</td><td>2 - Service desk agent picks up the issue.</td><td>3 - Customer and service desk agent discuss the problem.</td><td>4 - The customer is satisfied and the service desk agent resolves the issue!</td></tr>
</table>

Image source: `https://confluence.atlassian.com/display/SERVICEDESK/Getting+started+wi
th+JIRA+Service+Desk`

Installing JIRA Service Desk

JIRA Service Desk is a commercial add-on provided by Atlassian. JIRA provides an easy-to-use interface, called the **Universal Plugin Manager (UPM)**, for administrators to find and install third-party add-ons. Perform the following steps to install JIRA Service Desk through the UPM:

1. Log in as a JIRA administrator user.

2. Browse to the JIRA administration console.

3. Select the **Add-ons** tab and then the **Find new add-ons** option.

4. Search for `JIRA Service Desk` in the search box. This will locate the add-on.

5. Click on the **Free trial** button if you want to evaluate JIRA Service Desk before purchasing, or click on the **Buy now** link to purchase directly. This will prompt the UPM to start downloading and installing the add-on.

6. Click on the **Get License** button when prompted and follow the steps to either generate a trial license or purchase a full license.

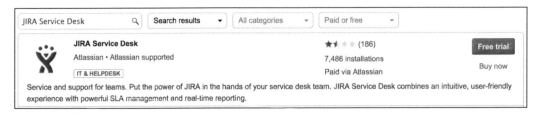

After you have successfully installed JIRA Service Desk, there will be a new item added to JIRA's top menu bar called **Service Desk**, as shown in the following screenshot:

Getting started with JIRA Service Desk

Before we start using JIRA Service Desk, it is important to understand that we familiarize ourselves with a number of new terminologies introduced:

- **Agents:** Agents are members of your service support team that will be working on customer requests. They are your normal JIRA users that can perform actions such as editing, assigning, and closing requests.

- **Customer Portal**: Customer portal is the main landing page for your customers. It is a simple, clean, and easy-to-use front interface for your service desk, without all the extra noise from the standard JIRA interface. The following screenshot shows the customer portal from Atlassian's support portal:

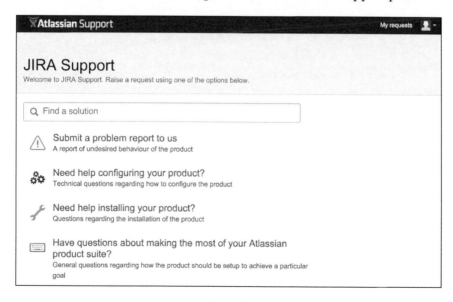

- **Queues**: Queues are like JIRA filters that show you a subset of issues that meet a certain criteria. Service desk agents use queues to prioritize and pick out requests to work on.

- **Requests**: Requests are what your end users (not agents), such as customers, submit to JIRA Service Desk. Under the hood, they are just normal JIRA issues. However, using the term request is less confusing in the context of a service desk environment.

As shown in the following screenshot, when customers interact with requests, the user interface is very different to what agents will see. It is much simpler to show only the key information, such as the request description and its status. Customers cannot make changes to the request details, and can only add new comments or attachments to the request.

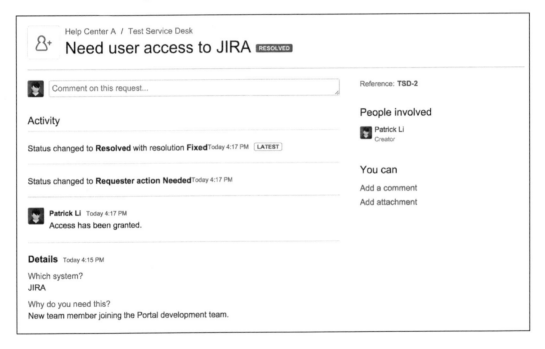

The key information of service desk are as follows:

- **Request Type**: Request types represent the different types of requests customers can make. These can be anything including a problem report, help request, or general inquiry. When you create a new request type, JIRA creates a new issue type behind the scenes. One major feature of request type is that it allows you to specify a user-friendly name for it. While the actual issue type is called problem report, you can rename it and display it as **Submit a problem report** instead.

- **Service Desk**: The service desk is what agents will be working from. Each service desk has a front, customer-facing portal. Behind the scenes, a service desk is a JIRA project, controlled by JIRA permissions, workflows, and other schemes.

- **SLA**: Service-level agreement defines the quality of service that is being guaranteed to your customers. In JIRA Service Desk, SLAs are measured in time, such as response time, and overall time taken to resolve issues.

Creating a new service desk

The first step to start working with JIRA Service Desk is to set it up. Since under the hood, a service desk is a JIRA project with a brand new user interface. You can either create a new service desk from scratch, or enable an existing project with service desk features. The second option is very useful if you have been using JIRA as a service desk in the past, and would like to *upgrade* the experience with JIRA Service Desk.

To create a new service desk, perform the following steps:

1. Bring down the **Service Desk** menu from the top navigation bar and select the **Create a Service Desk** option.

2. Select the **New Service Desk Project** option to create a new service desk from scratch. Enter a name and key for the service desk and click the **Create** button.

3. Select the **Enable for existing project** option to use an existing JIRA project. Select the project and click the **Enable** button.

If you choose to use an existing JIRA project for your service desk, JIRA Service Desk will review your project configurations such as permissions to make sure they will be compatible. If a problem is found, you will be prompted with the incompatibility, as shown in the following screenshot, where we have an issue with the existing permission scheme used by the project. You can click on the **Details of which permission need to be set...** link to review the details of the problem, and then click on the **Upgrade permission scheme** button for JIRA Service Desk to automatically make the necessary changes.

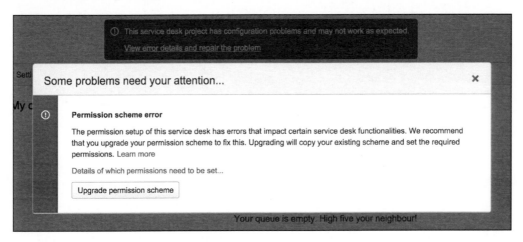

Once your service desk is created, you will be taken to your service desk user interface, as shown in the following screenshot:

Every service desk has two interfaces. One that will be used by you as the admin and members of your support team called agents. The second interface is called the **customer portal**, which is what customers will see and use to create requests and interact with agents. As you make configuration changes for your service desk, you can always preview the change by clicking on the **Customer Portal** link on the top right-hand corner, which will show you what the customer portal will look like.

Branding your customer portal

You can brand your customer portal for your service desk with:

- **Help center name**: The overall name for your help center. Think of this as the name for your JIRA instance.

- **Help center logo**: The logo for your help center. This is the logo that will appear on the top-left corner. Think of this as the logo for your JIRA. JIRA Service Desk will use this logo to automatically change and adjust the top bar color.

- **Customer portal name**: The name for a specific service desk portal.

- **Customer portal introduction text**: A welcome text that will be displayed for a specific service desk portal.

- **Customer portal logo**: The logo for a specific service desk portal.

The following screenshot illustrates each of these items on a sample customer portal:

To configure a specific customer portal's branding, perform the following steps:

1. Browse to the service desk you want to brand.

2. Select the **Settings** tab and then **Portal Settings** from the left.

3. Enter a name and welcome text in **Customer Portal name** and **Introduction text**, respectively.

4. Check the **Use a custom logo for this Customer Portal** option and upload a logo for your customer portal.

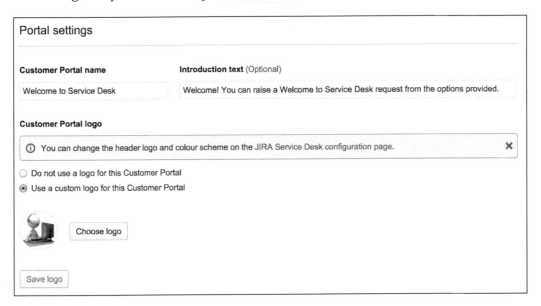

If you want to also set up the overall help center branding, perform the following steps:

1. Click on the **JIRA Service Desk configuration page** link from the **Portal settings** page. Please see the following tip if you do not see the link.

2. Enter a name in the **Help Center Name** field.

3. Check the **Customize theme and branding for Help Center** option and upload a logo for your help center.

> You can also get to the **JIRA Service Desk configuration** page by going to the JIRA administration console. Select **Add-ons** followed by **Configuration** under **JIRA Service Desk**.

Service desk users

JIRA Service Desk introduces a number of new user types. Under the hood, these user types are mapped to new project roles created by the add-on when it is installed:

- **Agent**: Members of the service desk team that works on requests. Agents are added to the **Service Desk Team** project role.

- **Customer**: End users that will be submitting requests through your help desk portal. Customers are added to the **Service Desk Customers** project role.

- **Collaborator**: Other JIRA users that are not usually members of your service desk team, but can help to solve customer problems. Collaborators are added to the **Service Desk Collaborators** project role.

Adding an agent to service desk

Agents are JIRA users that will be working on customer requests in JIRA Service Desk. These are usually members of your support team. Agents consume the JIRA Service Desk licenses.

To add an agent to a service desk:

1. Browse to the service desk you want to add an agent.
2. Select the **People** tab and then **Agents** from the left.
3. Click on the **Add an agent** button.
4. Search and select the user and click on the **Add this agent** button.

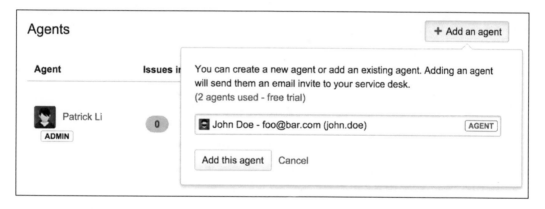

When adding an agent to a service desk, you can select an existing user in JIRA, which will grant the user access to the service desk. If the user you want to add as an agent does not exist, you can also create a new JIRA account and add him/her as an agent in one step by typing in the user's e-mail address. An e-mail will be sent out with a link to set his/her password. New user accounts created this way will be automatically added to the JIRA-users group, service-desk-agents group, and **Service Desk Team** project role. Refer to *Chapter 8, Securing JIRA,* for more information on groups and roles.

Adding a customer to service desk

Customers are end users that will be creating requests through your customer portal. You can manually invite customers or allow them to sign up themselves. JIRA Service Desk requires customers to have an account to submit requests. The good news is that customers do not consume the JIRA Service Desk licenses.

To invite a customer to a service desk:

1. Browse to the service desk you want to add a customer.
2. Select the **People** tab and then **Customers** from the left.
3. Click on the **Invite customers** button.
4. Enter the e-mail addresses of customers to invite and click on the **Send invites** button.

E-mails will be sent out to customers with details on how to access the customer portal and steps to create an account if necessary.

If you want to allow users to sign up themselves, you need to set your service desk to **Everyone can access** and enable the **Anyone can sign up** option, as shown in the following screenshot. If you want to restrict your service desk to only a list of pre-approved customers, then you need to select the **Only people on my customer list can access my Customer Portal** option.

Adding a collaborator to service desk

Collaborators are JIRA users that are not part of your support team, but have expert knowledge and understanding in the domain area that can assist support agents to diagnose and solve customer requests. In JIRA, collaborators are users in the **Service Desk Collaborators** project role, and adding a user as a collaborator is an easy way to grant that user access to your service desk project. Collaborators do not consume JIRA Service Desk licenses.

To add a collaborator to your service desk:

1. Browse to the service desk you want to add a collaborator to.
2. Select the **People** tab and then **Collaborators** from the left.
3. Click on the **Add collaborator** button.
4. Search and select the user and click on the **Make user a collaborator** button.

When making a user a collaborator, you are simply granting permission for the user access to your service desk, so he/she can view, comment, and add attachments to the request.

Request types

JIRA uses issue types to define the purpose of issues, while the JIRA Service Desk uses request types for the same purpose. In fact, each request type is mapped to an issue type behind the scenes. The one key difference between the two is that, a request type is what is shown to the customers, and a more descriptive display name is used. For example, an issue type is called **Incident**, and the corresponding request type will be called **Report system outage**. You can think of request types as issue types with a fancy display name.

Setting up request types

To create a new request type for your service desk:

1. Browse to the service desk you want to create a new request type for.
2. Select the **Settings** tab and then **Request Types** from the left.
3. Click on the icon to select a new icon for the request type.
4. Enter a name for the request type. You can be as descriptive as possible with its name, so your customers can easily understand its purpose.
5. Select the issue type that the request type is mapped to.

6. Enter an optional description. The description will be displayed underneath the request name to help your customer decide what type of request to create.

7. Select a group or groups this request type belongs to. We will talk about groups later in this section.

8. Click the **Add** button to create the new request type.

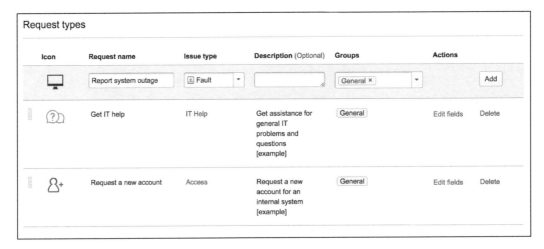

You can reorder the request types by dragging them up and down the list. The order you set in the list will be reflected on the customer portal. Make sure you put some thoughts into this. For example, you can order them alphabetically or by placing the most common request types on the top.

Organizing request types into groups

As the number of request types grows, you can group similar request types into groups. Therefore, when customers visit the portal, all the request types will be organized logically, making the navigation much easier. For example, as shown in the following screenshot of a customer portal, we have four request type groups: **Application Update**, **General**, **Infrastructure Change**, and **System Access**. When clicking on the **System Access** group, we have the four types of requests customers can raise.

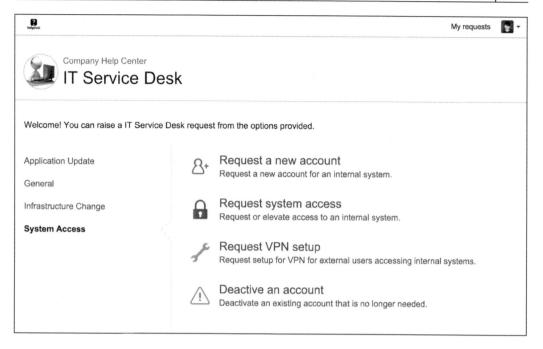

As we have already seen in the *Setting up request types* section, you can add one or more groups to a request type. You can select one of the existing groups or create a new group by simply typing in the new group's name. When a request type belongs to two or more groups, it will be displayed when each of the group is selected on the portal.

 You cannot reorder request type groups. One way to get around this is by adding a number in front of the group name, for example, 1 **General** and 2 **Application Update**.

Setting up fields

JIRA Service Desk lets you set up different field layouts for each request type. The important thing to note here is that, when you are setting up fields for JIRA Service Desk, you are not creating new custom fields (as you would in JIRA), you are simply adding and removing existing fields onto the request form when customers create a new request. You can think of this as adding fields onto screens. If you want to add a field that does not yet exist, you will have to create a new custom field first, as described in *Chapter 4, Field Management*, and then make it available in the request form.

One of the more useful features JIRA Service Desk allows you to do with fields is the ability to let you create a custom display name, independent to the actual field's name. This means you can give a more descriptive and user-friendly name to the field, when it is displayed to customers. For example, for the JIRA field Summary, you can give it a display name of `What is the problem you are having?`. Since the display name is independent of the field's name, your existing filters and search queries will continue to work as they are.

To set up field layouts for a request type:

1. Browse to the service desk you want to set up field layouts.

2. Select the **Settings** tab and then **Request Types** from the left.

3. Click on the **Edit fields** link for the request type you want to set up fields for. This will list all the fields that are currently displayed when customers create a new request.

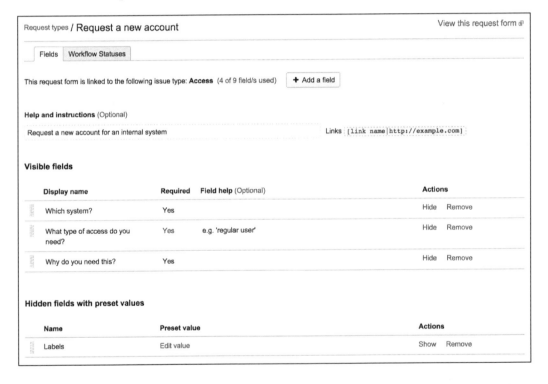

4. Click on the **Add a field** button to select an existing field (both system and custom) to the request type so that it will be displayed.

5. Click on the field's **Display name** to change what customers will see when the field is displayed. This does not change the field's actual name in JIRA, it only makes the display more user friendly.

6. Change the field's mandatory requirement by clicking on the **Required** column. Note that you cannot change this value if it is grayed out.

After you have set up your field layout for the request type, you can click on the **View this request form** link at the top to see a preview of the result. As shown in the following screenshot, we added the **Due Date** field to the form, but it is now displayed as **When do you need it by?**:

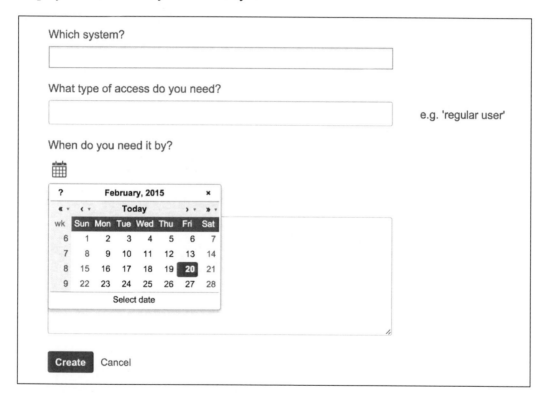

Setting up workflow

Just like with fields, you can also control how workflow statuses are displayed in JIRA Service Desk. Note that you cannot actually change the actual workflow, but you can make the workflow less confusing to your customers, so they know exactly how their requests are progressing.

To set up the workflow for a request type:

1. Browse to the service desk you want to set up a workflow for.
2. Select the **Settings** tab and then **Request Types** from the left.
3. Click on the **Edit fields** link for the request type you want to set up a workflow for.
4. Select the **Workflow Status** tab. This will list all the workflow statuses that are available in the workflow.

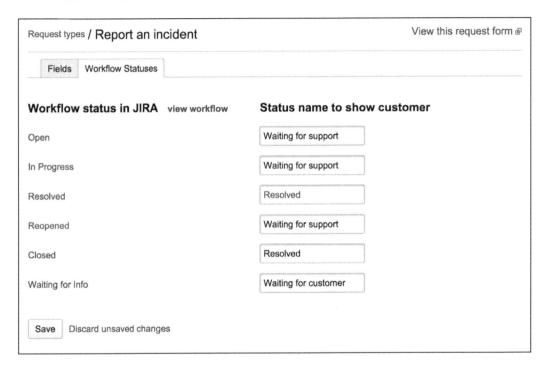

As we can see from the preceding screenshot, the actual JIRA workflow status names are listed in the left column. For each of the statuses, you can choose to give it a different display name that will be shown to the customers.

For example, the statuses **Open**, **In Progress**, and **Reopened**, are normal JIRA workflow terms, and represent that the request is currently with a support agent. However, these names can be confusing to customers, so we give them a new display name of **Waiting for support**.

You are not changing the workflow itself, you are simply making it more user friendly to your customers.

Service-level agreement

Service-level agreement or SLA defines the agreement between the service provider and end user in terms of aspects of the service provided, such as its scope, quality, or turn-around time.

In the context of support service, an SLA will define different response times for different types of support requests. For example, severity 1 requests will have a response time of 1 hour, and severity 2 requests will have a response time of 4 hours.

JIRA Service Desk lets you define SLA requirements based on response time. You can set up the rules on how response time will be measured and goals for each rule.

Setting up an SLA

JIRA Service Desk's SLA is divided into two components, the time measurement and goals to achieve. Time can be measured for a variety of purposes. Common examples include overall time taken for request resolution, and response time to customer requests. To set up SLA metric:

1. Browse to the service desk you want to set up the SLA on.
2. Select the **SLA** tab and then click on the **New Metric** button from the left.

A simple example will be JIRA Service Desk will start counting time as soon as the request is created. Every time an agent requests for more information from the customer, the count will be paused until the customer responds back. Once the request is finally closed off, the count will be stopped. The following screenshot shows you how to set up an SLA time measurement for the simple example:

*   For the **Start** column, we select the **Issue Created** option, indicating when it can start counting time as soon as the request is created

*   For the **Pause on** column, we select the **Status: Waiting for Info** option, indicating that counting can be paused when the request enters the Waiting for Info status

*   For the **Stop** column, we select the **Entered Status: Closed** option, indicating that counting will be stopped once the request is closed

As you can see in the following screenshot, for each of the three columns, you can select more than one condition:

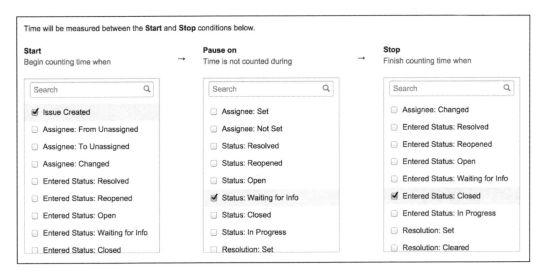

This allows you to set up multiple entry points for starting and stopping time. An example of this usage will be to measure response time. For example, you need to guarantee that an agent will respond to a new request within one hour. If the request is sent back to the customer for further information, a response time of one hour is also required as soon as the customer updates the request with the requested information. The following screenshot shows you how to set up the time measurement for this SLA:

- For the **Start** column, we select both the **Issue Create** option and **Entered Status: In Progress** option. Therefore, we will start counting when the issue is first created, and also when it is put back for our agents to work on.

- For the **Stop** column, we select both the **Entered Status: Waiting for Info** option and **Entered Status: Closed** option. Counting will stop when an agent sends the request back to the customer for more information or when it is closed for completion.

The difference between the two examples here is that, in the second example, we do not pause time counting when the request enters the **Waiting for Info** status; instead, we stop counting completely. This means that when the request enters the **Waiting for Info** status, the current counting cycle ends, and when the request enters the **In Progress** status, a new counting cycle will begin, as shown in the following screenshot:

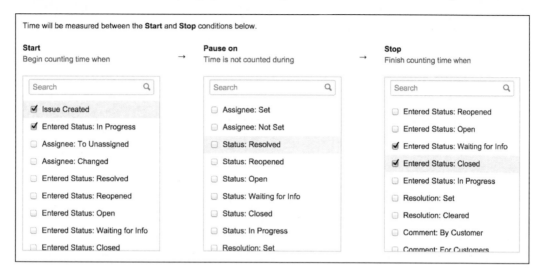

Once we defined how time can be measured, the next step is to set up the SLA goals. The SLA goals defines the amount of time allowed for each of the scenarios we have just set up. If we take the aforementioned response time example, we may set up our goals as shown in the following screenshot:

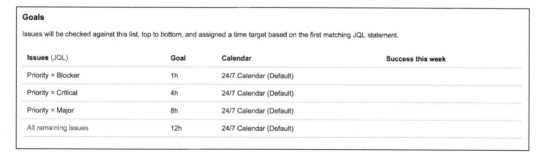

In our example, we defined that for requests with priority set to Blocker, the response time will be 1 hour, critical requests and major requests will have a response time of 4 and 8 hours, respectively. Everything else will be responded to within 12 hours.

As you can see, there are several components when it comes to define an SLA goal:

- **Issues**: Issues that will have the goal applied to them. Use JQL to narrow down the selection of issues.
- **Goal**: The time value for the goal. You can use standard JIRA time notation here, where 3h means 3 hours, 45m means 45 minutes, and 2h30m means 2 hours and 30 minutes.
- **Calendar**: Calendars define the working days and working hours SLA will be applied to. For example, **24/7 Calendar** means that time will be counted every hour of every day. As we will see later, you can create your own custom calendars to define your working day, hours, and even holidays.

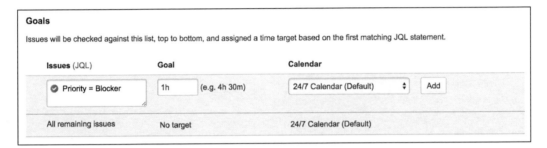

Setting up custom calendars

As we have seen, when setting up SLA, you can select a calendar, which defines the working days and hours that can be counted toward the goal. The JIRA Service Desk comes with two calendars out of the box:

- **24/7 Calendar**: This is the default calendar, where time will count around the clock
- **Sample 9-5 Calendar**: This calendar will only count the time between 9A.M. to 5P.M., from Monday to Friday

You can create you own calendars as follows:

1. Browse to the service desk you want to add a calendar for.
2. Select on the **SLA** tab.
3. Click the **Calendar** button from the left, and click the **Add Calendar** button from the **Calendars** dialog.
4. Enter a name for the new calendar and configure the options.
5. Click the **Save** button to create the calendar.

JIRA Service Desk lets you configure your calendar with the following options:

- **Time zone**: Select the time zone that will be used for the calendar
- **Working days**: Select the days that can be counted toward SLA
- **Working hours**: Hours of each working day that can be included in SLA
- **Holidays**: Add holidays such as Christmas to be excluded from SLA

As shown in the following screenshot, we have set up our calendar to have working time between 9A.M. to 5P.M., from Tuesday to Friday, and 9A.M. to 12P.M. on Saturday. We also added **Christmas Day** and **New Year Day** as holidays, so SLA will not be applied on those 2 days.

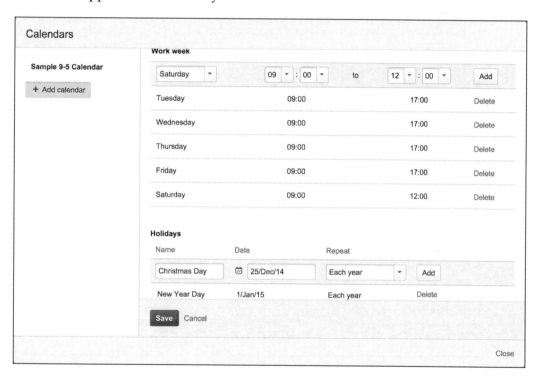

Queues

Queues are lists of requests with predefined criteria for agents to work through. You can think of them as JIRA filters. They help you and your teams organize the incoming requests into more manageable groups, so you can better prioritize them. JIRA Service Desk uses JIRA's search mechanism to configure queues, refer to *Chapter 9, Searching, Reporting, and Analysis,* for more details on JIRA search options.

Creating a new queue

You as the service desk administrator can create new queues for your team. To create a new queue:

1. Browse to the service desk you want to add a queue for.

2. Select on the **Queues** tab and click the **New Queue** button.

3. Enter a name for the queue. It will clearly reflect its purpose and types of requests that will be in it.

4. Enter the JQL that will return the requests you want for the queue. If you are not familiar with JQL, you can click on the **Basic** link, and use the menu selection to construct your search criteria.

5. Select the fields that will be displayed when the queue is showing the issue list. Click on the **More** option to find more fields to add. You can also drag the fields left and right to re-arrange them. You can select the fields that will display the most useful information.

6. Click on the **Create** button to create the queue.

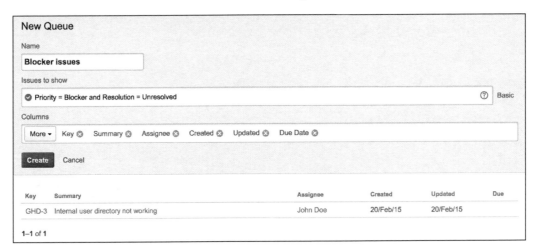

As shown in the preceding screenshot, when you make changes to your search criteria and field selection, there is a **preview** area at the bottom that will show you the result of your search and the field layout.

Creating knowledge base articles

As your team works diligently to solve problems for your customers, pieces of *gold nuggets* of knowledge will start to accumulate over time. These include things like common questions customers face and steps to troubleshoot them. JIRA Service Desk allows you to *extract* this information and create a knowledge base, which helps customers find solutions themselves. Out of the box, JIRA Service Desk only supports Atlassian Confluence for knowledge base creation, but it is possible to use other tools via third-party add-ons.

To integrate JIRA Service Desk with Confluence, you will first have to create an **application link** between JIRA and Confluence. If you have already done this, feel free to skip to the next section. To create an application link for Confluence:

1. Browse to the JIRA administration console.
2. Select the **Add-ons** tab and **Application Links** from the left.
3. Enter the fully qualified URL to your Confluence instance in the **Application** text box and click the **Create new link** button, as shown in the following screenshot:

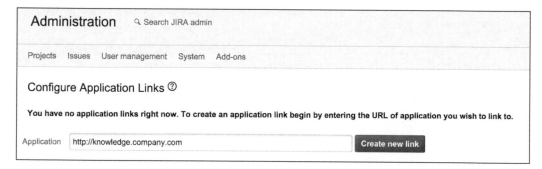

4. Follow the onscreen wizard to complete the linking process.

Once the application link is created between JIRA and Confluence, we can use it for JIRA Service Desk. Each service desk will need to be individually integrated with Confluence. To set up a Confluence KB for a service desk:

1. Browse to the service desk you want to set up a Confluence KB for.
2. Select the **Settings** tab and click on the **Confluence KB** option.
3. Check the **Link to a knowledge base** option.
4. Select the linked Confluence (it may be named as something other than Confluence) from the **Application** drop-down.

5. Select the Confluence space that the knowledge base article will be created in. If you do not have a space already, click on the **Create a knowledge base space** link.

6. Click on the **Link** button to complete the integration setup.

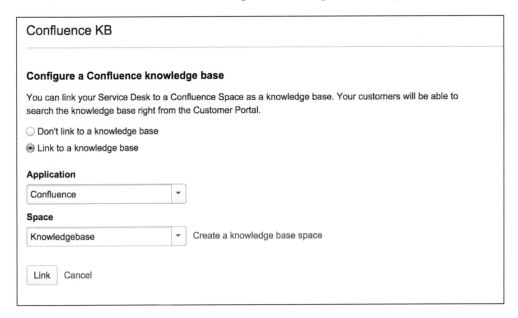

After the integration is in place, when an agent views a request, there will be a new **Create KB article** option available. Clicking on that will allow the agent to create a new knowledge base article in the preconfigured Confluence space, as shown in the following screenshot:

From the customer's perspective, a new search box will be available on the customer portal (for service desk with KB feature enabled). Customers will be able to search to see whether there is any information already available on their problems. As shown in the following screenshot, when searching for VPN, the service desk returns a knowledge article from past requests, and if this is what the customer is looking for, it will save valuable time for both the customer and the agent:

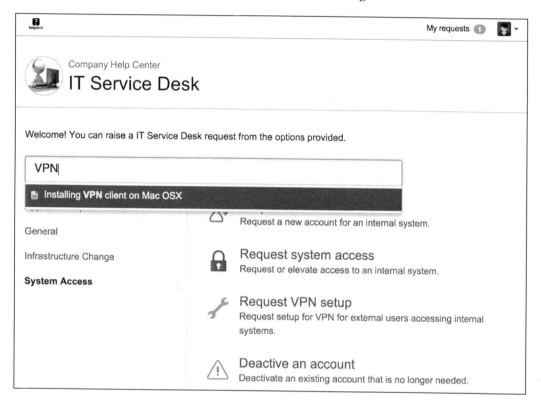

Summary

In this chapter, we learned how to use JIRA Service Desk to transform JIRA into a powerful service desk solution. The JIRA Service Desk add-on is built based on many of JIRA's out-of-the-box features, such as workflow engine and search query (JQL), and provides a brand new user interface to remove the friction caused by the old JIRA interface. This makes the overall experience a lot more pleasant for the customers.

In the next chapter, we will look at another add-on called JIRA Agile, to help you run projects the agile way.

11
Advanced Features

In previous chapters, we covered all the basic features of JIRA and showed how you can customize many of its out-of-the-box features to make JIRA work for you. In *Chapter 10, JIRA Service Desk*, we looked at the add-ons. Specially, the first major add-on that transformed JIRA from an issue-tracking system to a service desk solution. In this chapter, we will take a look at two more add-ons that can transform your JIRA to be more than just an issue-tracking system.

By the end of this chapter, you will have learned how to:

- Run agile projects in JIRA with JIRA Agile
- Collect feedback from visitors directly on your website with **Issue Collector**

JIRA Agile

So far, you have seen and used JIRA as a traditional issue-tracking system, where users can log issues and transition them through workflows. With the recent increased adoption of agile development methodologies, it is clear that JIRA by itself is not enough, and this is where JIRA Agile comes in.

JIRA Agile adds the power of agile methodologies to JIRA by providing a new user interface to help you and your team visualize user stories you have at hand. This also helps you prioritize your backlog. JIRA Agile is a separate product and does not come with JIRA. The first step for us is to install it via the Marketplace.

Getting JIRA Agile

JIRA Agile is a commercial add-on provided by Atlassian. As we have seen in *Chapter 10, JIRA Service Desk*, we first need to install JIRA Agile via the Universal Plugin Manager. Perform the following steps to install JIRA Agile via the UPM:

1. Log in as a JIRA administrator user.

2. Browse to the JIRA administration console.

3. Select the **Add-ons** tab and then the **Find new add-ons** option.

4. Search for JIRA Agile in the search box. This will locate the add-on.

5. Click on the **Free trial** button if you want to evaluate JIRA Agile before purchasing, or click on the **Buy now** link to purchase directly. This will prompt the UPM to start downloading and installing the add-on.

6. Click on the **Get License** button when prompted and follow the steps to either generate a trial license or purchase a full license.

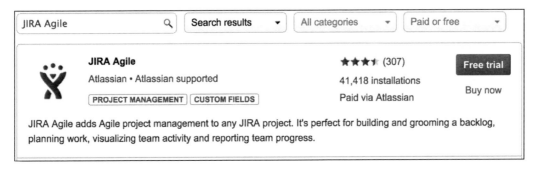

After you have successfully installed JIRA Agile, there will be a new item added to JIRA's top menu bar called **Agile**, as shown in the following screenshot:

Starting with JIRA Agile

Before we start using JIRA Agile, the first thing you need to understand is that it adds a new user interface to JIRA, allowing you to better visualize the data you already have in JIRA. For example, a story in JIRA Agile is the same as an issue in JIRA, and you can go back and forth between the two user interfaces.

Now that the relationship between JIRA Agile and JIRA is clear, we need to familiarize ourselves with a number of new terminologies that we will be using:

- **Scrum**: This is an agile software development methodology, where the development team plans and works on the project iteratively and incrementally to complete it. You can read more about Scrum at `https://www.atlassian.com/agile/scrum`.

- **Kanban:** This is a methodology where the focus is to visualize and limit the amount of work that is in progress. Kanban allows the project team to focus on delivering custom value. You can read more about Kanban at `https://www.atlassian.com/agile/kanban`.

- **Board**: This is what JIRA Agile uses to display and visualize issues in JIRA. You can think of it as a traditional white board, where you will have sticky notes representing the tasks to be completed. It helps you to visualize your backlog and plan your sprints (in the case of Scrum).

- **Card**: Following the preceding white board analogy, a card is the sticky note that represents the task to be done. With JIRA Agile, a card is an issue that is visualized differently, as shown in the following:

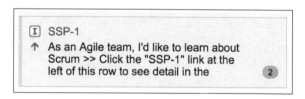

- **Story**: **Stories** or **user stories** represent requirements or features that are to be implemented. They are usually written in a nontechnical language and describe what needs to be done and whom the requirement is designed for (for example, the end user or the administrator) in a few short sentences. In JIRA Agile, a story is represented as an issue of type Story.

- **Sprint**: Sprints also known as **iterations**, are used in iterative agile development methodologies, such as Scrum. A sprint has a specific duration (that is, a start and end date) that is usually between 1–4 weeks. During this duration, the team works to deliver a portion or an improvement of the whole product or project, which is represented in JIRA as releases.

- **Epic**: An epic is a large user story that has not yet been broken down into smaller, more manageable stories. It is usually a group of related stories. Epics will be broken down into their component stories during the planning session, before becoming a part of a sprint. In JIRA Agile, an epic is represented as an issue of type Epic.

- **Backlog**: The backlog is an ordered list of all the issues that have not yet been included in a sprint.

Working with boards

To start working with JIRA Agile, you need to get familiar with boards. You can view and access boards from the **Manage Boards** page by pulling down the **Agile** menu and selecting **Manage Boards**. From the **Manage Boards** page, you will see all the boards that are shared with you. The following screenshot shows four boards, three are shared based on the project and one is shared based on the group:

Manage Boards					Create board
Board Name	**Board Type**	**Administrators**	**Saved Filter**	**Shares**	**Operations**
Critical Issues	Kanban	Patrick Li	Critical Issues	🔒 **Project:** Global Help Desk	Configure | Copy | Delete
DMS Review Board	Scrum	Patrick Li	Filter for New Scrum	🔒 **Group:** jira-users	Configure | Copy | Delete
Sample Kanban Project	Kanban	Patrick Li	Filter for Sample Kanban Project	🔒 **Project:** Sample Kanban Project	Configure | Copy | Delete
Sample Scrum Project	Scrum	Patrick Li	Filter for Sample Scrum Project	🔒 **Project:** Sample Scrum Project	Configure | Copy | Delete

There are three modes for JIRA Agile boards, namely **Plan**, **Work**, and **Report**:

- **Plan**: This is where you plan your sprints. This mode is only available with Scrum boards.

- **Work**: This is where cards (issues) are progressed (workflow transition) from one column (issue status) to another.

- **Report**: This contains a number of built-in reports and charts such as the Burndown chart (Scrum) and Control chart.

The following screenshot shows an example of a Scrum board in the **Plan** mode:

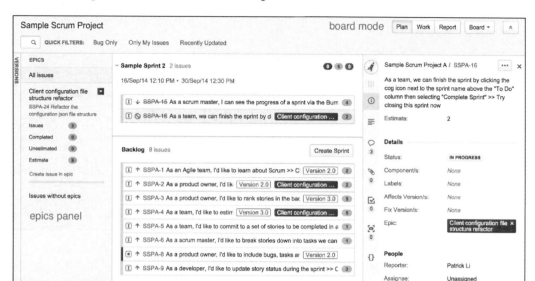

JIRA Agile has two types of boards, Scrum and Kanban. The **Scrum** board is designed to support the Scrum methodology, where teams plan and work in sprints. Scrum boards have access to all three aforementioned modes.

The **Kanban** board is designed to support the Kanban methodology, where teams focus on managing and constraining their work in progress. Since Kanban does not have a planning session like Scrum, its boards do not have the **Plan** mode.

Creating a new board

There are two ways to create a new board. You can create either a new Scrum or Kanban board. If you want to first try out JIRA Agile without impacting your existing projects, you can select the **Create a Scrum/Kanban board** option with a sample data link in step 3.

Perform the following steps to create a new board:

1. Bring down the **Agile** menu and select **Manage Boards**.
2. Click on the **Board** option at the top-right corner and click on the **Create board** button.

3. Choose to create either a Scrum or Kanban board.

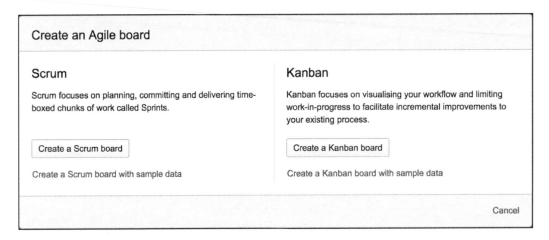

4. Select how you want to create the new board:

    °   **New project and a new board**: This will create a new JIRA project and a new agile board containing issues from that project only.

    °   **Board from an existing project**: This will create a new agile board for an existing project and its issues.

    °   **Board from an existing Saved Filter**: This will create a new agile board containing issues from a saved search filter. This option allows you to include issues from multiple projects in one board:

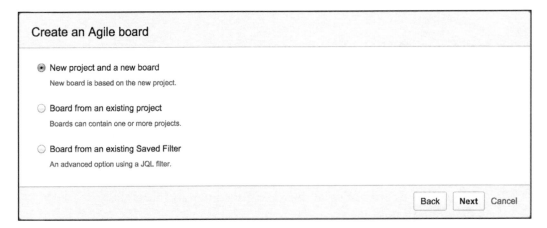

5. Enter the details for the board. The following screenshot shows creating a board from a saved search filter:

6. Click on the **Create board** button to create the agile board.

After a board is created, all existing issues are placed into the backlog. You will then be able to plan and add them to sprints if it is a Scrum board or start working on them and move them along the workflow if it is a Kanban board.

Working with Scrum boards

Teams that work with the Scrum agile methodology can use Scrum boards that, as we have seen, can be created for a specific project or search filter. Scrum boards have a Plan mode, which lets you create epics, add stories to epics, and set up sprints.

Working with epics

As you have already seen, an epic is a large user story which needs to be broken down during the planning session before the start of a sprint. You can create epics directly on your Scrum board in JIRA Agile. Perform the following steps to create a new epic:

1. Browse to your Scrum board and make sure you are in the **Plan** mode by clicking on **Plan** (or **Backlog** in newer versions) at the top-right corner.
2. Click on the plus **Create epic** link in the **Epic** panel to the left.
3. Enter a name and summary for the new epic. The epic name is what will be displayed on the Scrum board.

As shown in the following screenshot, the **Create Epic** dialog box looks very similar to the normal **Create Issue** dialog box. In JIRA Agile, when creating a new epic, you are creating a new issue of type Epic in JIRA. This means that you can create epics via the traditional method, as well:

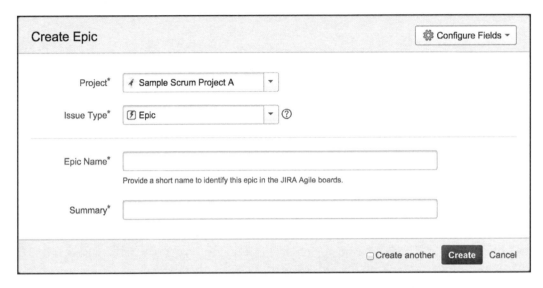

After you have created your epic, you can start breaking down your user stories and add them to it. Adding issues to an epic allows you to group similar stories together. You can add new as well as existing issues to an epic.

To create a new issue directly in the epic, perform the following:

1. Click on the expand arrow of epic you want to create a new issue in.
2. Click on the **Create issue in epic** link.
3. Create the issue as per normal. Note that from the **Create Issue** dialog, the **Epic Link** field is prepopulated with the current epic and is read-only. This will ensure that the new issue will be created in the correct epic.

You can also add existing issues to an epic by simply dragging the issue and dropping it onto the epic from the **Epics** panel, as show in the following screenshot:

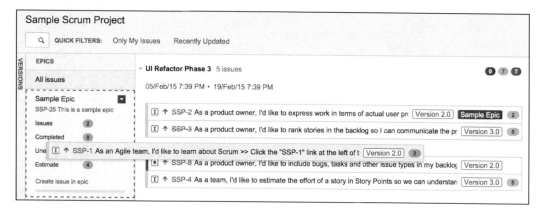

Working with sprints

During your planning sessions, you and your team will need to decide what issues will be in the backlog in your next sprint. To create a new sprint in JIRA Agile, all you have to do is to click on the **Create Sprint** button in your backlog.

After creating your new sprint, you can drag-and-drop issues from your backlog into the sprint, or you can add issues from your backlog by dragging the sprint marker or footer down. All issues that are above the marker will be automatically added to the sprint. You can add issues from the backlog or other sprints that have not yet started, but not issues that are part of an active sprint.

After creating your next sprint and including the issues to be completed, you are ready to start your sprint. Perform the following steps to start a sprint:

1. Browse to your Scrum board and make sure you are in the **Plan** mode by clicking on **Plan** at the top-right corner.

2. Click on the **Start Sprint** link. This will bring up the **Start Sprint** dialog. If **Start Sprint** is grayed out, it means that you already have an active sprint, and you can have only one sprint active at a time.

3. Enter a name for the sprint if you want to change it.

4. Select the start and end date for the sprint.

5. Click on the **Start** button to start the sprint and you will be taken to the **Work** mode of the board.

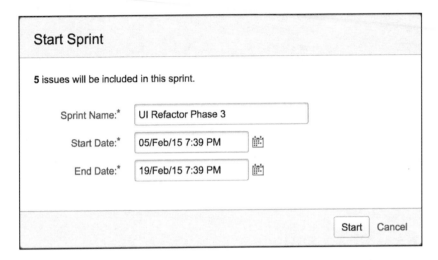

On the last day of the sprint, or if you have completed all stories in the sprint, you can end it. Any issues that have not been completed will be returned to the backlog or the next available sprint if there is one. Perform the following steps to end a sprint:

1. Browse to your Scrum board and make sure you are in the **Work** mode by clicking on **Work** at the top-right corner.

2. Bring down the menu next to the name of the sprint.

3. Click on the **Complete Sprint...** button.

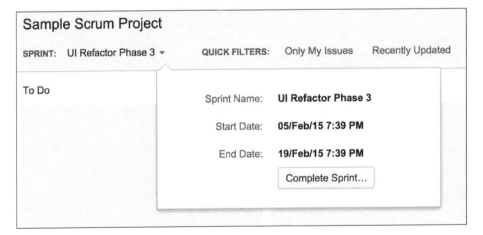

Working with Kanban boards

There is a no **Plan** mode in Kanban boards, so you will be starting in the **Work** mode directly. With Kanban, the focus is on visualizing and understanding what you and your team are working on, and also limiting the amount of work in progress.

With each Kanban board, you can set a minimum and maximum constraint on the number of issues that can be within each of the columns, and if the constraints are exceeded, the board will alert you of that. The following screenshot shows a Kanban board in the **Work** mode, and as you can see, the **In Progress** column is highlighted in red to indicate that the constraint placed on the column has been exceeded:

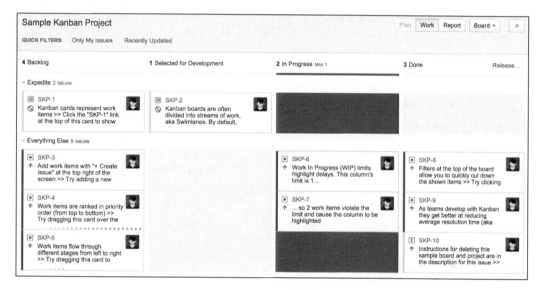

Setting up column constraints

Each column on a Kanban board can have its own minimum and maximum constraints. Perform the following steps to set up the constraints for a board:

1. Browse to your Kanban board and make sure you are in the **Work** mode by clicking on **Work** at the top-right corner.

2. Bring down the **Board** menu and click on the **Configure** option.

3. Select the **Columns** option from the left panel.

4. Select the type of **Column Constraint**.

5. Specify the minimum and maximum constraint values for each of the columns you want to place a constraint on. The constraints will be saved automatically.

The following screenshot shows that we are limiting the minimum and maximum number of issues that can be in the **In Progress** columns to 5 and 10, respectively:

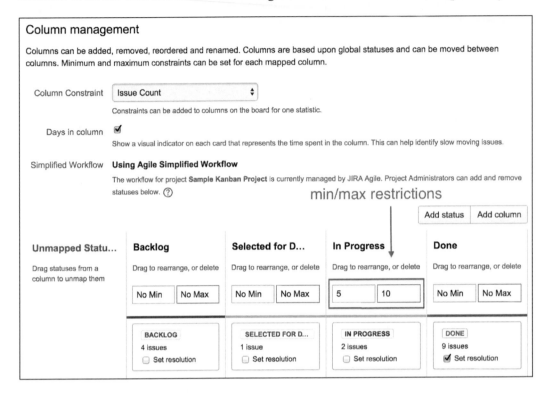

Releasing a version

Since Kanban does not have sprints, instead of ending a sprint in the **Work** mode, you release a version. While releasing a version from a Kanban board, a new version will be created in JIRA, and all issues that are released as part of the version will automatically have their **Fix Version/s** field set to the new version. Perform the following steps to release a version from a Kanban board:

1. Browse to your Kanban board and make sure you are in the **Work** mode by clicking on **Work** (or **Kanban board** in newer versions) at the top-right corner.

2. Click on the **Release…** link at the top of the **Done** column.

3. Enter a new name for the new release version.

4. Select the release date, usually today's date.

5. Enter an optional description for the release.

6. Click on the **Release** button.

Setting JIRA Agile as the home page

By default, the JIRA home page will be the dashboard. However, after a while, you may find that you are working in the JIRA Agile interface more and more and would like to default the home page to your board instead. You can do this by performing the following steps:

1. Click on the user profile icon at top-right-hand corner.

2. Select **Agile** under the **My JIRA Home** heading.

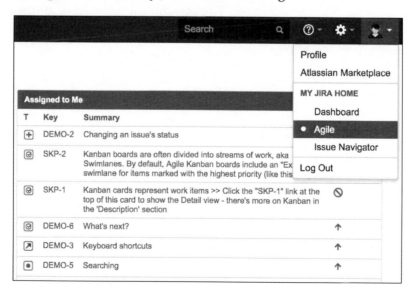

After setting your home to Agile, the next time you log in or click on the JIRA icon at the top-left corner, you will be taken to your last visited agile board instead of the standard JIRA dashboard.

Issue collector

JIRA is a great system for tracking and managing issues, but one of the challenges is that it can be overwhelming at times for users who are not familiar with JIRA to get started quickly. Another challenge is that there is no simple way of taking advantage of JIRA's issue-tracking capability and making it available to other websites, such as an Intranet. Just like JIRA Agile, a new add-on, the issue collector has been created to address these issues. Issue collector is another add-on from Atlassian and is bundled with JIRA.

With the issue collector, you can embed a feedback form directly in your website, collect feedback from visitors, and automatically push that feedback into JIRA. The major advantages of using the issue collector are as follows:

- Visitors do not need to have a JIRA account. The extra step of having to create a new account can be a turn off for some people.
- Visitors can provide their feedback on the spot without having to go to JIRA. In fact, they may not even know that JIRA exists.
- The feedback form is very simple to use, unlike the create issue dialog box, which can be complicated.

When embedded, the feedback form is accessed via a trigger, usually a tab positioned at the edge of the web page. You can control the position of the trigger while adding an issue collector in JIRA. The following screenshot shows an issue collector dialog when triggered:

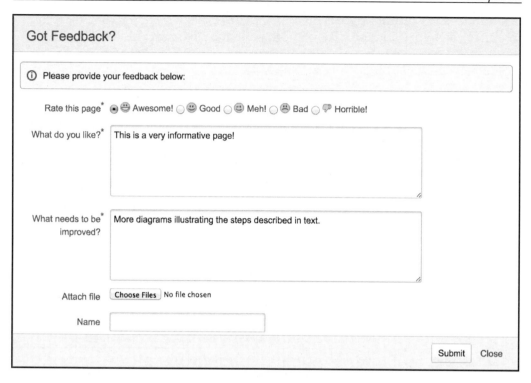

Setting up an issue collector

Issue collectors are created on a per-project basis, so when a user submits his/her feedback with the form, JIRA will know which project to create the issue in. Perform the following steps to set up a new issue collector for a project:

1. Browse to the **Project Administration** console for the project you want to use an issue collector with.
2. Select the **Issue Collectors** option from the left panel.
3. Click on the **Add Issue Collector** button.
4. Fill in the form (see the following table) and click on **Submit**.

The **Add Issue Collector** page is divided into three major sections. The first section requires you to provide some basic information for the issue collector. The most important parameter is **Issue Type** and **Reporter**. The following table lists all the parameters needed to create a new issue collector:

Field	Description
Name	This specifies the name of the issue collector. You should use a name that conveys the purpose of the issue collector.
Description	This specifies more descriptive text about the issue collector.
Issue Type	This specifies the issue type for new issues created via the issue collector form.
Reporter	This specifies that the default user that will be used to create issues when issues are created.
Match Reporter	This specifies whether new issues should always be created with the issue reporter, or if JIRA should try to match the user with an e-mail, or if there is an active session with JIRA.
Collect Browser Info	This option specifies, if you want to collect additional information from the user's browser.
Trigger Text	This specifies the text that will be displayed on the **Trigger** tab.
Trigger Style	This decides where you would like the **Trigger** tab to appear on the page. If you choose the **Custom** option instead of creating a **Trigger** tab, you will get a JavaScript code snippet that will let you control and use other elements on the page as the trigger, by replacing the `#myCustomTrigger` text.
Template	This chooses what the feedback form will look like. You can also create your own form by choosing the **Custom** option.
Message	This specifies the message that will be displayed in the info panel on the feedback form.

There is also a **Template Preview** section at the bottom to help you visualize the final issue collector dialog.

Embedding the issue collector

After creating the new issue collector, you will be able to embed it in your website. JIRA offers two options to embed an issue collector, either through HTML or JavaScript.

Embedding through HTML requires you to have the ability to modify the HTML page you want to embed your issue collector into. If you want the issue collector to appear on every page on your website, you will need to have a common HTML page that can be included in all the pages such as a header HTML.

Embedding via JavaScript allows you to add the generated code as a part of an existing JavaScript file that has already been included in the page. Again, this requires you to have the ability to modify the JavaScript file. This option also requires the jQuery library to be available, so you will need to make sure you have included jQuery before calling the generated code, as follows:

```
<script src="http://code.jquery.com/jquery-latest.js"></script>
```

Perform the following steps to embed your issue collector in your website:

1. Select either the **Embed with HTML** or **Embed with JavaScript** option under the **Embed this Issue Collector** section.

2. Copy the contents from the **Installation instructions** text area and paste the code snippet into the appropriate location of your page.

You can also click on and expand the **More Instructions** section to get more details and examples on how to do this. The following screenshot shows an example of an issue collector embedded in Atlassian Confluence, an enterprise wiki solution:

The issue collector shown in the preceding screenshot contains the **Summary** and **Description** field, and also a custom field called **System** from JIRA.

If you do not have Atlassian Confluence or another website handy, but still want to try out the issue collector, you can test this directly in JIRA using the announcement banner:

1. Browse to the JIRA administration console.

2. Select the **Systems** tab and then the **Announcement Banner** option.

3. Cut and paste the issue collector code into the **Announcement** text box and click on the **Set Banner** button.

After you save the announcement banner, the issue collector will be displayed in normal JIRA pages such as the dashboard. It will not be displayed in the administration console.

Summary

In this chapter, we learned to expand JIRA beyond being just a simple issue-tracking system. Note that both JIRA Agile and issue collector simply built based on the JIRA platform, takes advantage of its already robust issue management features and presents the users with new interfaces and ways to interact with and use JIRA. There are many other great add-ons available in the **Marketplace** option that will make using JIRA a much more enjoyable and productive experience for you and your team.

This is the last chapter and the end of our journey. Throughout this book, we looked at the various out of the box features JIRA has. We also looked at how you, as an administrator, can install, morph, and adapt it to your environment and use cases. Features such as custom fields and workflows make JIRA a very flexible application. In the last two chapters, we also introduced add-ons that bring even more capabilities to JIRA, and they are just a few out of thousands more available. It is now your job to discover and try other add-ons to enhance you and your users' experience using JIRA and to make it a success.

Index

Symbols

21 CFR Part 11 E-Signature plugin 105

A

AD/LDAP connector directory type
  about 235
  permission options 235
  using 235
advanced fields, custom field types
  Group Picker (multiple group) 104
  Group Picker (single group) 104
  Hidden Job Switch 104
  Job Checkbox 104
  Project Picker (single project) 104
  Text Field (read only) 104
  User Picker (multiple users) 104
  Version Picker (multiple versions) 104
  Version Picker (single version) 104
advanced search, JQL 280
Apache's Velocity template language
  URL 208
Atlassian
  URL 23
  URL, for documentation 301
Atlassian JIRA
  URL 14
attachments
  about 87
  enabling, in JIRA 87, 88
autocomplete feature 282
autocomplete renderer 120

B

backlog 338
basic search 279
board 337
built-in fields 102
built-in share feature 286
business processes
  mapping 161, 162
  workflows 162

C

CAPTCHA
  enabling 243
card 337
comments
  about 85
  creating, on issue 85, 86
  managing 86
  permalinking 86
  reference link 87
common transition 174
components, JQL
  about 280
  Fields 281
  Functions 281
  Keywords 280
  Operators 281
Components tab, Project Administration
  about 52
  component lead 53, 54
  components, creating 53
  components, managing 53
  default assignee 53, 54
  fields 52

condition group **176**
conditions **166, 167**
CSV
  data, importing through 41-46
custom calendars
  24/7 Calendar 328
  configuring options 329
  creating 328
  Sample 9-5 Calendar 328
  setting up 328
customer portal
  about 314
  branding 315, 316
custom event
  adding 210
  firing 210, 211
custom field context
  about 105
  creating 112
custom fields
  about 102
  configuring 111
  creating 107-109
  default values, setting 114
  deleting 109-110
  editing 109-110
  managing 106
  select options, configuring 113
custom field types
  about 102
  advanced fields 104
  standard fields 103
custom issue type 91

D

dashboard
  about 297
  configuring 299
  creating 298, 299
  deleting 299
  editing 299
  layout, setting 300
  managing 297
  sharing 299
data
  importing, into JIRA 40

  importing, through CSV 41-46
default groups
  jira-administrators 245
  jira-developers 245
  jira-users 245
default issue types 91
default text renderer 120
distributed version control system
    (DVCS) 50

E

e-mail
  in JIRA 196
  sending, manually 204, 205
epic
  about 338
  working with 341, 342
error queue 203
events
  about 206, 207
  custom event, adding 210
  custom event, firing 210, 211
  custom events 206
  mail template, adding 207-209
  system events 206

F

field
  about 35
  renderers, setting for 121
field configuration
  about 114, 115
  copying 117
  creating 116
  deleting 116
  editing 116
  field description 118
  field rendering 120
  field requirement 119
  field visibility 119, 120
  managing 117, 118
  screens 122
field configuration scheme
  about 122
  adding 123
  associating, with project 126, 127

configuring 125
copying 124
deleting 124
editing 124
managing 122
files
attaching, to issue 89
filters
about 286
creating 287
deleting 291, 292
editing 288, 289
managing 287
ownership, changing 292
sharing 288, 289
subscribing 290

G

gadgets
about 300
deleting 304
editing 303, 304
moving 303
placing, on dashboard 301, 302
global permissions
about 253, 254
configuring 255, 256
deleting 257
granting 256, 257
JIRA system administrator, versus JIRA
administrator 255
revoking 257
groups
about 244
adding 246
default groups 245
deleting 248
Group Browser 245
membership, editing 246, 247

H

Help Desk project
components, creating 59
custom events, setting up 229, 230
custom field, setting up 128, 129

dashboards, setting up 305
field configuration scheme,
setting up 129, 130
field configuration, setting up 129
filters, setting up 304
gadgets, setting up 306
groups, setting up 273
implementing 60, 61
issue type scheme, creating 99
issue type screen schemes, setting up 157
issue types, creating 98, 99
mail servers, setting up 229
new project, assigning to category 59
new project, creating 58
notification scheme, setting up 230
notifications, setting up 231
permission schemes, setting up 274
permissions, setting up 274, 275
project category, creating 57
requisites 273
screen schemes, setting up 156, 157
screens, setting up 154-156
setting up 57
summarizing 231
user group association, setting up 273
workflow, implementing 192-194
workflow schemes, implementing 192-194
workflow schemes, setting up 191, 192
workflows, setting up 189-191
hierarchy, JIRA
field 35
issue 35
project 35
project category 34
high-level architecture, JIRA
about 2
application services 3
data storage 3
URL 2
web browsers 3
home directory, JIRA 4

I

incoming e-mails
about 221
benefits 222

mail handlers 223
server, adding 222, 223
in-line editing 69
installation directory, JIRA 3
installation
Java 10, 11
JIRA 9, 14
JIRA Service Desk 310, 311
MySQL 12
issue
about 35, 64
assigning, to users 74, 75
cloning 80
comments, creating on 85, 86
creating 66-68
deleting 69, 70
editing 68, 69
files, attaching to 89
key aspects 64
linking, to other issue 78
linking, with remote contents 79
moving, between projects 70-72
notifications, receiving on 73, 74
screenshots, attaching to 90
sharing, with other users 75
vote, casting on 72, 73
working with 66
issue collector
about 348
advantages 348
embedding 350-352
setting up 349, 350
issue linking
about 76
enabling 76
issue navigator
about 278
advanced search 278
basic search 278
sections 278
issue priorities
about 97
creating 97, 98
issue security scheme
about 266
adding 267
applying 271

configuring 267, 268
default security level, setting 270
security level, adding 268
security level, deleting 270
users, adding to security level 269, 270
Issue Summary 64
issue types
about 90
creating 92
deleting 92
issue type screen scheme
about 148
adding 149
associating, to screen schemes 151, 152
associating, with project 152, 153
association, deleting 152
association, editing 152
configuring 151
copying 150
deleting 150
editing 150
iterations 337

J

Java
installing 10, 11
Java Development Kit (JDK)
about 7
URL, for installing 10
Java Runtime Environment. *See* **JRE**
JEditor plugin 122
JIRA
architecture 1
attachments, enabling 87-89
data, importing 40
e-mail 195, 196
home directory 4, 5
installation directory 3
installation options 8
installing 9, 14-19
MySQL driver, installing 19
obtaining 14-19
post-installation configurations 27
request types 319
screen management 133
search interface 277

search options 277
security 233
server 5
service desk 309
setup wizard 19-26
standalone distribution 8
starting 26
stopping 26
system events 206
system requisites 5
URL, for database switching 3
WAR distributions 9
JIRA Agile
  about 335
  backlog 338
  board 337
  card 337
  epic 338
  installing, via UPM 336
  Kanban 337
  Scrum 337
  setting, as home page 347, 348
  sprint 337
  stories (user stories) 337
JIRA Agile boards
  creating 339-341
  plan mode 338
  report mode 338
  working with 338
  work mode 338
JIRA architecture
  about 1
  high-level architecture 2
  home directory 4
  installation directory 3
  URL 2
JIRA Cloud
  URL 5
JIRA Enhancer Plugin 104
JIRA installation
  about 9
  Java, installing 10, 11
  MySQL, installing 12
  MySQL, preparing 12, 13
JIRA issue summary
  about 64
  Attachments 66

Comments 66
Date Fields 66
Issue Details / Fields 66
Issue Operations 66
Issue Summary 66
Issue View Options 66
Project / Issue Key 66
User Fields 66
Vote / Watch Issue 66
Workflow Options 66
JIRA Misc Workflow Extensions
  about 187
  URL 187
JIRA Query Language. *See* **JQL**
JIRA Service Desk
  about 309, 310
  agent, adding 317
  agents 311
  collaborator, adding 319
  creating 313, 314
  customer, adding 318
  customer portal 311
  customer portal, branding 315
  installing 310, 311
  queues 312
  request 312
  request type 313
  service desk 313
  SLA 313
  user types 316
JIRA Suite Utilities plugin
  about 187
  URL 187
JIRA Toolkit Plugin 104
JIRA Workflow Toolbox plugin
  about 187
  URL 187
JQL
  about 280
  components 280
  query 281
  URL, for syntax reference 281
  versus SQL 280
JRE 7

K

Kanban
about 337
URL 337
Kanban board
about 339
column constraints, setting up 345
version, releasing 346
working with 345
key format, project
modifying 39, 40
keytool 30
knowledge base articles
creating 331-333

L

LDAP Connector 235
link types
creating 76, 77
listeners 206

M

mail handlers
about 223
adding 226-228
comment, adding 224, 225
comment, adding before separator 226
comment, adding before specified
marker 226
comment, adding from non-quoted
e-mail body 225
comment, adding with entire e-mail
body 225
deleting 228
editing 228
new issue, adding 224, 225
mail queue
about 202, 203
flushing 204
viewing 203
mail servers
incoming 196
outgoing 196
mail template
adding 208, 209

HTML template 208
registering, with JIRA 209
subject template 207
text template 208
MySQL
about 12
preparing, for JIRA 12, 13
URL 12
MySQL driver
installing 19
URL 19

N

nFeed 105
notifications
about 212
receiving, on issue 73, 74
troubleshooting 220, 221
notification scheme
about 213, 214
adding 214
assigning 218, 219
copying 215
deleting 215
editing 214
managing 216
notification, adding 216-218
notification, deleting 218

O

outgoing mails
disabling 200
server, adding 197-200
SMTP, enabling over SSL 200, 201
test mail, sending 201, 202
working with 197

P

**permission options, AD/LDAP connector
directory type**
Atlassian Crowd 235
Atlassian JIRA 235
Internal with LDAP authentication 235
Read only 235
Read only, with local groups 235

Read/Write 235
permission schemes
about 260
adding 261
applying 265
configuring 263
copying 263
deleting 262
editing 262
managing 261
permission, granting 264, 265
permission, revoking 265
permissions
global permissions 254
hierarchy 253
issue security 266
project permissions 258
troubleshooting 271
plugins, custom fields
21 CFR Part 11 E-Signature 105
JIRA Enhancer Plugin 104
JIRA Toolkit Plugin 104
nFeed 105
SuggestiMate for JIRA 105
post functions 167
post-installation configurations, JIRA
about 27
context path, changing 29
HTTPS, configuring 29-31
memory, increasing 27, 28
port number, changing 29
project
about 35
creating 37-39
field configuration scheme, associating
    with 126, 127
key format, modifying 39, 40
user interfaces 46
Project Administration
about 50, 51
Components tab 52
Fields tab 57
Issue Types tab 56
Notifications tab 57
Permissions tab 57
Roles tab 57
Screens tab 56

Summary tab 51
Versions tab 54
Workflows tab 56
Project Browser
about 47, 48
Change Log tab 48, 49
Components tab 48, 49
Issues tab 48
Labels tab 48
Reviews tab 50
Road Map tab 48, 49
Source tab 50
Summary tab 48
Versions tab 48, 49
project permissions
about 36, 253, 258
Administer Project permission 36
attachments permissions 259
Browse Project permission 36
comments permissions 259
issue permissions 259
JIRA Administrator permission 36
list 258
permission schemes 260
time tracking permissions 260
voters and watchers permissions 259
project roles
about 248
adding 249
administrators 248
default members, managing 250, 251
deleting 250
developers 248
editing 249
members, assigning 251, 252
Project Role Browser 248
users 248

Q

queue
about 329
creating 330
quick search
about 283
queries 283
running 283

R

remote contents
  issue, linking with 79
renderers
  autocomplete renderer 120
  default text renderer 120
  select list renderer 120
  setting, for field 121
  wiki style renderer 120
reports
  about 293
  Average Age Report 294
  Created versus Resolved Issues Report 293
  dashboard 297
  gadgets 300
  generating 294-296
  Pie Chart Report 294
  Recently Created Issues Report 294
  Resolution Time Report 293
  Single Level Group By Report 293
  Time Since Issue Report 294
  Time Tracking Report 294
  User Workload Report 293
  Version Workload Report 293
request types
  about 319
  fields, setting up 321-323
  organizing, into groups 320, 321
  setting up 319, 320
  workflow, setting up 323, 324

S

screens
  activating 158, 159
  adding 137
  configuring 138
  copying 138
  deleting 137
  editing 137
  field, adding 139
  field, deleting 140
  screen tabs, using 140
  tab, adding to screen 141, 142
  tab, deleting 142, 143
  tab, editing 142
  working with 133-136

screen schemes
  about 134
  adding 144, 145
  association, deleting 148
  association, editing 148
  configuring 146
  copying 146
  deleting 145
  editing 145
  issue type screen scheme 148
  screens, associating to issue operations 147
  working with 143, 144
Script Runner
  about 188
  URL 188
Scrum
  about 337
  URL 337
Scrum board
  about 339
  epic, working with 341-343
  sprints, working with 343, 344
  working with 341
search interface
  about 277
  issue navigator 278
search options
  advanced search 278
  basic/simple search 277
  quick/text search 277
search results
  column layout, customizing 285, 286
  exporting 284, 285
  result views, switching 284
  sharing 286
  working with 284
security, JIRA
  about 233
  groups 244
  Help Desk project 273
  permissions hierarchy 253
  permissions, troubleshooting 271
  project roles 248
  user directories 233
  users 238
  workflow security 272
Security levels 267

select list renderer 120
simple search 279
SLA (service-level agreement)
  about 325
  custom calendars, setting up 328, 329
  setting up 325-328
software requisites, JIRA
  about 6
  application servers 8
  databases 7
  Java platforms 7
  operating systems 6
Split Regex, regex expression 226
sprint
  about 337
  working with 343
standard fields, custom field types
  Date Picker 103
  Date Time Picker 103
  Labels 103
  Number Field 103
  Radio Buttons 103
  Select List (cascading) 103
  Select List (multiple choice) 103
  Select List (single choice) 103
  Text Field (multi-line) 103
  Text Field (single-line) 103
  URL Field 103
  User Picker (single user) 103
standard issue link 78
step 165
stories (user stories) 337
Structured Query Language (SQL) 280
subdirectories, JIRA_HOME
  caches 4
  data 4
  export 4
  import 4
  log 4
  plugins 4
  tmp 4
subtasks
  about 93
  creating 94
  enabling 93
  issue type schemes 94
  issue type schemes, creating 95, 96

SuggestiMate for JIRA 105
system events, JIRA
  Custom Event 207
  Generic Event 207
  Issue Assigned 206
  Issue Closed 206
  Issue Commented 206
  Issue Comment Edited 206
  Issue Created 206
  Issue Deleted 206
  Issue Moved 206
  Issue Reopened 206
  Issue Resolved 206
  Issue Updated 206
  Issue Worklog Deleted 207
  Issue Worklog Updated 207
  Work Logged On Issue 206
  Work Started On Issue 207
  Work Stopped On Issue 207
system fields
  about 102
  Assignee 102
  Component/s 102
  Description 102
  Due Date 102
  Effects Version/s 102
  Fix Version/s 102
  Issue Type 102
  Priority 102
  Reporter 102
  Resolution 102
  Summary 102
  Time Tracking 102
system requisites, JIRA
  about 5
  hardware 5, 6
  software 6

T

time tracking
  about 81
  configuring 81, 82
  original estimates, specifying 83
  work, logging against issue 83, 84
transition
  about 165

conditions 165, 166
post functions 165, 167
transition screen 165
triggers 165, 166
validators 165, 167
triggers 166
troubleshooting
JIRA permissions 271

U

Universal Plugin Manager (UPM) 310
User Browser 239
user directories
about 233
accessing 234
Active directory (AD)/LDAP 235
JIRA internal directory 234
LDAP, connecting to 236-238
managing 235, 236
user interfaces, project
about 46
Project Administration 46
Project Browser 46
users
about 238
adding 240, 241
CAPTCHA, enabling 243
issue, assigning to 74, 75
issue, sharing with 75
public signup, enabling 242, 243
User Browser 239
user types, JIRA Service Desk
agents 316
collaborator 317
customer 317

V

validators 167
Velocity
URL 208
Versions tab, Project Administration
about 54
fields 54
options 55
versions, creating 54, 55
versions, managing 55, 56

View Issue page 64
vote
casting, on issue 72, 73

W

wiki style renderer 120
workflow, authoring
about 170-174
condition, adding to transition 175
post function, adding to transition 178, 179
trigger, adding to transition 174
validator, adding to transition 176, 177
workflow designer
about 168
using 168-170
Workflow Enhancer for JIRA
about 188
URL 188
workflow plugins
about 187
JIRA Misc Workflow Extensions 187
JIRA Suite Utilities 187
JIRA Workflow Toolbox 187
Script Runner 188
Workflow Enhancer for JIRA 188
workflows
about 162, 163
existing workflow, updating 179, 180
extending, with add-ons 187
issue status 165
managing 164
transition 165
workflow designer, using 168, 169
workflow schemes
about 180, 181
activating 186, 187
association, deleting 185, 186
association, editing 185
configuring 182, 183
creating 182
issue type, assigning to workflow 183-185
managing 181
viewing 181
workflow security 272

Thank you for buying
JIRA Essentials
Third Edition

About Packt Publishing

Packt, pronounced 'packed', published its first book, *Mastering phpMyAdmin for Effective MySQL Management*, in April 2004, and subsequently continued to specialize in publishing highly focused books on specific technologies and solutions.

Our books and publications share the experiences of your fellow IT professionals in adapting and customizing today's systems, applications, and frameworks. Our solution-based books give you the knowledge and power to customize the software and technologies you're using to get the job done. Packt books are more specific and less general than the IT books you have seen in the past. Our unique business model allows us to bring you more focused information, giving you more of what you need to know, and less of what you don't.

Packt is a modern yet unique publishing company that focuses on producing quality, cutting-edge books for communities of developers, administrators, and newbies alike. For more information, please visit our website at www.packtpub.com.

About Packt Enterprise

In 2010, Packt launched two new brands, Packt Enterprise and Packt Open Source, in order to continue its focus on specialization. This book is part of the Packt Enterprise brand, home to books published on enterprise software – software created by major vendors, including (but not limited to) IBM, Microsoft, and Oracle, often for use in other corporations. Its titles will offer information relevant to a range of users of this software, including administrators, developers, architects, and end users.

Writing for Packt

We welcome all inquiries from people who are interested in authoring. Book proposals should be sent to author@packtpub.com. If your book idea is still at an early stage and you would like to discuss it first before writing a formal book proposal, then please contact us; one of our commissioning editors will get in touch with you.

We're not just looking for published authors; if you have strong technical skills but no writing experience, our experienced editors can help you develop a writing career, or simply get some additional reward for your expertise.

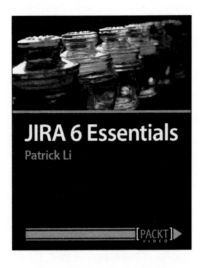
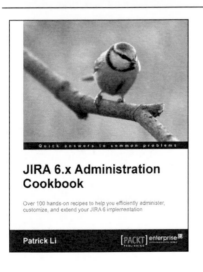

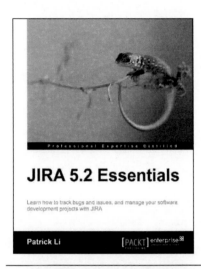

JIRA 5.2 Essentials

ISBN: 978-1-78217-999-3   Paperback: 396 pages

Learn how to track bugs and issues, and manage your software development projects with JIRA

1. Learn how to set up JIRA for software development.

2. Effectively manage and handle software bugs and issues.

3. Includes updated JIRA content as well as coverage of the popular GreenHopper plugin.

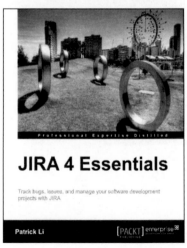

JIRA 4 Essentials

ISBN: 978-1-84968-172-8   Paperback: 352 pages

Track bugs, issues, and manage your software development projects with JIRA

1. Successfully manage issues and track your projects using JIRA.

2. Model business processes using JIRA Workflows.

3. Ensure only the right people get access to your data, by using user management and access control in JIRA.

4. Packed with step-by-step instruction, screenshots, and practical examples.

Please check **www.PacktPub.com** for information on our titles